THE RACE TO TRUTH

THE RACE TO TRUTH

*Blowing the Whistle on Lance Armstrong
and Cycling's Doping Culture*

EMMA O'REILLY

with Shannon Kyle

BANTAM PRESS

LONDON · TORONTO · SYDNEY · AUCKLAND · JOHANNESBURG

TRANSWORLD PUBLISHERS
61–63 Uxbridge Road, London W5 5SA
A Random House Group Company
www.transworldbooks.co.uk

First published in Great Britain
in 2014 by Bantam Press
an imprint of Transworld Publishers

A CIP catalogue record for this book
is available from the British Library.

ISBNs 9780593074060 (cased)
9780593074077 (tpb)

Addresses for Random House Group Ltd companies outside the UK
can be found at: www.randomhouse.co.uk
The Random House Group Ltd Reg. No. 954009

The Random House Group Limited supports the Forest Stewardship
Council® (FSC®), the leading international forest-certification organisation.
Our books carrying the FSC label are printed on FSC®-certified paper. FSC is
the only forest-certification scheme supported by the leading environmental
organisations, including Greenpeace. Our paper procurement policy can
be found at www.randomhouse.co.uk/environment

Typeset in 11½/15½pt Sabon by
Kestrel Data, Exeter, Devon.
Printed and bound by
CPI Group (UK) Ltd, Croydon, CR0 4YY.

2 4 6 8 10 9 7 5 3 1

To Terry.
Gone way too soon, but always there.

Our lives begin to end the day we become silent about things that matter.

Martin Luther King, Jr.

Contents

Foreword
by Lance Armstrong

When Emma asked me to write the foreword for her book, I was surprised. But even more so, I was both humbled and happy to do it. Our shared history has been a very interesting one, to say the least, and there was a time I didn't expect to hear from her again.

Prior to my admission, I had tried to reach out and apologize but understandably didn't hear anything back. Then months later I got a message out of the blue. My former soigneur had taken her time to consider events and wanted to talk again, which was incredible for me to hear.

Before meeting Emma in Florida in November 2013, all those years later, I was thinking: 'Shit, is this going to be totally awkward?' But within sixty seconds we were totally at ease, a testament to the friendship we'd once shared. We haven't stopped speaking since.

All credit to Emma, as she's always been a very direct no bullshit kind of girl, even if 90 per cent of the time I cannot understand what she's saying, she speaks so fast in her thick

Irish accent! She says what is right and what is wrong and for a time that worked against the lies I was telling the world. Overnight my story as sporting hero and Tour de France champion went from a lilywhite picture to jet black. But, unlike many others, Emma doesn't view it like that. She wasn't going to sit there and say: 'It's black or it's white.' She sees the cool shades of grey.

From the start, when Emma spoke up to try and clean up cycling, she showed enormous courage. Without a doubt I was the brashest when it came to defending myself and the sport and I took it too far. However, while others, who'd also got hurt, danced on my grave, Emma did not join in and I really respect her for that.

On the US Postal team, we got on very well together and it was an extraordinary thing that Emma was given the role of soigneur in such a male-dominated sport. She was a vocal, outspoken, fun person and we got on just great. When she left the team we didn't keep in touch but after she spoke out about doping, the lawyers rolled in and our positions were staked out. On both sides things became aggressive and I said words no man should ever say about a woman. We'd never fallen out personally, but publicly it got nasty.

Today the Lance Armstrong story has become a cottage industry, with many books, movies and a whole lot of drama out there for people to see. And while a lot of it's true, some of it's been completely embellished and exaggerated. Yes, I doped, but from what I can tell, so did many pro-cyclists and while I've been banned for life, hundreds of others involved will go unpunished. The half-truths and varying accounts frustrated Emma. She was a member of our team at the time and now finally she gets to share the eyewitness account of her story.

For ten years, when my image as sporting icon was that

lilywhite colour, nobody wanted to listen to Emma, the whistleblower, talking about the dark side. And now she's staked out another position, centred round forgiveness and reconciliation, some don't want to hear this either. But Emma O'Reilly doesn't give a shit. She just marches to the beat of her own drum and she's fine with that. I admire her deeply, as I've come to appreciate just how tireless she is in the face of naysayers.

Since those days of fighting for my corner and career my life has changed considerably. Not only from the outside but also from the inside. Although I am still under plenty of stress, I am beholden to nobody, no sponsors, no teams, and in some ways feel happier than ever. If I could sum my life up in one word it would be 'fearless', not in a cavalier, crazy way, but it's neat to be free. Being forgiven by people like Emma only adds to my peace and humility, something I'm hugely grateful for.

Of all the characters in this saga, Emma has handled her experience completely differently to most. In spite of what she went through, she took her time and came to a very mature and reasoned place. This position is one most people involved in this story will never reach. I honestly don't know if I'd have the courage and character to do what Emma did. This won't come as a shock to anyone but this woman is a much better person than I am or ever will be.

Lance Armstrong
Austin, Texas

May 2014

Acknowledgements

I'm writing these acknowledgements from the very first bike race I did as a soigneur, the Rás Tailteann (an eight-day stage race in Ireland). It's reminding me of all that's great about cycling: the decency, love of the sport, enthusiasm and sincerity. I'm here because one of my best friends, Tony, runs it. TC, thanks for always mouthing off for me – together with Alasdair, we were some motley crew. All I can say is that no wonder I ended up in so much trouble with you two looking after me.

Mike, without whom I'd never have been able to speak out, and for your unwavering support throughout all the crap – thank you from the bottom of my heart. You're my hero.

My buddy Sharon, where would I be without you? You're my calm reasonable side, my sounding board for everything. I'm a lucky person to have a BBF like you. I'm never alone with you in my life, thank you.

My brother Norbert, as contrary as me but so much more fun. Thanks for always being there, for always looking out for me and for always having my back.

Really this book would never have been written if it wasn't for a certain Irish journalist who came into my life in the summer of 2003. David, you've played way too big a role in my life, thank you for the journey.

Niall, thanks for all your help behind the scenes. Much respect to the choices you made as an athlete and for having the strength of character to create a successful life after.

I couldn't write these acknowledgements without mentioning the peace, confidence and joy I've got since Lance and I have buried our hatchet. To anybody who's got people to forgive, go ahead and do it. It's one of the best feelings in the world. Love Lance or hate him, he's done so much for cancer and that's more important than any bike race.

Shannon, thank you for making this book a pleasurable experience, you've been brilliant. Here's to many more Friday night dinners!

Giles and everyone at Transworld, thanks for all your help and support.

All the staff and patients of The Body Clinic, thank you for all your help and support. To Jean et al, thanks for making sure the place ran while I disappeared at short notice. To my patients for listening to me going on and on about my favourite subject, and for rescheduling appointments at short notice.

Prologue

JUST LIKE THE FIRST time we'd met, I heard him before I saw him.

'Uh, do you guys have my room key?'

Loud. Texan. Alpha. Unmistakable.

I spun round and, bang, I was staring back into the eyes of Lance Armstrong. My former work colleague and friend. The great sporting icon who sued me for £1 million. The man who labelled me a money-grabbing, alcoholic whore. The man who repeatedly called me a liar when he knew all along I was telling the truth.

The man I'd helped bring down.

'Hello Lance,' I said, smiling.

Clear lines framed his intense blue eyes and I saw that he looked tired. A deep-rooted tiredness from somewhere within.

We were standing in the air-conditioned lobby of a Florida hotel. Lance was wearing golfing clothes: chinos, white shoes and a V-necked argyle sweater, all a far cry from his cycling Lycra. He ambled over.

'Hi Emma,' he said.

We had a stilted hug – the first contact between us since I'd worked as his masseuse fourteen years ago. We had exchanged a fair few phone calls in recent months and had planned to meet a bit later that evening, but a mix-up meant that he hadn't known where I was and vice versa, leading to us meeting now, earlier than expected. What was clear, though, was that we were both wary. Understandably. Neither of us trusted the other. Not yet.

I had travelled to Florida with Matt Lawton, the chief sports reporter for the *Daily Mail*, who would cover our reunion for the newspaper and so avoid an influx of other requests for stories. The past decade had made me media-savvy, something I most definitely wasn't at the start of this journey.

After shaking hands with Matt, Lance puffed out his chest a little and suggested we all sat down. He hadn't asked to meet Matt beforehand or tried to control this interview. For him, a control freak, that was new.

I watched as a change moved across Matt's face while he spoke to Lance. Matt was a lifelong cycling fan who had covered this story for years, but I spotted a reaction in him that I'd noticed many times when people came into contact with Lance. He was nervous, awestruck.

We ordered wine and I sat back, happy to let the lads do their thing. Lance talked about the Union Cycliste Internationale (UCI, the sport's governing body), about the unfairness of his lifetime ban, about his sorrow.

'When it comes to the ban from competitive sport, people don't want to hear Lance Armstrong complaining that he has been treated unfairly,' he said. 'I made my bed. I have to sleep in it. And I have to get to grips with that.'

After the photographer got his pictures, Lance wanted to go for dinner privately, just the two of us. This was the real reason

I'd agreed to come all this way. To get away from the cameras, away from journalists, leave the circus behind and just be two people again. Face to face.

We headed out of the hotel. Lance being Lance, he had plans already. 'There's a great place twenty minutes' drive away,' he said.

'Hey, let's just go somewhere close by instead?' I suggested.

Stepping into the warm night air, Lance glanced down at my feet. 'Sure glad I'm not a girl, so I don't have to wear heels,' he joked.

I found myself laughing. 'It's really good to see you again,' I admitted.

By the time we'd walked the block to a restaurant called Mama Louis it was as if all the subpoenas, court cases, affidavits, accusations and name-calling had melted away. It was as it always had been between me and Lance. Easy.

When we walked into the restaurant, I sensed heads turn and diners nod at each other behind menus.

Look! Is that Lance Armstrong? God, yeah it is.

'Wine, Emma?' Lance smiled.

'Go on then.'

Lance looked at me. 'You know, I *am* sorry—' he began.

I held my hand up. Lance had already apologized by text. We'd spoken on the phone and he'd said that he was sorry then too.

'Lance, I didn't come all this way to have you apologize again. I'm not here to have you humiliate yourself. I don't need my ego placated. To be quite honest, I feel as if I should say sorry to you too. I feel bad for the way things happened, the way it worked out. You were not the only bad guy in this . . .' I trailed off, thinking of all the painful years I'd endured.

We avoided each other's eyes and looked down at our menus. Neither of us liked warm, fuzzy conversations that much, I remembered.

'Whatcha havin'?' Lance asked. 'I'm starving.'

With food on its way we relaxed.

'What about your girlfriend? How's she coping?' I asked. Anna Hansen and Lance now had two children together.

'Yeah, she's great, managing just fine,' he said. 'I'm getting on well with my ex, Kik, too.'

'And the kids?' I asked, thinking of the part in Lance's *Oprah* interview where he had described how he had to tell his eleven-year-old twin girls and thirteen-year-old son that he'd lied. 'Stop standing up for your dad now,' he'd said to his son Luke.

'They're resilient. It was hardest on Luke, but nobody's bullied him. None of their friends' parents have stopped them from coming on play dates. We're lucky.'

A ripple of emotion passed across his face.

'You know, if Luke ever came home and said those words I called you, Emma – like I say, there'd be a fucking war in our house.' He stopped himself from going further.

There and then I realized Lance had not wasted the past year. He genuinely had done some soul-searching. His contrition wasn't an act, I could tell. For Lance, this was deep.

'Thank you,' I said quietly.

We each took a large swig of wine.

'You know, the person this was hardest on was my boyfriend at the time. Mike,' I said. 'He has MS, Lance, and the stress made his health suffer terribly. A month after you sued me he was walking with a stick; six months later he was in a wheelchair. And if someone had said those things about your girlfriend, you'd want to thump them.'

Lance looked visibly shocked. 'MS? I'd no idea, Emma,' he said. 'I'm sorry. How's he doing now?'

When our meals finally arrived one salad was far bigger than the other and I assumed it was Lance's until it was placed in front of me.

'Ohhhhh,' he said, his face falling. 'I thought that was for me!' He glanced up at the waitress. 'Can I change my order and have one of those, please?'

I laughed. Lance wanting the best. Nothing had changed.

'Certainly, Mr Armstrong – and just to let you know, it's a pleasure to have you here, and if there is anything else you need please let me know,' she said, almost curtseying at the end.

'Wow,' I whispered as she walked away. 'Is that the response people give you still? Nobody has a go at you?'

'Nope,' he said. 'Not out on the street anyway. I get a lot of stick on Twitter and email, but thankfully to my face people are really supportive still.'

The empire Lance had built up quickly crumbled after he was branded a serial cheat in the United States Anti-Doping Agency (USADA) report that, in 2012, called the actions of the US Postal team in which he rode and for which I worked, 'the most sophisticated, professionalized and successful doping program that sport has ever seen'. He was currently being chased for $100 million in a series of legal cases, including one brought by the US Justice Department, which had teamed up in a 'whistleblower' lawsuit with a former teammate, Floyd Landis.

'We're having to pay for inflation too,' Lance explained. 'I've offered a huge sum to Floyd but he says it's not enough.'

Lance's face fell as he talked about the closure of Capital Sports and Entertainment, the company he had set up with his long-time manager, Bill Stapleton. 'It's the collateral damage done by the USADA report,' he sighed. 'Fifteen people lost their jobs. Gone. And having to leave Livestrong was the toughest thing for me.'

I waited for him to speak again.

'I understand, Emma, why people hate me,' he said eventually. 'I was a monster who got out of control.'

This wasn't the old Lance I knew, with his fists up against the whole world. This flicker of what I felt was genuine regret and introspection told me he had changed since being stripped of his seven Tour de France titles. This was a man who knew he'd done wrong and deserved to be punished. This was a man who knew he'd acted like a complete prick.

'In many ways, Lance,' I began, thinking of all the people who had let me down, or who had manipulated me for their own purposes, 'I bear you less ill will than many others in this whole sorry story.'

He cast his familiar intense gaze at me, and I hoped he understood the depth of my forgiveness.

'I don't deserve that, Emma, but I thank you for it,' he replied.

1

The Beginning of the Race

'GO ON, GET IN! I'll help you!'

His emphasis on the word 'help' told me this was the last thing my older brother, Norbert, planned to do. A shove between the shoulder blades confirmed my fears as I plopped like a stone into the freezing water of the River Dodder, near our home in Tallaght, Ireland. Cycling my legs frantically, I bobbed to the surface.

'Norbert! Help!' I screamed.

'C'mon then,' he laughed, swiftly pulling me out. 'You're such a girl, Emma O'Reilly!'

Spluttering, I went to give chase, but he was off, running across the fields, knowing full well I'd never catch up. I couldn't be annoyed for long, though. He was my much adored big brother and, growing up in Tallaght, a sprawling working-class area of estates in south Dublin, having an older brother could only be a bonus.

Way before me, Norbert learned to ride a bike, teasing me mercilessly when I couldn't join him. Not until I was seven did I pluck up enough courage to try – a ripe old age for a kid in

7

our area to learn. But I was a 'chicken' – I didn't take risks that might involve getting hurt.

In the end it wasn't Norbert but our dad, Nobby O'Reilly, who coaxed me on to a piece of 1970s junk and wheeled the bike halfway down the hill near our estate one Sunday morning.

'You still holding on, Da?' I screamed as we picked up speed.

'Sure, Em, I'm still holding on,' he replied, his voice dissolving into the distance. The split second of realization that he was no longer holding me turned my terror into joy: suddenly I could ride a bike by myself.

'Wheeeeeeeeeeeeeee!' I cheered. It's a sound only a child can make after discovering a new form of freedom.

And freedom it was. Shortly afterwards, Norbert got a Chopper for his birthday and most weekends we would take off, racing around roads that back then were much quieter than they are now. We were true kids of the seventies.

I'm the middle child of three. My sister Clare arrived four years after me. Mammy and Dad had married in 1965 and even as kids we could see how much they were in love. My dad liked a pint of Smithwick's and was a law unto himself, bless him. Rules were 'guidelines' in his eyes. If there was a double yellow line, he'd park on it; if he could get away without getting insurance, he'd not pay for it. Once he was stopped by a copper for drink-driving – an incredible feat considering drink-driving wasn't a crime in Ireland at the time. No, Nobby answered to nothing and nobody, except our mammy, Terry. What Mammy said went and Nobby never crossed her. He daren't, but besides, he loved her too much.

For Mammy, family was everything. She was a traditional housewife, so the moment Dad returned home from work, dinner landed on the table of our utterly spotless three-bed semi. But that wasn't her only role in life. Mammy drove a car – rare for a woman in those days – and helped run Dad's catering business. Back then venues needed to serve food in order to obtain a late bar licence, so my parents had a chip van and would travel for miles to events. They were a good team: Dad was the ideas guy while Mammy grafted next to him. We were far from rich, but we kids had the best they could afford – the best clothes, the best food, the best of everything.

Mammy's sisters all lived in more upmarket parts of Dublin and didn't approve of her decision to settle in Tallaght to bring up her family. We were the black sheep, but to Mammy all that mattered was that we were happy, be it in Tallaght or wherever. To me, she was my hero and I never wanted to leave her side.

'Will you go and play, Emma, and leave me be?' she'd laugh, as I followed her from room to room. A quiet child, I liked routine, and that meant having her close. With her skin soft as sand, I loved sitting on her lap to have a cuddle, although she'd never let me touch her shoulder; she had a birthmark there so sensitive it made her shudder.

We were brought up Catholic, although neither Mammy nor Dad practised the faith at home, leaving all lessons in fire and brimstone to the strict nuns at our primary school.

One Saturday morning, Norbert was told to take me to school for running practice, but instead we stopped to play on the seesaw in a local park. Bumping me up and down, higher and higher, my brother laughed his head off until my screams of fear turned to pain as I bounced headfirst on to the seesaw handle.

'Emma!' Norbert cried, switching back into protective big brother mode, fearing he'd get the blame. I was bloody and bruised, but he begged me not to tell Mammy or Dad. On the Monday, when the nuns spotted my swollen eyes, one particular witch known as Sister Brenda had little sympathy.

'You deserved that,' she scolded. 'You defied us, skipping your running training like that. And now you've been punished by God.'

I hung my head over the desk, riddled with self-pity and guilt, wondering if I should mention this in confession later.

Mammy often went into hospital for ulcers and gallstones, and she complained of headaches. After one visit to the doctor she came home grumbling.

'I don't want to be taking high-blood-pressure pills,' I overheard her complain to Dad. 'They'll do no good.'

'Okay, if you can manage without them,' Dad agreed. He was never going to disagree with her anyway.

Soon after, I was watching her pack up boxes to go and work at the Tallaght Festival. 'Mammy,' I said, tapping her arm. 'Can I come?'

'No, Emma! It'll be a late night.'

'Can *I* help then?' asked Norbert.

'Not you, Norbert, either,' she chided.

'But why?' I protested. Mammy was letting one of the neighbours' kids down the road help out and he was the same age as my brother.

'Ah,' said Mammy, looking me straight in the eye. 'No child of mine is serving chips at a festival and let that be the end of it.'

With Mammy's decision made clear, we said goodbye as she and Dad left for the evening. 'See you tomorrow,' she said.

The next day, I woke to a strangely quiet house, with no Mammy clattering in the kitchen making breakfast. As I went back upstairs to look for her, Dad told me she had fallen ill on the way home last night and was in hospital.

'Will she be okay, Dad?' I asked.

'I hope so, Emma,' he replied.

When I was dressed, I found Norbert outside with Dad on the driveway, wiping away tears.

'What's wrong?' I asked.

'Nothing,' replied Dad. 'Norbert's hurt himself, that's all.'

My big brother was always falling out of trees or grazing himself coming off his bike, yet I'd never seen him cry before. Soon after, the doorbell went and in streamed various aunties, all anxious to get the kettle on, all with the same expression as Dad.

Two days later, Dad came home from hospital, his eyes hollow with a pain I'd never seen before.

'Mammy has died,' he announced. 'She had a brain haemorrhage while we were walking the mile home from the Tallaght Festival and then another one the next day. There was nothing the doctors could do.'

I stared, dumbfounded, as Dad's eyes welled up.

'Before the doctors switched off her machine,' he cried, 'I squeezed her birthmark hard and she didn't so much as flinch, so I knew she must be gone, Emma.'

Mammy. Gone.

I was eight years old and it was as though a heavy fog of grief had dropped on me from a great height, its dark cloak numbing my world.

For us three kids, the next few days were a blur of aunties and neighbours coming and going, bringing over casseroles and helping Dad in the house. Our poor dad. He'd his work cut out for him. He had no clue how even to use the oven. His working life also changed drastically, because he had to give up travelling to and from festivals to be home for us. For a while he took a job as a chef in a hospital instead.

Mammy's clothes disappeared and soon there was almost nothing left but memories. We kids never spoke about what had happened. It was too painful. Thankfully, though, Dad made sure we never forgot. As I grew up, missing Mammy terribly, Dad would tell me how much I reminded him of her.

'Terry knew her mind, Emma, so she did. You're so much like your mam.' When he said it, his face was full of the memory of their love.

My training as a *soigneur* began early. The word means 'someone who takes care of things' and, as the oldest girl in the house, my mornings started with making breakfast, the fire and the beds. After school it was dinners, washing, tidying, shopping. Dad needed me and I was determined to be there.

With Mammy gone, we grew closer to Dad, and I developed his and Norbert's love of professional cycling. Every July for half an hour a day we were glued to the Tour de France on TV, enthralled by the drama of each stage, the agony of the climbs, the beauty of the backdrop. How envious we were of the crowds who got to stand so close to see the riders in the toughest race in the world fly by.

Money was very tight, which we knew full well every time Dad asked us to push the car up the hill when it ran out of petrol, or hide from the milkman when he tried to get us to settle our bill. Determined to buy his own racing bike, however, Norbert saved up from his Saturday job, then immediately joined the Irish Road Club, one of the best-known and longest-running cycling clubs in Ireland.

By now, aged eleven, I'd joined Cuchalann Running Club with my best friend, Sharon, but as soon as I was old enough I followed Norbert into cycling, joining a club called Rentokil. From there we moved to the Emerald-sponsored Carlsberg team, landing ourselves cool jerseys to wear. The club was run by the McQuaids. Pat McQuaid, who went on to be UCI president, was one of ten kids and they were a larger-than-life, cycling-obsessed family, determined to put Ireland on the map.

For me, running and cycling were social activities rather than competitive sports. I was never very good at dealing with the pain every cyclist experiences; when lactic acid burned my muscles and my chest felt as if it would explode, I always slowed the pace. Although I did well running the 800 metres and managed to win a couple of cycling races and medals now and then, I definitely saw myself as Miss Average.

Eventually, I fell more in love with cycling than with athletics, as there was a democracy in the sport and no sense of hierarchy. Unlike in running, winners and losers hung out together after cycling races; it was a true team sport. I had posters of Sean Kelly above my bed instead of Spandau Ballet, but I didn't care that this made me a geek. My sister, Clare, gave up on me in disgust when she realized I'd much rather lust after a man on a bike than a man with a guitar.

'You're just a pair of squares,' she cried when Norbert insisted on catching up with the Tour on TV instead of watching soaps.

Cycling at weekends was a wonderful way to spend my teenage years and I much preferred mashing pedals up and down to sitting in a classroom. In 1984 we watched in amazement as Greg LeMond rode the Tour and came third in support of his team leader, winning the white jersey for Best Young Rider. The Tour de France was no longer just for Europeans. America had arrived, and Greg's poster joined my other heroes on the bedroom walls.

My running coach was well connected, though, and managed to secure me a couple of scholarships in America, one in Eugene, Oregon – the place where Nike started – and another in Villanova, Pennsylvania. Dad was beside himself with excitement.

'It's a great opportunity, Emma,' he said proudly. But when I shrugged my shoulders his face fell.

'Aw, Dad, I prefer cycling,' I explained.

Poor Dad was furious, especially with Norbert. 'This is your fault,' he cried. 'Getting Emma into cycling when she could've made something of herself with running.'

Turning down the opportunity felt easy, but I needed to think of something else to do. When I left school at sixteen there was no way Dad could afford for me to go to college so, after rattling through various options in my mind, I settled on applying to be an electrician. You got free training and a guaranteed job – perfect. The fact that the industry was dominated by men never entered my head.

Without telling Dad, I did an aptitude test; there were only four women taking it out of a total of five hundred people. I passed with flying colours and broke the news back home.

'An *electrician*!' Dad cried, his eyes rolling almost into the back of his skull. 'You can't be a tradesman, Emma!'

'No?' I smiled. 'But Dad, I've got a place on the course.'

Incensed, Dad brought his friend Eddie Byrne round and thrust his chapped, dirt-stained hands in front of me. 'Look, Emma,' he said. 'See what happens when you take up a trade.'

'But being an electrician isn't a dirty trade,' I argued.

Dad had to admit I was right. As much as he was appalled by my career choice, out of all the trades it was the cleanest.

Straight away I settled into a year of training at a government centre, working entirely with lads after the only other girl on the course dropped out. It never bothered me, as I loved the craic. They were all like big brothers. I had my own rules: don't curse or tell dirty jokes yourself and then you can tell the lads off for doing it. My philosophy seemed to work. I could banter with the lads, but always got shown respect.

A year later we were transferred to Davenham Engineering in Dublin to complete our training. I suspected I wasn't going to be the world's best electrician, but I knew I'd have a job at the end, so I carried on. One afternoon we were all working over electrical board panels on a big desk when some of the lads began looking over my shoulder and laughing. I turned to see that a load of Page Three posters had been pinned up on the wall behind me. Taking a deep breath, I rolled my eyes and stood, hands on hips.

'Okay, lads,' I said. 'Yous all have a good gawp at the wall behind me, then go move them elsewhere, like in the toilet, so's not to embarrass me, okay?'

Jokes were made about never coming out of the loo, so I laughed along, and an hour later the posters had vanished and my faith in the guys had been restored.

By the time I was nineteen, I longed to go away on holiday, something aside from the caravan to Wexford where we usually went as a family. But with no money to spare after helping Dad with the household bills, it was out of the question. Then I hit on the idea of volunteering as a massage therapist for a cycling team, so I could see a bit of the country.

I found a college with a massage course held at weekends and signed up. While other girls on the course were training to work in gyms or beauty clinics, I was aiming for cycle races, hoping someone would take me on. And my plan worked. After getting my certificate, I managed to wangle a place volunteering at a nine-day amateur race called An Post Rás with the Telecom team. Afterwards their manager, Kevin Eccles, kindly got on to Alasdair MacLennan from the Irish National team to say, 'Take Emma, she's great!'

So, initially on an ad hoc basis, I became the soigneur for the Irish Nationals – a bit of a coup. Their mechanic was Tony Campbell, whom I always knew as TC, and the two of us became our own little dysfunctional but tight team. Put simply, the soigneur is the person on a cycling team who really does everything that needs doing. Not only was I massaging around six riders a day, but I'd be washing up water bottles, preparing food and clothes for races and booking hotel rooms. Whatever they needed, I'd do it, and I loved every minute. If behind the scenes it was organized chaos, on the track we were doing very well, even surprising a lot of people at the World Championships in 1991 in Stuttgart, doing better than expected for a team that wasn't very prominent in international cycling at the time. Not only was I having fun but, more importantly, I was also getting to travel abroad for the first time.

But however comfortable I felt with the lads, at times it was mortifying being the only girl. At a five-day amateur race, called the ESSO Breton Tour, in 1992, we found ourselves having to stay in an old barracks, with dorms to sleep in and communal showers. Cringing inside, I had to ask TC to stay and hold the shower-room door shut while I nipped in for a panicked wash alone.

Being part of the pro-am racing scene was an eye-opener. Years earlier, probably as soon as I was old enough to understand what doping was, I had realized taking performance-enhancing substances was an underground part of the sport. There were even whispers about our hero Sean Kelly, but nobody talked much about it. Naturally you knew there would be more doping among the pros, especially on the European teams. Lads who rode for French amateur clubs always raised eyebrows. If they'd made it in France, something was very likely going on, because competition was so fierce there that it was just assumed their riders were doping. This was all suggested, although none of it was either proven or disproven. The on-going joke about any champion was: 'They must know a good pharmacy.'

We referred to this as 'not normal'. If a rider took off like a rocket, or behaved in some strange way, we knew what was likely to be behind it. One year during the Milk Race, the pre-cursor to the Tour of Britain, I heard how a particular rider, unable to control an aggressive rage, came to fist fights all over the shop with various staff. We knew full well it was likely to be amphetamines behind his sudden mood swings.

'Not normal,' the lads muttered on the massage table after-wards.

'Yep,' I agreed. There was always plenty of talk about doping, but I wanted to keep out of it. Drugs held no interest for me.

During another race everyone talked about a UK rider test-ing positive for Ecstasy, a new drug on the scene, but nothing came of it. That was the thing: it was brushed away as fast as the subject was brought up. It was so easy to ignore.

In 1992 the Irish National team were doing exceptionally well in the Milk Race. Our main rider, Conor Henry, won the yellow jersey and just had to hold on to it for a few days to win the race. As he sped across the finish line in Lincoln after the final stage, the feeling was both surreal and incredible. Our team had won, the lads had done it. As excited and proud as I was, I always saw victory as belonging to the riders. They did all the training and hard work. We were just there to support them.

At that Milk Race, I also made a promise to myself never to get involved with any of the riders. I had got a bit friendly with a few of them, only to hear back some stories about myself that were nuts. Learning to keep a distance then can only have been a good thing.

It was a year later, at the 1993 World Cycling Championships in Norway, that I heard about a new boy wonder, a brash, cocky Texan who'd been tipped to win gold at the Olympics the year before and now, at twenty-two, was slaughtering the opposition. We all heard stories of how he'd even turned up at races with 'Mum' written unapologetically on his T-shirt as a sponsor. I listened to other riders speaking of his phenomenal energy, drive and arrogance.

'He doesn't shut up,' said one of them. 'You should hear him sounding off about being the next big thing.'

'He sounds like a character,' I said.

His name was Lance Armstrong.

2

Another Planet

I FELT HIS PRESENCE BEFORE actually seeing him for the first time. Lance's drawl echoed in the hotel dining room as he asked for an extra portion of pasta and chicken. He then swaggered to his seat, talking and laughing louder than anyone in the room.

'Alpha male,' I thought, as I scuttled past him clutching my plate, head down, shy as ever.

At five foot eight, Lance was on the small side, but stocky with it. His chest was always a little puffed out and he never seemed still, talking non-stop. My instinct was: avoid. Like I did all the so-called rising stars or new champions of the sport. If you sucked up to the riders you were known as a 'chamois sniffer' and that wasn't my scene. Many of the staff on cycling teams were frustrated ex-pro riders, or fans who'd got a lucky gig. As much as riders were like rock stars to me when I was younger, I saw them in a different light now. Chatting over a massage, you got to know their personalities, their likes and dislikes, their human side.

Sometimes I'd crack up inside, smiling to myself as I observed this crazy little planet I'd landed on. The circus of men in Lycra, clipping around in their cleats, taking themselves and winning so very seriously. As much as I loved racing, it was only ever riding a bike to me. I always rooted for my team, but it could never be more than a sport.

Besides, I knew my place as the geeky, quiet soigneur girl who needed to get on with her job. It was a tough job, too, always thinking ahead, making preparations for the next day. Several times TC yelled at me after I'd left the water bottles soaking in Milton bleach solution in the bath after a race and he'd been desperate for a wash after getting in late. Although we would have a chuckle about it later, I wanted to get everything right. Being a soigneur was just a hobby, but I was still anxious to do the best job I could.

The massage part of my work I found enormously satisfying. Where else can you get a captive audience for an hour in one room? I liked the sociable side of it, but there was more to it than that. I liked the power of a massage: it feeds the system and takes away the waste – by which I mean it helps create new blood cells and drains the lymphatic system. All from human touch. By manipulating the muscles, not only do you increase the blood circulation, but also there's the side effect of slowing the heart rate and breathing, so the body starts to relax, even involuntarily.

I always did the riders' legs first, then, depending on what type of race stage they'd done, I focused on other parts of the body. For time trials they'd need attention on their hamstrings. If they were doing a climb, their arms were tired. By the end of races, they were more tired from straining over the handlebars and braking, so shoulders and backs needed pummelling. The muscle tells you so much. Without asking, I knew just by touch whether they'd had a bad day. If the muscle felt empty, it meant they had nothing left for the next day. If there was something left, they had more to give.

I only ever gave them forty minutes' attention. Sometimes the lads would keep me talking to get me to do more, or they'd even say, 'Emma, I think you've cut me short!' but actually I had to be vigilant on time for a reason. Any longer than forty minutes and the muscles would start to need extra time to recover from the massage itself, leaving them sluggish the next day. Recovery in a bike race is everything: how fast you recover is the key to enduring a race, especially, as I would soon discover, a three-week Grand Tour.

The final day of the 1993 World Championships was incredibly miserable, wet and dreary. Lance Armstrong, though, rode with a ferocious energy, and he roared with victory at the finish. A cocky twenty-two-year-old kid wasn't meant to win, not the senior Worlds, not on such a filthy dirty day, but he'd done it.

'Fair play to him,' I thought. And, as thoughts go, that's as far as mine went on the new champion. Never in a million years would I have dreamed that our paths would even cross again, let alone the rest of what was to come.

By 1993 I'd been working for the Irish National team for about four years part-time, covering the Milk Race, the Tour de l'Avenir (the race for the stars of the future), ESSO Breton Tour and the Worlds. It was then that a mechanic called Brian Davies, who had just joined the LA Sheriff team in California, recommended me to them. It was a year-long contract, paid, and it meant travel in the States. A dream come true. I accepted.

Before my flight, I had to sort out a visa; at that time you couldn't even go from Ireland to the USA on holiday without one. After everything to do with the job was signed and sealed, all I needed was the formality of the stamp. I gave up my electrician's job and rented flat, then merrily wandered down to the visa office to see to the last bit of red tape. But as the lady there eyed my application, she pursed her lips. 'An electrician *and* a massage therapist, are we?' she asked, eyebrows shooting to her hairline.

'Er, yeah . . . ?' I began, not liking her tone.

She shoved my application roughly back at me. 'Pull the other fast one,' she laughed. 'Next!'

I stood there, cheeks flushed, wondering what on earth had just happened, but I could see there was no point in arguing with a jobsworth. The visa lady had made her decision not to believe that I was a masseuse and it was too late to get the paperwork over from LA Sheriff before the start of their season. It felt like my American dream was over before it had begun.

For the next few months I stayed with my Auntie Kathleen, but thankfully it wasn't long before the dream was rekindled. Brian got a job with another pro-am team, Shaklee, and recommended me for a second time, and just at that time I won a US Green Card in a lottery. So that spring of 1994, a few weeks before I turned twenty-four, I found myself on a flight to Boulder, Colorado.

It was a scary move. I had no money to speak of and in this job I wouldn't be getting paid either, but the lads were generous, giving a full split of their winnings to the rest of the team. At first I stayed in Brian's house, but then one day the phone rang. I couldn't get to it in time before it went to answerphone, so I called the number back. The voice I heard was that of a lad I'd been seeing back in Ireland.

'Emma!' he gasped as I picked up the receiver. 'Where've you been? I've been worried sick!'

'What do you mean? I've been working,' I replied.

'But I've left loads of messages and nobody ever got back to me!' he insisted.

Starting to feel a bit sick, I apologized, then confronted Brian, who rolled his eyes. 'Oh, those calls,' he said. 'I thought he was some weirdo bugging you.'

One of the riders then told me that his girlfriend Sarah had a spare room in her apartment, and the next morning I was standing with my worldly goods, which consisted of a suitcase and a massage table, outside her house in Boulder. Luckily she welcomed me with open arms and became my treasured room-mate for four years.

Boulder was a fabulous place to be in your twenties. In be-tween working hard as the lads trained, the team staff cycled, hiked in summer and skied in winter. We ate out loads and spent half our time in coffee shops when we weren't working. It was as if the sun was always shining.

Two years later, a rider called Michael Engleman moved to Montgomery-Bell, a team sponsored by Montgomery Securities – a burglar alarm company, I assumed – and put in a good word for me there. 'You're efficient and cool, Emma, I'm sure they'd love you on board,' he said. They were bigger than Shaklee, so I happily agreed.

The move to Montgomery-Bell – which would soon become the US Postal Service Pro-Cycling Team after they'd signed a $4.5 million deal – would be a massive promotion. This was a serious business, run by the former Olympic champion Mark Gorski along with an investment banker and entrepreneur called Thom Weisel. Compared to the other teams I'd worked with so far, the difference was night and day.

That Christmas I was going home to Ireland and wasn't due to return to the States until the date the training camp for the team now known as US Postal Service was supposed to start, but I still hadn't heard anything from them about an interview. Taking the bull by the horns, I sent a message, leaving my number in case they wanted to get in touch. A day later someone from US Postal rang.

'We've arranged a flight to San Francisco for you and a taxi to pick you up,' a voice said. No messing. Very professional.

Luckily, before I flew to California I got chatting to a mechanic who'd also had an interview with the team. I mentioned my plan to wear jeans for my interview. Casual was best, I thought. He laughed out loud. 'Emma, you'd better smarten up for this interview, dude. Montgomery Securities is a bank, not a burglar alarm company.' Pre-warned, I raided Sarah's wardrobe.

When the taxi dropped me off, I smoothed my skirt and jacket gratefully. Here I was, standing outside the most iconic, coolest building in San Francisco, the Transamerica Pyramid. 'Oh. My. God,' I thought, squinting up as the sun glinted off the glass. 'I'm just a girl from Tallaght.'

This vibrant, exciting city was everything I'd ever dreamed America could be and I made a vow to myself that once I'd finished with cycling, I'd move here.

A lift whisked me from reception to the company office on the twenty-first floor, where Mark Gorski, the team's general manager, and Diana Sangston, Thom Weisel's right-hand lady, introduced themselves. I recognized Mark from when he'd won his gold medal for track cycling in Los Angeles in 1984. We shook hands, and Diana showed me the staggeringly beautiful view from her office window.

'It's amazing,' I said. Money talks and wealth whispers, I thought, and this was whispering to me.

We sat down and, with a quiet confidence, Mark told me about their new venture and the high hopes he had for this US

Postal team. Twenty-five men strong, the new team planned to send their best riders to compete in Europe. The aim was to accumulate enough points in the UCI system to qualify for the Tour de France. Getting the green light for the toughest race of them all would mean that US Postal would be a serious rival to America's current biggest team, Motorola.

I was impressed.

Mark also mentioned a women's team, but I knew I'd rather work with the men. At Shaklee I'd never been much good with hormonal tears. 'Don't say anything, Emma,' I thought to myself. 'You might not even get the job.' As usual, though, I wasn't able to keep quiet for long and I told Mark that I'd prefer joining the lads.

He nodded, and then, with the team's PR manager, Dan Osipow, took me out to lunch in the smart financial district. As much as I liked Mark, I couldn't fully warm to a guy who was going to control my destiny, so I remained polite and enthusiastic, minding my Ps and Qs. At the end he said he'd be in touch.

Two days later, Dan rang me. 'We'd be delighted to have you on board, Emma,' he said.

'I'd be delighted to join you,' I replied.

This was a life-changing moment – even if back then, as I put the phone down, I could never envisage just how much.

Back home, it was a huge relief to be telling Dad I had a proper paid job to return to. He and Norbert said they were proud too because I was working in a sport they loved. Some of my aunties weren't as impressed.

'A swan what?' asked one.

'A "*swan–your*",' I joked, helping her pronounce it. 'A soigneur. It's French for looking after people, and I will look after the riders.'

'But Emma, are you going to get paid enough to live off doing this?' worried another.

I laughed. True, it wasn't the greatest wage in the world, but it was enough to pay my way. Alasdair and TC were happy for me too. 'It's all thanks to your tutelage, guys,' I told them.

So in January 1996 I flew back to Boulder and then straight out again to a training camp in a one-horse town called Ramona, about an hour's drive from San Diego near the Mexican border. I was nervous meeting all the big names – not just the riders, but also the *directeur sportif* (DS), Eddie Borysewicz, who was a legend I'd read about as a child. Even just saying hello to him was something to me. This was a man who had worked with Greg LeMond and it didn't get much bigger than that.

Known as Eddie B, because the Americans couldn't pronounce his surname, he was a real character and had largely been responsible for bringing the States to world prominence back in the 1980s, even though he spoke barely a word of English. Originally from Poland, Eddie's Eastern-Bloc style of management changed the face of American cycling. He was the first person to point out when riders were overweight, or weren't pedalling efficiently. Eddie started the revolution.

Back in 1990, it was Eddie B who had signed a nineteen-year-old Lance Armstrong to join what was then the Subaru-Montgomery team, but after clashing with Thom Weisel the young rider didn't last long. Rumour had it that the pair were just too alike, too hot-headed. Now our biggest name was Andy Hampsten, a tough climber, and with him and other potentially world-beating riders like Tyler Hamilton, Eddy Gragus and Sven Teutenberg, our hopes of breaking into Europe were real. To begin with there was also another female soigneur on the team: Alison, the sister of rider Darren Baker, although she was to stay for only one season.

During this time I got to know some of the riders very well. Tyler Hamilton was a favourite, a handsome guy from Marblehead in Massachusetts with a willingness to 'dig in' like I'd never seen before. 'Digging in' is the expression used when you watch a rider keep going long after they've hit the wall of exhaustion, of pain. Tyler wasn't just a committed athlete, he was an all-American boy with a naturally sunny, polite nature. He was good fun to hang out with, and a group of us would all go to the pictures together.

Cycling is a tough sport – broken bones and bruises are common – so every team has a doctor and ours was a cheerful guy called Dr Prentice Steffen. Along with soigneurs, doctors aided the riders' recovery after races, sometimes by injecting vitamin supplements, a practice that was par for the course in Europe. It was also an open secret in the cycling world that doctors on the biggest teams led 'medical programmes', the subtext being that they provided riders with 'help', in other words banned stimulants. As we were just an up-and-coming team, I didn't think we'd follow that route, or at least I hoped not.

We stayed in the cheesy Ramona Inn alongside Sizzler, a generic barbecue joint where we ate every evening. A few days into camp, Thom Weisel turned up, resplendent in a sharp suit. With his swept-back grey hair and hard stare, Thom wasn't the most remarkable-looking man in the world, but he made up for it in the way he carried himself and spoke. I've always said Thom Weisel makes Lance look like a pussy cat. A powerful financier, he'd set up a new bank at the age of fifty-four, sacking investors who offered even half a million dollars because it 'wasn't enough' for him. He was also good mates with Steve Forbes, a guy who that year was running as a presidential candidate.

When Thom started talking, a hush fell over the restaurant.

'We're here. We've arrived. We're gonna do this,' he began, punching the air. According to Thom, we were set to be the biggest team in the States, in Europe, in the world. Looking the riders individually in the eyes, he said he wanted one day to win the biggest race of them all, the Tour de France. As we sat there with wafts of spare ribs and grease under our noses, success in the likes of the prestigious Tour felt a million miles away. Yet with Thom's words ringing in our ears, anything seemed possible.

'Go get 'em!' he cried, wrapping up his speech. 'You're gonna be big!'

'Frigging hell, Emma,' I thought to myself. 'If this guy says it's gonna be big, it's gonna be big.'

3

The Missing Link

'I'M GOOD AT PAIN' are the opening words of Tyler Hamilton's award-winning book *The Secret Race*. He goes on to give a fascinating explanation of how hard an endurance sport cycling is. And how hard a pro rider needs to be.

Cycling doesn't pound the joints like other sports, so this means muscles and aerobic fitness can be pushed to their limits. It's tougher than climbing Mount Everest. A pro cyclist will ride enough miles in training alone to circumnavigate the globe, reaching the edge of human capacity. So what sort of athlete elects to put themselves through this? In Europe, traditionally it was working-class kids who grew up using cycling as a cheap form of transport, but for these American lads it was a wealthy sport to get involved with. This was because it was costly to travel to different cycle events across the States, and of course the equipment was expensive too; a decent racing bike didn't come cheap. Although Lance was an exception, most of the boys were from fairly middle-class backgrounds.

Only certain personality types choose such a painful sport. Whether it's been the loss of a parent or another life-changing incident, many riders have something to prove, either to themselves or to others. The nerdy image of cycling belies the tough interior you need in order to survive. There is no doubt that it was also a macho world, and when you then throw in a few old-school characters it's no surprise that sexism was part and parcel of it.

As much as I respected him, I quickly learned that Eddie B was one of those types, as well as being a nutcase of a manager. I decided he meant nothing by it, but he would constantly shout 'Lady! Lady!' as he ushered me over for a lecture on something or other. 'Now listen, Lady!' One day as he was lecturing me on my driving I decided I'd had enough.

'I'm not your fucking lady. My name is Emma. Just remember to call me Emma in the future,' I shouted back at him.

He flinched, then grinned and wisely changed the subject. 'Emma, I know what it is you need, he-he-he . . .' he hinted.

I just laughed in his face. 'Yeah, Eddie B. Yeah, yeah.'

Another time he approached me while I was on my way to the washing machines, laden with laundry.

'Listen, Lady, I've a good joke for you,' he said.

'Go on then,' I sighed.

'Do you like sex?'

I sighed again. 'I've heard it's okay.'

'You like hiking?'

'Yeah, sure, I love hiking.'

'Well go take a fucking hike.' He erupted with laughter.

I laughed along. God love him, I could do nothing else. Only in cycling could a boss tell you a joke like that. He was one fearsome coach, however, with a focus on team effort rather than individuals.

In February we all set off for Uruguay, travelling in the back of a battered 1930s open-topped van that acted as our 'tour bus'. It was a memorable experience. We performed well and spirits were high, until it became clear that the Uruguayan team managers weren't going to let us win the race. We ended up demanding the win money up front in exchange for allowing the home team to claim they were champions. Insane!

The travel made me long even more for Europe, and in April that year I got my chance to go to Belgium for six weeks. For me, Europe was the place where the most exciting, elite races took place, with riders at the top of their game; plus I longed to see the world, and in Europe there was a sense of romance and culture I missed in the States.

As much as I was determined to travel and fit in, there was nothing I could do to tolerate the team's head soigneur, Waldek Stepniowski. A tall Polish ex-cyclist, he had an interesting story of how he had escaped his communist homeland, running from a hotel in the night while on tour and claiming political asylum in the United States. But as big as his heart was, he was also an enormous sexist, albeit in a different way to Eddie B.

One afternoon I was walking past the team truck while he was chatting to another soigneur in Polish, and I could see him weighing me up, his eyes rolling up and down my legs. Cheeky beggar, I thought.

'Right,' I said, determined to face him. 'Don't you *ever* talk like that about me again.'

'Hey, whaddya mean?' Waldek cried, his palms high in the air.

'I know what you're doing,' I continued. 'If you're going to speak about me, then do it behind my back at least.'

'No idea what you're on about,' he hissed, making it obvious he did.

A few days later he was giving me more sideways glances as he stood with some other lads.

'Emma, I need to talk to you,' he said.

'Yes?'

'I need to know what time of month it is for you, so if you're hormonal we can understand it.'

'Waldek,' I began, 'at least if I'm in a bad mood I've a reason. What's your friggin' excuse?'

Wanting to nip all of this in the bud, if not for my own sake then at least for the reputation of the team, I rang Mark Gorski to explain the situation.

'I don't want to kick up a fuss,' I said, 'but at the end of the day American women wouldn't tolerate Waldek speaking to them like that, you know what I mean?'

Mark listened intently and after that Waldek never said another word to me.

Inevitably, I ended up back on the rota to cover smaller races stateside. Aside from Motorola, we were the strongest team in the US, doing well in the CoreStates, as the US National Championships are known, and also in the Tour DuPont. This was a big razzle-dazzle affair, set up as North America's answer to the Tour de France, and it attracted a certain crowd with it. One of the pretty girls who was volunteering in the riders' areas caught Tyler's eye and he fell in love with her. She was a petite brunette named Haven Parchinski, and he ended up marrying her.

Although DuPont was fun, I still longed to be in Europe where the big races were – at least until I heard how badly our lads were doing there. When teams get crushed, the saying is that you are 'getting your asses handed to you' and this was precisely how everyone described what was happening to us there. Things hit a new low in the Tour de Suisse, where I heard that Thom was so angry at their poor showing that he ignored racing etiquette and just roared off in the director's car rather than following protocol and driving behind his losing team. This was a huge reality check. The big American dreams we'd hatched in California were not translating into success across the pond.

Then came grumblings. Word returned that riders were asking for 'more' than vitamin B injections from Dr Steffen.

I liked Prentice; he was a nice guy, but something told me he was too 'holistic' for the cycling world. During one stage of the Tour DuPont he was in my passenger seat and when I braked hard my arm automatically shot out across his chest to protect him.

'Oh Emma,' he said, 'you've a natural maternal instinct.'

I laughed. 'Not much maternal about me, Prentice.'

Over a massage, when one rider mentioned others asking for 'something more', I just laughed. 'Ah, it's not my scene.'

'Y'know, Emma, that's the best way – you just stay out of it.'

'I plan to!' I said firmly.

I meant it. I'd never so much as smoked a cigarette. Yeah, I knew the rumours, I knew doping happened on the big cycling teams, and many soigneurs got involved, as 'looking after' the riders' needs was all part of the role. It was the job. But so far it had been simple enough for me to keep out of it and that's what I fully intended to continue doing. My work ethic has always been if you're going to do a job, do it properly, so from massages to cleaning I gave a hundred per cent. Surely if I kept my head down and did my best nobody could ask for anything more?

I felt a little nervous when we went off for the Volta a Portugal – the Tour of Portugal – in August as, phenomenal coach as he was, Eddie B seemed to be incredibly disorganized. Everything that could go wrong did go wrong. Our car broke down and we stayed in horrible places where the food was almost inedible. By now it was becoming clear that we wouldn't even finish in the top twenty teams. A disaster. I didn't fancy being in the riders' shoes. There seemed little to celebrate, until news broke that Motorola had withdrawn sponsorship and so their team was finished. This meant there was potentially an open slot in the Tour de France for us and if we had a good season in 1997, then we'd get in as the wild-card team. We had a chance to ride in the world's toughest race; all we needed to do was improve, drastically.

With this exciting development came rumours that top brass were now looking for a European doctor. Prentice Steffen, apparently, wasn't cutting the mustard, or much else. Our American team and bosses had the will, the drive and the talent, but as yet one major piece was missing. The drugs. Once again I closed my ears to it. For all I knew, it was just talk.

It was at the end of the season, at some races in Japan and China, when I heard more rumours; this time about me. Apparently there were plans not to keep 'the girl' for the following year. This was no huge surprise; after all, I knew Waldek didn't want me, a girl, doing Europe. I was bitterly disappointed, as I loved life on the road, so I spoke to Mark and agreed to a $2,000 pay cut in order to stay on, but it was made clear I'd be covering the US races only.

Around this time another, even more shocking, rumour was doing the rounds, and sadly it turned out to be true. We heard news that the boy wonder, Lance Armstrong, had been diagnosed with testicular cancer. Stunned that such a fit young man could be struck down with the disease in his prime, it was all the riders talked about.

'Poor lad,' I thought. While the riders spoke of how frail and thin he apparently looked as he underwent treatment in an Indiana hospital, I tried not to dwell on it. I can't stand voyeurism when folk are sick or dying. The situation reminded me a bit of the jockey Bob Champion, whose book I'd read years ago. He had also contracted cancer at the peak of his fitness, but then went on to win the Grand National at Aintree. His story inspired me.

That winter of 1996, I bumped into John Hendershott, a former soigneur from Motorola, after a race and we got chatting. He'd acted as Lance's soigneur, but I wasn't especially interested in that. 'Shott' was someone who always made me laugh, with his awkward gait and conversation. For some reason I've always got on with klutzy types. Standing six foot four inches tall and about the same wide, he wasn't to be messed with, but he was decent to me. At his place in Erie, Colorado, we bonded over a few bottles of Bud as Shott sounded off to me about cycling.

'I'm outta here, Emma,' he told me. 'Retiring to this ranch. Right now, I feel as if I never want to touch another bike again.'

Tired and jaded myself, I listened to Shott bitch and moan. 'It's too intense, Emma,' he said. 'Pro racing is too much of a mad, crazy world.'

He'd mainly worked for Lance, and I guessed Shott would have given out 'shots' of his own, as he was on $80,000 a year. But he knew me as a clean soigneur and respected that I didn't want to know. Talking to him reinforced my own view that I was never going to make a full-time career of being a soigneur. I was planning to leave the sport by the age of thirty, when I would still be young enough to start a new career, whatever that might be.

I looked at Shott, such an alpha male, and thought to myself how similar he was to the Lance I'd seen so far. Then Shott admitted they'd not kept in touch since the cancer diagnosis and I could imagine he didn't do feelings very well.

While I sympathized with Shott, I couldn't imagine ever feeling the same way about cycling that he did. Sure I'd begin to think of our life on the road as crazy 'planet cycling', isolated for weeks, living and breathing the daily battles, desperately trying to win; but it was also an exciting life and a chance to see the world. We parted ways, thanking each other for a great night. Shott said he hoped to see me soon but was bowing out of the races for ever.

Back in the camp, things were looking up. By late January 1997 we'd inherited all Motorola's trucks and infrastructure and, with new sponsorship on board, Thom brought in new and more expensive riders. As part of the shake-up, I was one of a number of staff who were moved to Girona in Spain, the heart of the European cycling scene. I still wanted to be based in Ireland, but I rented a room in Girona near the service course, a fancy name for the lock-up where we kept all our equipment.

Before we left America, however, Thom Weisel summoned all staff to his beach house in Oceanside, California, for another of his now infamous rah-rah talks. My God, his house was something else. I walked in feeling as if I'd stepped into a glossy magazine advert. After we had been served champagne from silver trays, we gathered to hear Thom speak. As usual, when he spoke, we listened.

'We're going to Europe to do one thing and one thing only – win!' he announced.

The all-new Postal team was bigger, better and turbo-charged. He had overhauled the staff, bringing in the veteran mechanic Julien DeVries, who'd worked with legends like Eddy Merckx and Greg LeMond, and a host of new riders including Viatcheslav Ekimov, the Olympic gold medallist (known as Eki, as nobody could pronounce his name) and George Hincapie.

Eddie B, bless him, was replaced by a Danish directeur sportif, Johnny Weltz, and Dr Steffen had been let go for a Spaniard, Dr Pedro Celaya, who brought his own soigneur called José Arenas. I'd heard grumblings that Dr Steffen wasn't happy about being ousted, but in all cycling teams when it came to staff it was a revolving door.

The riders seemed to like Pedro, with his soft brown eyes and direct, approachable manner, but I avoided him. I already on principle disliked European doctors and what they stood for.

My boss was now head soigneur Freddy Viaene and we had more European riders than Americans, but still enough to call it an American team, determined to break into Europe. Postal, Thom said, would focus on all the major tours. We would intensify our campaign at the prestigious one-day classic Liège–Bastogne–Liège, go all out for the Tour de Suisse again and then, all being well, compete in the pièce de résistance: our very first Tour de France. For both myself and the team the pressure was now on and I was thrilled to be part of this fabulous ride.

4

A Testing Tour

BY APRIL 1997 OUR new directeur sportif, Johnny Weltz, was already at loggerheads with Waldek, so reluctantly he sent for me to cover the Ronde van Vlaanderen – the Tour of Flanders – leaving me in no doubt I was Plan B. But who cared? I was going to cover a big race I'd only ever read about or watched on TV before.

The day before the race, I faced having to get all the equipment across from Denver to Ghent, taking planes, trains and taxis all on my own. With three bike bags, mechanical stuff, a suitcase and a massage table this was no mean feat, but I thought to myself, 'Emma, just get it done. You can't be asking for help already.' The last thing I wanted was a reputation as the needy girl.

I managed to get the plane from Denver to Brussels, waddling with dead-weight bags, dumping half, then walking for a hundred yards and going back, hoping each time nobody would run off with them. Somehow I made it to Ghent station, but no taxi would take me with all that luggage.

'Oh frigging hell!' I mouthed, as the last cabbie zoomed

past, so I rang the team hotel and after much chat (the Belgians are worse than the Irish) they agreed to send two cabs. When I arrived, head mechanic Julien watched incredulously as I dragged equipment from taxis like a magician pulling handkerchiefs from a sleeve.

'Emma,' he said, in his gruff Flemish accent, 'how did you do this?'

I laughed. 'Where there's a will there's a way.'

He sent me off for a shower and lie-down. 'You deserve it,' he said.

Impressing Julien was a positive step; if you were all right by Julien, you were all right with everyone. I heard he even went to Johnny to say, 'Look what Emma did. Would Waldek do this?'

There was only one way to work as a soigneur. Throw yourself into it. So I did. The job was 24/7, exhausting and frenetic from the moment you woke up. Not only did you prepare the riders, making sure they were fed, watered and clothed, but you had to be there at the start and end of the race and make sure they got a bag of food in the middle. Afterwards, of course, it was time for a rub, then clean everything up and prepare it all again for the next day.

One big deal was the bottles. Washing them, filling them, handing them out and making sure there were enough of them was a constant battle. Riders drink two to three bottles an hour, more if it's hot. And it wasn't just water we worried about; they needed a special energy mix as well to top up calories. All bottles and food were prepared the night and morning before the race, and then the next worry was getting to the feeding zones, of which there was at least one during each race, sometimes two or three in the classics. Every night I'd get my map out to plan the route, because, whatever happened, I had to make it to that zone in time. Soigneurs from other teams would sometimes laugh when I pulled up in the car.

'Ah, it's the mad lady driver,' one or two would 'joke', even though I was just doing my job, the same as the male soigneurs.

The fact was, I was terrified of missing handing an exhausted rider his feed bag. Those lads would have suffered enough already. Often I'd have to fight my way through crowds of fans too. Belgian fans were especially bad, running like hell from one point of a race to another, not leaving room for staff. In winter races I'd time my arrival at the zone to the last minute, so that the heavily syruped tea we'd made would still be warm enough to heat frozen hands.

After reaching my allotted place by the side of the road, I would stand with the musette bags on my arm, each filled with two bottles of water, a can of Coke, peanut butter and jam sandwiches, frangipane, rice cakes and maybe some chopped kiwi to freshen the riders up. Dr Pedro insisted on unprocessed foods, as they were easier for the body to digest, although this seems rather ironic when you think about it. We would buy the frangipane fresh from the bakery; it was the perfect cake for a race, keeping moist for days. Not only did I need to be a racing driver with sharp elbows, but being an expert in the longevity of cakes was also on the rapidly growing list of soigneur skills on my CV. I would have just a split second to get the bag of food to the lads as they whooshed past, so there was no room for error. Two moving targets didn't work, so I'd stick out my arm as far as it could go. Then it was up to riders to spot me and snatch the musette as they shot past. Woe betide me if they or I missed.

After feeds, I'd race back to the hotel or to the finish line, depending on the rota. Following the massages, I'd finally be able to relax and have dinner before the evening's prep kicked off. Often I hung out with the other soigneurs, including Ryszard Kielpinski, Freddy, José Arenas, or with Julien. Over the next few months Julien introduced me to his family. Vera, his wife, was a real lady and his sons were good craic too. They insisted on calling me Emmatje, the *tje* part being a Flemish term of endearment, and in turn they became my Pepe and Meme.

Working with new soigneurs was a learning curve. While Ryszard was obsessed with laundry, José Arenas, as lovely as he was, struck me as being unbelievably sloppy. In the cycling world, everyone is paranoid about germs and bugs; a simple common cold can destroy a race for a rider. Even air conditioning was banned in case it spread an infection. Tutting to myself, I'd trail behind José, redoing jobs as he cut corners, a fag always hanging from his lips. One morning I looked at the way he'd packed the sandwiches and had to say something.

'José!' I chided. 'The lads' sandwiches are gonna look like squashed mush by the time we've elbowed through the crowds. Can you not at least make them look nice to begin with?'

José shrugged and lit up yet another cigarette. I waved my hand in front of my face. 'And you know the Americans hate smoking!'

As much as I liked him, it baffled me why José had been brought in. He was good at cracking jokes, sure, but his abilities as soigneur seemed to me to be sorely lacking. Then, one afternoon, at the Circuit de la Sarthe in Le Mans, all became clear. As I stuck my head round the door of one rider's room to check his kit, I saw José flicking a syringe. In one deft movement he gave the guy an injection, pressing the plunger with more confidence than any doctor I'd ever seen.

I walked blankly past, pretending I'd seen nothing. Okay, I thought, so that's what José excels in . . .

The quote 'None so blind as those who will not see' is apposite here. I knew of banned drugs that riders could be using, but only vaguely and on the grapevine. I'd heard of EPO (erythropoietin), cortisone and testosterone. EPO was known as a drug cyclists could get away with, as no test had been developed for it at that time. Its effect was to increase the amount of oxygen in the blood, with the result that a rider's endurance threshold was raised: you could ride for longer with less pain and your recovery was quicker. As well as this, it raised the haematocrit level, or the volume of red blood cells. A test did exist for this, and the UCI said if a rider's haematocrit level was over 50, it was likely the blood had been tampered with and the result would be a suspension. However, riders were able to manipulate their levels very quickly by drinking lots of water or inserting a saline drip, or timing when a test was likely to occur. EPO stayed in the system for only four hours.

Cortisone had a strong physiological benefit, making riders feel better and acting as an anti-inflammatory, speeding up the recovery rate, while testosterone was used to build muscle mass and also to aid recovery. That was as much as I knew. While riders still used the phrase 'not normal' for signs of doping, they also used '*pan y agua*', Spanish for 'bread and water', or sometimes 'spaghetti and water', for when you were riding clean.

The next obvious sign that something was going on in the team came shortly afterwards, during the notoriously hard one-day Paris–Roubaix race. I noticed Pedro and José disappear into the kitchen at the back of the truck with the door shut firmly behind them. Then, as the riders emerged from their rooms after a shower, they all headed over. As I passed by with some bottles, I saw Pedro and José open the doors and hand out white bags to a couple of the big riders. I watched as they walked off, bold as brass, with the bags swinging in their hands. Averting my gaze, I grabbed a J-cloth and went to wipe up after José's bad job cleaning the water coolers.

'Okay, well that's that then,' I thought, scrubbing madly. I was no fool; I knew exactly what the point of Pedro was. The action plan was now in place, although goodness knows what was in the white bags. Also obvious was that none of the Americans on the team was getting one. That afternoon, as I passed Tyler and Darren their energy mix, I felt almost apologetic.

'Thank you,' said Tyler, ever polite, always smiling.

'Well, some energy mix is hardly the same,' I thought. 'But every little helps, I guess.'

In June, we arrived at the Tour de Suisse with a reinvigorated sense of hope. This would be nothing like last year; this year we were going places. On the first morning at the hotel, our busy day had only just begun when the UCI drugs testers arrived. They always gave twenty minutes' to half an hour's advance notice so that riders were ready in their rooms to have a urine sample taken. It was all very civilized until our head soigneur, Freddy Viaene, appeared to morph into a mix of Mr Bean and Basil Fawlty as he ran up and down corridors fussing.

'What's the matter?' I asked him, baffled.

'Nothing!' he snapped.

Dr Pedro, meanwhile, swanned around, hands in pockets. He gave me a little smile and I managed to stop myself from wrinkling my nose.

'We're a clean team, Emma,' he said, smoothly, brushing an invisible hair from his jacket. 'We've nothing to hide.'

Yeah, right, I thought, as I stalked off to help Ryszard with the endless washing. I didn't believe a word of it. Thankfully, the testing came to nothing and we could all relax, although Freddy was known as the 'walking heart attack' after that. He was stress on legs.

Whatever Pedro was up to, the fact was that Eki was the only Mr Consistent with his race results; the other riders still struggled. With the Tour de France looming, we needed some sort of miracle to get everyone up to speed. Hard work and determination didn't seem quite enough. Despite this, excitement was mounting. We were going to the Tour, my very first one, and as nerve-wracking as it was, I couldn't wait.

After all the years watching the Tour on TV, I was gobsmacked by the sheer scale of it when we puttered up in our old camper vans. It had grown into a smooth corporate machine, with everything running on time, everyone knowing their place; in many ways it was far easier than other races, as we were told what to do and were shepherded around. With an entourage of over three thousand people, thirteen thousand gendarmes, and helicopters constantly circling above, not to mention a million fans thronging on the roadsides, this was racing at its most accessible and spine-tingling. The Tour was a battle, not just of who could cycle the fastest but of a man's spirit. Riders' hearts could beat two hundred times a minute – something the human body is not designed to do day in, day out – so they had to be in as good shape psychologically as physically.

While other big teams, like the Spanish ONCE or the French Festina, arrived to a fanfare in huge, luxurious, tinted-glass coaches, we parked our campers as the obvious newbies, with little sponsorship or press attention. Some spectators had nicer vans than our clapped-out roadsters. But being the rookies, not expected to get anywhere – or as an Irish saying goes, the 'gyp bags' – nothing mattered. We were here and determined to give it our best shot, staff and riders alike; spirits were high, as was our adrenalin.

For the first few days a strange, nervous energy bristled through the camp and the lads were more edgy over breakfast than usual. My early-morning duties were my least favourite parts of the job. To wake a rider, a soigneur had first to knock, then stand at the door waiting to hear the rider shout back, which always made me feel so rude. Then at breakfast I didn't like acting as a waitress. To avoid being tutted at, I'd try to spot when milk or bread or whatever had run out before the riders did.

Once the lads had got as many calories into themselves as possible (they burned off up to nine thousand calories per day) I made sure they were kitted out for the start line and had their sun block, their chamois cream, their arm-warmers, their bottles – but inevitably someone had forgotten something. 'Emma, have you a . . . ?' was the regular cry.

Next we kitted out the DS's car, which followed the riders with spare rain jackets, helmets, shorts, and the extra bottles. So many bottles. We'd started out with five thousand, but Julien used his contacts to get more. He made our lives a hell of a lot easier. So many in cycling kept their contacts to themselves, but not my Pepe.

Then, as the race went on, we waited, had a drink, or carried on organizing the next day, before meeting the riders at the finish line. My God, that's when you saw what it took. They would fall off their bikes, looking like zombies.

Once a rider had a go at me over dinner. 'Emma!' he cried. 'You didn't tell me where our camper van was at the end of the race!'

'I did! I pointed it out!' I protested.

Riders were always so utterly spent, many could barely see straight, so I would grab their slack jaws and point them in the right direction. 'See that van, with Postal written all over it? That's where you need to go, okay?' I would tell them, as they barely mustered the strength to nod, let alone walk.

Within twenty minutes of the end of a race, the lads had to have a doping test. If you didn't show up, it was an automatic fail, meaning you could be out of the race. After this, the priority was to get them back to the hotel as soon as possible. Rest was all-important. The saying was always the same: 'Why stand when you can sit and why sit when you could lie down?' – a rule the lads stuck to obsessively. I'd drop them off at the very door of the hotel, within feet if I could, as every step counted. Then I'd rush inside to get more calories into them, something carb-heavy like fruit, yoghurt and muesli, or sandwiches. At this point we didn't have a chef, so it was simple stuff and they'd fall on it like wolves.

Once they were done, the lads turned into old men, shuffling around to their rooms for a shower, massage, then dinner. They didn't want to expend a single calorie of extra energy, and indeed many didn't have it. Human bodies are not designed to tolerate punishing pain day in and day out for three weeks. By Day Seven you could see lads starting to break.

At the end of the soigneurs' day, we'd long for our beds too, although sometimes I'd have a coffee and catch up with Pepe. His son Steffan was a character too. 'I think at some point we need to throw you in the pool,' he kept saying, grinning at me, a few days into the Tour. It became a bit of a catchphrase,

'Throw Emma in the pool', but I just laughed it off: 'Just you try, lads.' Let them have their fun.

Inevitably I became the butt of many jokes. One afternoon I was driving to the airport to pick someone up when my tyre blew while I was overtaking a lorry on the *périphérique*, or ring road. I narrowly escaped a serious accident, but if I expected any sympathy back at work I was wrong.

Eki thought it was hilarious. 'You're Emma O'Rally from now on,' he boomed over dinner.

I liked Eki, with his mullet and hardcore mentality. He was old school, brought up in Russia, sent away for three-month training camps in Siberia from the age of twelve. He told stories of 6 a.m. starts, where kids were screamed at by coaches riding mopeds with megaphones. One morning, desperately tired, Eki and his friends sneaked into the canteen to steal sugar to pour into the petrol hub of their despot coach's moped. 'Just carry on without me!' the coach screamed when his bike didn't start. They waited until he'd gone off to the staff room before slipping back to their dormitories, desperate to catch up on sleep. The brutality shocked me.

'Eki, that's sadistic. I can't imagine little kids being sent away so young,' I cried.

'Ah, but it was an opportunity for a better life,' he mused. 'A way out.' Eki rarely spoke, but when he did everyone listened. He also had the softest skin on his legs that I've ever known.

As the race progressed, the change in the riders was incredible. From Days Seven to Ten things went rapidly downhill. Lads aged, their faces pinching and hardening as they struggled to cope with the demands on their bodies. Confronting this hardship, we were a team in every sense of the word; the riders were the stars and we circled in their orbits, giving them everything they needed so that all they had to do was cycle for their lives. As the Tour wore on, however, one staff member above all others was clearly becoming a focal point.

Dr Pedro. I quickly cottoned on to the fact that, if I saw Pedro sitting on the edge of a rider's bed, that was the sign to keep walking; or if I got to the camper van and the door was shut, not to knock. It was blatantly obvious he was up to no good. I was no idiot. The cupboards and fridge in the truck were now packed with plain boxes, but I just ignored them. As long as there was enough room for water, frangipane and yoghurts, then it remained none of my business. I didn't want to know about it. I could be blind, deaf and dumb. The only time I stepped in was when I felt I had to.

Injections were a common sight in cycling, even for kosher supplements like vitamins to help recovery, but when I spotted needles left in hotel-room bins or in the baths, I had to say something.

'Aw, c'mon lads,' I chided one evening. 'You can't leave dirty needles lying around like this! A chambermaid might prick herself.'

They could do what they liked, but they had to think of other people too.

After one stage, all fifteen teams descended, turning the hotel into chaos. As we bustled around, sorting out equipment, I happened to be walking past the swimming pool when Steffan bolted over and in a split second had me tight in a fireman's lift.

'Emma's going in the pool,' he yelled.

I screamed, mortified. I was only wearing a tiny pair of shorts and a T-shirt.

'Nooooo!' I cried, as Steffan held me firm.

'One . . . two . . .' he began, as I imagined eyes boring into my backside. I felt myself blushing all over, wondering how the hell to get out of this. I couldn't let myself be seen soaking wet in what I was wearing. I'd die of embarrassment. Then I thought of something.

'Steffan,' I whispered urgently into his ear, 'I. Can't. Swim.'

Now it was his turn to pause, as riders and staff cajoled him onwards.

'Dunk her in!'

'Get her wet!'

'Uh, really? Uh, okay Emma,' he whispered. He put me down gently on the poolside as jeers turned to boos. Relieved I was off the hook, I hurried away from the scene, only to bump into a nice-looking lad.

'You got away with that,' he winked.

'Yeah,' I laughed.

'I'm Simon Lillistone and I work for Giro in their marketing team,' he said, holding out his hand. Giro, an American company, is a leading bike-helmet manufacturer, so he was at the Tour representing the firm. We chatted for a while before I had to rush off to sort logistics for the next day, having no idea I'd just bumped into my future husband.

Incredibly, as the Tour wore on it became clear our riders were going to finish; this was miraculous compared to the previous year. After one good stage finish, when we were back at the hotel eating dinner, a mechanic from Rabobank cocked his eyebrow at me. 'You must have a good doctor,' he said. 'Because it takes a good one to get all nine riders around.'

I knew exactly what he was insinuating. Doping was rife within the European teams. Riding on spaghetti and water would have been suicide for us this year.

On Stage 14, we watched in awe as the Festina team led by Richard Virenque zoomed, as if on motorbikes, to the top of an Alpine climb. There was no way I could believe they were doing it *pan y agua* either.

But we finished the race. The riders had done their job, we had marked our place in the Tour de France, and we'd definitely be invited back next year. The first stage of Thom Weisel's master plan had worked. The Americans had finally landed.

5

Man on a Mission

JUBILANT AT HAVING FINISHED the Tour, and as part of the team ritual, we went for drinks that Saturday night, staying at EuroDisney for the final blow-out. The wife of a champion rider, whose name I'll change to Tracy, was near me. I'd been asked out by a mechanic a few days earlier and was wondering aloud whether to go.

'Why would you go out with a staff member when there are so many riders around?' Tracy asked, genuinely baffled. 'At least riders make money!'

She looked away when Simon came over.

'Emma, I see a pool and think you'd look great in it,' he said. I jumped up to escape, but as I did so, Simon tripped, bringing me down with him and I smashed my face on the paving. As blood poured down my T-shirt, everyone was killing themselves as they tried to stem the flow.

'Can we just leave the pool alone now?' I laughed.

There was little time off between races and we hit the road again soon after. By September 1997 we'd been on the move for months and I was exhausted; it was a strange, discombobulating, bone-tiredness that I'd never experienced before. By bedtime – midnight at the earliest – I'd fall on to the duvet, face down, and be asleep before I hit the pillow. Often we'd have to get up during the night too, especially for the laundry. If the dryer was in use in the evening, I'd have to put the clothes on to wash late, then get up at 3 a.m. to stick them in the dryer for the morning. There's nothing like going to bed knackered, knowing you have to get up in two hours, for self-pity to set in.

Inevitably, with tiredness came frayed tempers. One evening I was getting the lads' shirts ready to wear for dinner when Pedro knocked on my hotel-room door as I was throwing them into piles. Eki pile, Tyler pile, etc.

'Emma, do you have a spare shirt for my friend?' he asked. Everyone had to wear the same team denim, but although providing for the doctor was in my job description, looking after his mates wasn't.

'Sorry, Pedro, I only have a few spares and I need them for riders,' I said.

His face fell. 'Why can't I have one?'

'Because they're for the riders!' I repeated. He skulked off.

I thought nothing more of it until another staff member told me later Pedro had run to Johnny and tried to get me sacked.

'The little toerag!' I exclaimed.

Tensions arose in strange ways, but as a woman I realized they were sometimes out of my control. One of the French riders had stopped getting massages from me recently because his wife had received calls and faxes claiming I was having an affair with him. It was all total rubbish and I'd no idea who was behind it, but the riders came out in my support and told him I didn't have a crush on him. He was not my type, but he avoided me anyway. All rather bizarre, and not very amusing.

Later that month we arrived in San Sebastián for the Worlds, and there I came across David Millar, British cycling's pin-up boy. Dark-haired, with a wide, engaging smile, David was young, attractive and had a reputation as a clean rider, someone who openly didn't approve of any programme – well, as openly as was possible. Nobody ever came out and said 'I am clean', but at races word got out. At just twenty, David was the big rising hope, the one to watch, and how I admired his goal of doing it *pan y agua*.

Towards the end of the Worlds, Freddy Viaene called me from the team hotel, sounding far more excited than usual.

'Emma, I've news,' he bubbled. 'Lance is coming! We've signed Lance Armstrong.'

'Whoa!' I agreed. 'Okay, this is big.'

We'd all heard how Lance had miraculously recovered from cancer, beating the odds to survive after the disease spread to his brain. Riders hadn't expected him to return to pro cycling, not after such radical treatment as chemotherapy and brain surgery. He'd been left with scars like Frankenstein, someone said, after doctors cut the lesions away in a pioneering method of treatment. Whether or not he went on to return to the sport, he'd beaten the odds already.

After Motorola folded, Lance had been signed with the French team Cofidis, but the contract fell through due to the team's doubts that he'd be able to return to his original pre-cancer form. He'd now signed to US Postal for the relatively modest amount of $150,000 plus bonuses.

I'd never heard of a cyclist overcoming a major illness to come back and compete. Somehow it didn't seem possible, especially not for big races where the human body is pushed to the limit even for those in robust health. If nothing else, Lance already impressed me with his bottle.

'Things are gonna change around here, that's for sure,'

Freddy said excitedly, and that afternoon the staff were buzz-
ing with the news.

Lance is coming. The champion. The biggest cyclist in
America. The Texan with the big mouth. The even bigger ego.
The one who came back from cancer. The one who they said
would never ride again.

His imminent arrival wasn't the only gossip. Everyone
assumed Lance wouldn't get on with Johnny Weltz, with
whom he'd already worked years ago at Motorola. Lance likes
the way he likes things, riders kept saying. He won't like the
disorganization. I was intrigued, wondering what was to come.
By now I'd come across Lance a few times at races, but I was
no chamois-sniffer even for the likes of him.

Before the Christmas break, Freddy resigned. He'd had enough
after locking horns with Johnny too many times and was off
to be star rider Frankie Vandenbroucke's soigneur, a great gig
for him. Left without a head soigneur, I became chief lackey by
default. From being the girl almost dropped from the team, I
was now heading it.

Following our improvement in 1997, expectations for the
team were even greater for 1998 as we set up training camp in
Ramona. Thom and Mark's master plan was working: bigger
sponsors were showing interest, money was piling up and
Lance Armstrong was coming.

Other new riders also joined, and I was introduced to
Jonathan Vaughters (known as JV), a young rider fresh out
of med school, whip smart and kooky with it. Road captain
Frankie Andreu was also on side; he was a former teammate of
Lance's who called a spade a spade. Christian Vande Velde was
a bright-eyed twenty-one-year-old rookie and Kevin Livingston
was another of Lance's old teammates.

I was happy to be back working with Ryszard, not just because we got on, but because he loved the job I loathed – laundry. Whoever potty-trained that guy sure did one good job, I joked.

Getting things up and running at the camp was hectic as usual, and by the first evening I caught sight of myself in the mirror and groaned. 'Oh, Emma, you're such a scruff.' Any sign of femininity was swallowed by our regulation, oversized clothing of team fleece and cargo trousers. As a nod to being female, my shoes had a slight heel and I wore my hair down, but without much make-up, just a rub of foundation, I felt far from attractive.

Strangely, that didn't stop riders from other teams occasionally asking me out. Sometimes a slip of paper would appear under my room door with an anonymous number scribbled on it; the only clue to who had delivered it was when a rider or mechanic ignored me the following day. More than anything, it made me laugh. That's not to say I wasn't looking for love, but I wanted something a bit more than just a thing for the road, which I assumed lots of lads were after.

One guy, whom I'll call Sebastian, a director for a big team I cannot name, had asked me out a few times, but I always said no. He just seemed so ridiculously out of my league. Sebastian had had a successful career as a pro rider (I even had his picture on my bedroom wall in Ireland) and now he was the owner of a phenomenally successful team, but when he'd asked me out at the Worlds the previous year, I actually thought it was a joke.

So on our first evening back at Ramona I restyled my hair a little, washed my hands and went to grab dinner with the lads, telling myself not to be so vain.

Around 9 p.m., I heard a car pull up into the darkness next

to my motel room, so I went to greet the new arrivals with their keys. First of all a smiling young guy jumped out.

'I'm Christian Vande Velde,' he said, shaking my hand enthusiastically.

'Hello,' I replied with a grin, jangling his key. This young dude looked like fun. I imagined he'd soon fit into the humour of the team, which was often at my expense. We'd all had a laugh the previous evening when the owner of the motel asked me if I wanted to join her for a 'bong' after we had finished work. Confused, I'd politely said 'No thanks.'

'I'll have just eaten,' I explained. She gave me a funny look and walked off. Later, when I recounted the story, the riders who'd already arrived cracked up laughing. Not knowing a bong was cannabis was apparently hilarious.

Now Christian nodded towards the passenger seat. 'Lance is here, Emma,' he said.

The door swung open and half his body emerged, the other half still leaning into the car. I assumed he was on the phone, so I turned away.

'Hey, Emma, Lance is trying to say hi,' Christian said, a little awkwardly.

'Aw fuck,' I thought, cringing. I must have looked pretty rude. Not a great start. I swung back to see an outstretched hand and a pair of intense eyes looking straight into mine.

'Good to meet ya,' said Lance.

'Hello. Emma,' I said, as his strong grip shook mine.

Lance bowled across the car park, a man on a mission. Something about him, the way he spoke, the way he moved, reminded me of a rock thrown into a pond. I wondered how quickly the effects of the ripples would be felt on our team and how far-reaching they would be.

6

Aftershocks

I DIDN'T NEED TO wonder for long. The next morning at breakfast the atmosphere was already noticeably different. Everyone was eating a little faster, was a little less talkative, and was watching the clock. As I went to check if anyone needed anything, once again I heard him before I saw him. Yes, Lance had landed.

'What the fuck's this?' he ranted, shaking a little cardboard box of cereal in the air.

'Okay, yeah, sure, we can change it,' Ryszard was nodding.

'Too right. Yeah, we need to look at all this crap,' said Lance. 'Crunchy muesli is all sugar. We need proper muesli, less sugar, more slow-releasing carbs. That's the shit, not this stuff.'

While most of the team were waking up with their coffee, Lance was demanding what was this, what was that, dead-cert opinions thrown in every direction. I wasn't sure where I'd stand with this guy, but at the same time I admired his tenacity. A mini whirlwind, he would shake things up and I wondered how it would all look when the dust settled, or indeed if it ever would.

The normal routine after breakfast was for riders to tinker with their new bikes, fuss over gears and brakes, adjust seats and get themselves ready for the 10 a.m.-ish roll-out for training. But with Lance around there was significantly less tinkering. Lads seemed to snap into gear that little bit faster, and Lance shot out of the door at 10 a.m. on the dot.

When they returned, after a seven-hour training ride, I gave Lance his first massage. Like the other riders, he was ready and waiting, wearing just a towel around his waist. Unlike the others, he wasn't relaxed; he was barking on his mobile.

'Yeah, we've got it covered, yeah we're hitting the roads at ten a.m. I wanna see a fair few changes though. We need . . .'

Fizzing with energy, this guy didn't even want to waste a few minutes' peace on my massage table. He was still getting his full fitness back, but I could tell Lance was in extraordinary shape already.

Over the next few weeks, I learned Lance's version of tiredness. He was no ragdoll, but I could feel in his body how hard he'd worked. Of all the riders, Lance's muscles were always the most empty. It's hard to describe, but a full muscle feels firm like a grape, and after a long ride they become almost like raisins. But Lance's muscles totally disappeared, almost on touch, after he'd powered through a training session.

As we started chatting, I found him easy to talk to. Like me, he was pretty direct and to the point. Things were black and white, right or wrong, in a way that, as an Irish girl, I respected.

From then on, Lance came only to me for his forty-minute massage, never to the other soigneurs. At first I was flattered, but soon my old angst crept in. After all, I wasn't a 'proper' soigneur. Everyone knew I was clean; everyone knew I turned the other cheek when it came to drugs. Unlike most of the European soigneurs, I wasn't a walking pharmacy; I couldn't give a rider 'extras', and by that I mean stimulants of the banned kind. This had never been an issue before, but I suspected it would be now. A fear that was soon realized when I overheard Lance ranting in his room.

'I need a fucking proper soigneur. Where's the fucking proper ones?' he raved.

I crept past his door, not knowing if he was criticizing someone else or thinking of me, or if I was being paranoid. Later on during the massage, Lance was on his mobile.

'God, I could do with Shott here,' he was grumbling. When he hung up, I confessed I had Shott's number.

Lance's ears pricked up. 'You do? Well how's about you give it to me then, huh?'

I was crestfallen at the idea of being replaced; after all, he'd seemed to forgive the fact that I wasn't fulfilling the role of a 'proper' soigneur.

I fiddled with my phone. 'Oh yeah, okay, it's here somewhere,' I began.

'You know,' Lance said, 'Shott never kept in touch. After the cancer diagnosis. No phone call. No nothing.'

I looked up from my phone. His eyes were cast down to the motel carpet, his jaw stuck out a little as he mused. Suddenly he looked a lot younger. I thought of Shott downing the beers that evening we'd hung out. No, I couldn't imagine him being especially in touch with his feelings. He'd probably had no idea what to say to Lance.

'Guess people react in different ways,' I said. 'Okay, found the number. It's . . .'

The next day after training I half expected Shott to be in Lance's room, pummelling away at his calves, but instead Lance leapt on to my massage table and we chatted like the Shott conversation had never happened.

As I kneaded his exhausted frame, I began to get to know Lance the person, not the rider. Without a doubt, cancer had been a big motivating factor in his life. He had always been extraordinarily driven, of course, initially to escape from his relatively poor upbringing, but almost dying and then being rejected by Cofidis appeared to have sent him into overdrive. His little black book was full of sponsors, directors to whom he wanted, needed to prove himself.

His cancer wasn't just part of his history either. While other riders would be going back to the States every three months to renew their visas, Lance would be going to hospital for tests to see if the life-threatening disease had returned. Of anything he'd been through, he openly said chemo was the hardest thing. He never spoke of it with a victim's mentality, however; he was matter of fact. It was all about the here and now.

I loved Lance's non-politically correct sense of humour too, examples of which I'm afraid I'm too embarrassed to share in a book. He wasn't as conservative as I find many other Americans can be (although the riders on the team were open-minded in many senses, having travelled the world from a young age), and he could be so absurd. If anything, he was a breath of fresh air, both for the team and for me to work for.

He had just got together with his girlfriend, Kristin, whom he called Kik. She had given up her job in PR to move into their apartment in Cap Ferrat, halfway between Monaco and Nice. He spoke of how proud he was of her, embracing life in this foreign land to the max, learning the lingo and immersing herself in the culture.

'That's nice, Lance. You're lucky to have a good woman behind you,' I said.

'You betcha,' he agreed. He never asked me about my love life, thankfully. I didn't fancy going into the whole saga about being asked out by a team director; somehow I didn't expect Lance would understand. The only rider I'd discussed that with was JV, Jonathan Vaughters, with whom I'd already shared several deep and meaningful conversations about my disastrous love life.

Training camp wasn't a place for wives and girlfriends, so they stayed at home, but during the rest of the year many tried to carve out lives around their men. Tyler's partner, Haven, moved nearby too, and would often hang out with Kevin Livingston's wife, Becky. I'd heard they often left Kristin out, but I'd no idea why, as I really liked her. The first time I met her, in fact, I was rather dazzled. Not only was she pretty, with perfectly blow-dried hair, but she was also feisty, intelligent and humorous – a great match for Lance, I thought. Just standing next to her made me feel like a frump. Once when I was cleaning out the team truck, she pulled up in a car, wearing white skin-tight jeans, her beautiful blonde hair tumbling 'just so' over her shoulders.

'Hey Emma!' she beamed, waving me over.

'Hey Kristin,' I mumbled back, wiping some sweat and oil off my face with the back of my fleece sleeve. I needed a shower. 'Ah Jaysis, Kristin, you make me feel like such a short little dumpy thing.'

'No, Emma, you look just fine,' she assured me generously.

I laughed. Inside I was thinking, 'Kristin, I bet you'd look good even in what I am wearing, dragged through a hedge backwards, first thing in the morning.' But ah well, she was fun with it. I liked her humour; she could be a bit raucous at times, but respectful with it.

Along with Lance also came his manager, Bill Stapleton, who reminded me of the lawyer in *To Kill a Mockingbird*. He was the money man and that's all he spoke about. But Lance also had people around him like Jeff Garvey, the successful businessman who helped him run his Lance Armstrong Foundation to raise money for cancer survivors. There was no doubt about how much this charity meant to Lance. I often heard him on the phone making decisions or chatting to cancer patients in his room after the massage. He did all of this with little fanfare, often alone in the evening.

By now I'd already heard one of Lance's nicknames floating around, although of course never to his face. The Lion King. 'How apt,' I mused. Lance didn't walk into a room, he bowled, his eyes roaming around, alert for spotting something out of place, something to be improved. He was always on to something, exploding with enthusiasm: 'This is The Shit! This is The Bomb!' He might be hankering after better-quality food, a better bike, a better hotel. Other riders parted like the Dead Sea as he entered the room, some avoiding, some gravitating towards him. He seemed to pick up on those who tried too hard, however; it was quite extraordinary to see.

I could see how infectious this force of nature was, yet he didn't intimidate me. If anything, I was entertained by him and by others' reactions to him. Lance didn't have to scare you.

The five-day race in Spain called the Ruta del Sol was his first pro race back in the saddle, but I was still working in the States and missed it. In his book *It's Not About the Bike*, Lance recalls it as a media circus, the big comeback gig for the cancer boy, but he finished up fourteenth. A position he didn't find acceptable.

I'd seen at first hand how much losing hurt Lance. Occasionally when he'd had a bad day training, not meeting his target time or whatever, he'd steam into my room with a heavy brow. Once he sat on my bed, still wearing his cycle clothes, unprepared for a rub.

'I don't deserve a massage,' he shrugged. 'Not today. My legs didn't do what they needed to do.'

'Lance, in that case,' I said, 'if you feel like that, you deserve one even more. Lie down.'

He did as he was told, but I could tell that this guy didn't just dislike losing, he positively loathed it, as if it hurt him in a physical way.

Losing wasn't the only 'issue' either. There was always something that was the Big Issue with Lance. Weight was an ongoing one. Being as skinny as possible was something to which most pro cyclists aspired, and I started to notice Tyler struggling too. To be a good climber, the less you weighed, the faster you'd ride; it was that simple. Keeping weight off when your body was screaming out for food after training was less simple. Riders were constantly watching what they ate, leaving food on their plates and talking about it. Often they would glug water in between meals to stop themselves from snacking. Being obsessed with weight and not walking anywhere made pro riders pretty dull people at times.

The season's first big race was Paris–Nice. This was the fruition of months of training for Lance, but I was sent to cover some races in California instead so wouldn't be there to see him. I didn't wish him luck. That wasn't what staff did, but on the quiet I had all my fingers crossed for him.

I was crouching down outside near the truck, stacking the never-ending bottles in a crate, enjoying the sun on my back when one of the mechanics cast a shadow over me.

'Emma, have you heard? Lance has abandoned Paris–Nice,' he said.

I stood up a little too fast, the hot sun suddenly making me feel dizzy. 'What?'

After all the hope, all the sheer grit and determination, I couldn't quite understand how this could have happened.

Lance. Quit. Those two words just didn't go together.

Cycling is one big gossipfest and I soon heard all the details of the day. Tupperware-grey skies, thrashing rain, dangerous roads slippery with water. I knew how hard these winter races in Europe were, knew how the other soigneurs would be busting a gut to make sure they could keep the syrupy tea hot enough to warm the riders' hands – the least anyone could do to help.

'Frankie saw Lance's face as he pulled his bike off the road,' Geoff Brown, one of the mechanics, told me. 'He says he's never seen him looking like that before.'

I felt for Lance, I really did. It was as if the gods were truly conspiring against him if, even with all his determination, he hadn't made it to the finish.

Later I heard that Lance had gone off to Boone in the Appalachians with Kristin and an old training buddy, Bob Roll. I'd no idea if we'd ever see or hear from him again, but I did know that Postal were willing to be patient. Meanwhile, I got on with the job in front of me. That evening, as I leaned up against the truck nattering away with Julien, a mechanic I'll call Paul turned up. He'd asked me out on a date earlier and had come to pick me up.

'Okay, I'll quickly get ready and be back,' I said, slipping off to slick on lipstick and check my hair. 'Not bad,' I thought half-heartedly, peering into the loo mirror. Better now the fleece was off, anyhow.

But when I returned my date had vanished.

'Where's Paul gone?' I asked Julien, suspiciously.

'Oh, I've sent him off to have a shave. He shouldn't be taking a lady out with stubble!' Julien roared with laughter.

'Thank you, Pepe,' I laughed, feeling sorry for Paul. I hoped it hadn't scared him off. Thankfully he did return, all clean shaven, and we went for a few drinks, but there weren't any fireworks.

I didn't have to wait long, however, before fireworks did occur, even if not in quite the way I was hoping. A few weeks later, on the final night of the Critérium du Dauphiné Libéré race, a rider from one of the competing teams knocked on my door at 2 a.m. On my second 'No! Get out!' he turned heel, but it then occurred to me that he was the third member of the same team to try it on. 'This is probably a friggin' bet: "Who can lay her first?" or something,' I thought grimly.

Incensed, I marched out of my room, went upstairs and banged with my fist on the door of this team's director, Sebastian, the same one who'd asked me out several times. He opened it with a surprised look on his face, but ushered me in. In pigeon French, I ranted at him with an anger you can only feel able to justify when you're half-cut at 2 a.m. Sebastian gazed at me, listening intently to every word.

'I'll make sure this never happens again,' he said in his perfect English. 'Here are my numbers. Give me a call.'

He handed me a card with the details of his mobile, his office and his PA as I started to curl inside with embarrassment. What had I been thinking? I thanked him and went back to bed, but woke with a sore head and groaned at the memory, burying my head in the pillow. How embarrassing had I been?

Despite, or perhaps because of, our altercation, I went out with this director a few times. Sebastian was a cool guy and I liked him. Ryszard wasn't so sure, as he didn't approve of the twelve-year age gap. 'It's not right, Emma,' he raved. 'You need a younger man. He's too old.' Johnny Vaughters, as usual, listened patiently through our massage, as every spit and cough of what I was thinking and feeling was shared. After half an hour, he suddenly spoke. 'Emma, you just need to sleep with him and then see what happens.' I laughed my head off. Now there's some straight-talking advice for you.

In May 1998 I heard that Lance had married Kristin in a Catholic church and afterwards he appeared at the Ride for the Roses, a now yearly charity cycling event to raise money for his foundation. Whether he would come back to win any races or not we still didn't know, but I had to admire the guy. His life was on track again.

There is a phrase in Tyler's book in which JV eloquently describes a crash in cycling: 'If you want to feel what it's like to be a bike racer, strip down to your underwear, drive your car at 40mph and leap out the window into a pile of jagged metal.' That was what it looked like at a race in Dunkirk, when I saw Eki get caught in the peloton and, like dominoes, they all went down.

The crashes these lads had to endure were hideous and often caused by nothing more than random bad luck. Once one rider toppled, the knock-on effect was impossible to avoid. In this instance Eki came off and skidded for metres on his shoulder and knee, grit and metal flying, making me physically shudder. This was a bad one. He limped back to the car, his face the colour of stone. Glancing down, my stomach turned over. The anatomy of the inside of his kneecap was on display, a raw wound filled with flecks of ground road grit. Just looking at it made me wince. Eki's face was immovable and he said nothing as we drove back to the hotel.

I helped him to his room, then ran for the first aid kit. 'Right Eki,' I said, as he sat on the side of the bath. 'I'll get the nail-brush.' It had a sponge on one side, so I dipped it in Betadine, an antiseptic lotion, to clean the wound. Eki stared down at it, his face unreadable, whereas I was recoiling and hurting enough for both of us. As gently as possible I picked into the wound, grit clinking into the bath. Sucking through my teeth, I glanced up at him apologetically. 'Sorry, Eki! Sorry!' As I pulled a deeply embedded piece of tarmac out, bile rose in the back of my throat. 'Sorry Eki – oh, urgh, I just can't.' He nodded, his face still expressionless, then he took the nailbrush himself. Here was a brave, pragmatic man who saw what needed doing and did it.

Afterwards I wrapped a bandage around his knee and drove him to hospital to have his shoulder X-rayed. As he struggled out of the car, I took his bag.

'No,' he barked. 'I'm not having a girl carry my bag for me.'

'Eki!' I insisted. 'If you bash it against your knee it'll make it even worse. Let me carry that bag.'

He harrumphed, hopping along in front of me as I marvelled at how rare old-school, macho men like Eki are.

7

Bonds

Later that month, while I was folding towels in preparation for a massage, George Hincapie walked into my hotel room.

'What's up, Switzerland?' I asked.

Now we'd been a team for five months, we'd all got close; it was, I imagine, like the Big Brother house – a bit mad. I was 'Chicken' to Lance, an Irish term of endearment, while I called him 'Cotton Picker'. Frankie Andreu was 'Ajax' after the blue bits in cleaning products because he could be so searingly abrasive, and George was 'Switzerland' because this New Yorker always tried to remain neutral in arguments.

'Um, I've heard you're going to Ghent,' he said. 'Can you do us a favour and pick something up from Freddy for me?'

'Sure thing,' I shrugged.

By now I'd learned to recognize the look on a rider's face when he wanted something. Even at a hundred yards I could see a question mark hovering above their heads like a halo. Demands were constant. Eki liked kiwi juice, even if we were in the middle of nowhere, and the Americans liked peanut butter, but it had to be a certain brand. The French liked Nutella. Often I told them 'No!' but they knew I couldn't resist. I liked to keep them happy. A few weeks earlier they'd all fallen in love with the cake in Belgium, so I cut them a few slices and froze it to dole it out later on. Not having time to ask the specifics of what George wanted from Freddy, I agreed, sticking it on my never-ending 'To Do' list.

The next morning, in Ghent, Freddy dropped by and passed me a small, tightly wrapped brown package, which I dumped into my bag. 'Cheers,' he said, turning to go.

'Okay, fine,' I said. 'I'll get it to George in Girona, but if I don't catch him there I'll give it to him when I go back to the States.'

Freddy stopped dead in his tracks and turned back.

'No!' he blurted out. 'Don't do that, Emma. Give it to George. It's testosterone. You don't want to be transporting it yourself.'

I felt a little sick as Freddy's eyes bored into me.

'Erm, Freddy – why would George need testosterone?' I asked. I felt hot. I knew it was a banned substance, but I also knew how ignorant I must sound.

'Because it's good for long events and gives the rider enough energy to sprint to the finish,' he explained. He went on to describe how pro riders also used other things to regulate their temperature so they didn't get too hot or cold. I was glad he'd told me, as I stood there with the banned substance in my hand, my head spinning. I was a clean soigneur; how was this happening? I quickly hid it in my bag and couldn't wait to get rid of it to George a few days later.

When we met, he snatched the package from my hand.

'Thanks,' he said, looking rather sheepish.

I didn't know what to say. Inside all I could think was 'never again'.

By now I'd also noticed the boxes piling up in the back of the truck. Many had the word 'Knoll' on them, and I'd heard of Knoll products because I had an uncle who was a pharmacist. I didn't want to know what was in them, however, so once I flung open the doors I would tell the lads to help themselves and go and busy myself with something else.

Meanwhile, Lance returned with Kristin and a Maltese dog they'd named Boone after the place he'd found his mojo again. Lance was back fresher than ever and made his official return at the US Pro Championships with Kristin by his side.

One afternoon he came into my room; as always, my hotel door was constantly revolving as I always had food and extra stuff the lads wanted.

'Wassup, Cotton Picker?' Sometimes I'd rib Lance about his new nickname a bit mercilessly. 'If you'd lived back in the times of slavery you'd have been the overseer's son,' I'd laugh at him. 'A big ole bully in the fields . . .' He'd laugh it off, shaking his head at my audacity in being so un-PC, as I pummelled away at him. This time, though, by the look on his face I could tell something was up.

'Hey, you got any, er, period-pain tablets for Kik?' he asked.

Not much makes me blush, but I felt myself go red. Could Kristin not have asked me herself?

'Oh, sorry Lance, no, I don't,' I said. The last thing I'd want to discuss with him was my periods.

'Uh, okay,' he shrugged.

Some demands I had to draw the line at.

*

The CoreStates went well, with George winning and Lance coming fourth, a good place for him after his break. Then, when he joined the team for the Tour de Luxembourg in June 1998, he performed better than ever. During our massages, he was stoked as I worked away at his thighs and calves, chatting about his goals and how training was going and what he needed to improve.

'I've worked for this,' he said. 'Boone was good for me.'

The enthusiasm of this guy who did everything to the nth degree was infectious.

After five days, on the Sunday, I found myself waiting with anticipation at the finish line, desperate to watch Lance succeed. And he did. Flying in first, his hands in the air in victory, his face lit up like the sun. It was a tremendous sight to behold.

'He friggin' did it!' I thought, mentally punching the air. I'd never felt happier about any win to date. As usual, it was chaos at the finish line, but as Lance was taken off his bike I grappled for my phone. It was so unlike me, but I had to call someone and spread the incredible news, so I dialled Mark Gorski's number. It must have been 4 a.m. in the States, but I didn't care.

'Mark!' I cried. 'Lance did it. He won. He won!'

'Oh, fantastic!' he replied, laughing.

He'd never heard me like this before, but I just needed to share the moment.

Lance was being pulled in all directions by happy staff and riders, so I waited in the car to drive him back.

'Jeeez,' he said, as he fell on the back seat, his face glowing. I just smiled; I didn't need to say anything.

As we pulled out of the car park to drive back to the hotel for a shower and massage, Lance was punching numbers on his mobile. 'Thom,' he barked, 'I've made the hundred points. You'll be hearing from Bill.'

Wow, I thought. Lance doesn't waste a single second. These UCI points meant a bonus, and that alone was enough to please him. He was, in fact, obsessed with money. During his chemo, to while away the hours productively (everything with Lance always had to be productive), he'd learned about stocks, shares and how they worked. Often he'd be on the phone to traders of some financial sort or other, checking how 'things were doin'', as they'd become a major part of his income. Among other things, he invested heavily in Dell computer products.

A mechanic once said, 'The only true friend Lance has is George Washington on dollar bills.' I understood. Like Lance, I knew what it was like to grow up without enough money. Whereas some might have seen his obsession with finance as greed, I viewed it as insecurity. Lance still had an awful lot to be insecure about. Not long ago he'd faced selling off everything he'd earned from cycling, thinking he'd never ride again. And his clean bill of health could be snatched away in the time it took to give a blood sample. Lance might have swagger, but that meant nothing in the face of those tests.

'Yeah, fingers crossed,' he'd say. 'That's all there is. Crossed fingers.'

At the end of the race we had to move hotels, but logistic-wise things went wrong again so I had to dart in and out of hotels in Metz to see if we could book rooms for the night. Leaving Lance and Frankie Andreu in the car, I had just ducked into the Campanile to check for vacancies when I heard a commotion outside. I rushed back out to find a French driver waggling his finger at Lance and Frankie. 'You disrespectful people!' he shouted in broken English. 'Living in our country like pigs. Littering, throwing your rubbish. Who do you think you are?'

'It's orange peel,' yelled Lance. 'It's fucking biodegradable!'

'Yeah, what's your problem?' Frankie added.

Both Lance and Frankie could start a fight in an empty room, so between them I didn't fancy this guy's chances.

'Can I not leave you lads for five minutes?' I joked, jostling them away. 'C'mon, I've got a room. Forget the peel, we'll pick it up.'

I gave them their keys and told them to go and wash and I'd meet them at dinner.

Fifteen minutes later, Frankie was downstairs and we were choosing what to eat. Our usual: chicken and salad one day, fish and salad the next. Another five minutes went past and I wondered what had happened to Lance. Finally he bowled in, looking chuffed.

'Where've you been?' I asked. 'It doesn't take half an hour to wash your hands!'

Lance's face fell in confusion. 'Have you not sorted out your rooms? What if that fucking asshole from outside comes a'lookin' for us?'

'You what, Lance?' I cried.

Frankie started laughing. 'Lance, what you on, man?'

'Yeah, well,' he said, a smile curling his lips. 'I've set up a nice little trap in case that old fella did decide to come after us. I'll know exactly if anyone has been in my room who shouldn't have been because he'll trip over!'

Frankie and I looked at each other and shook our heads.

'Oh my God, Lance, you're so not normal,' I laughed. 'The poor dude has probably forgotten all about you. You freak!'

'Yeah, well I've not forgotten him,' he shot back.

That night Lance even put a chair up against his door – another of his wacky security measures.

*

By now Johnny Weltz had been heading up the team for two years and nobody was especially happy. He seemed to me to be out of his depth and in denial about it. For soigneurs, everything is a race against time. You needed to know lists of races and flights, to book hotels and get the shopping done as early as possible, yet working under Johnny meant everything appeared to me to be on a wing and a prayer. Of course, if anyone was going to notice that things were not running smoothly it was Lance. He hadn't thought much of Johnny when he worked as a second director for Motorola and now he was on to him big time.

'Fucking Johnny Weltz,' he cussed, when I explained over a massage that I'd not had the timetable through for the following week.

Over dinner, Lance started pulling up more examples of why 'Fucking Johnny' deserved his nickname until within days it was a catchphrase in the team alongside Lance's other favourites, 'choad' and 'troll', for someone who was doing something he didn't like. By now even if the evening meal was over-salted, Johnny was going to get cussed.

My own issue with Johnny was what I thought were the unreasonable demands he placed on us. Sure, we soigneurs worked 24/7 and had to travel extensively, but at times there were simply not enough hours in the day. Especially infuriating was Johnny's stock reply: 'No worries, yeah yeah yeah, it will all be fine.'

One day, I walked in on a row José and another soigneur, Crespo, were having with Johnny in the truck about their pay. They thought he was unfairly questioning the money they were spending on medical stuff.

'It's not on!' José yelled.

'No worries,' Johnny sighed. 'It's being dealt with in the States. It'll all be fine.'

José and Crespo were so annoyed, they decided to walk out.

After racing in the States, then Luxembourg, we were off to the Volta a Catalunya, the Tour of Catalonia. Ryszard and I were so exhausted with jet lag we could hardly stand, but Johnny insisted he needed us in Spain, despite not having any proper timetable. Hearing that soigneurs were now walking out made me see red, so I went to confront him in the back of the truck.

'Johnny, can I have a word please?' I asked, noticing in my peripheral vision other soigneurs and mechanics take a step back.

'Look,' Johnny insisted, prepared with his stock answer, 'it will all be *fine*! No worries.'

'No worries, Johnny? No fucking worries? There are plenty of friggin' worries, Johnny, believe you me. Let me just *start* on the list of things we have to worry about,' I cried, my face burning with fury.

I reeled off a list of everything that had gone wrong and potentially could go wrong as he just stood there. He said quietly he'd sort it, as I tried not to scream with frustration.

Unexpectedly, Ryszard and I managed to wangle a day off in Spain after all and, determined to make the most of it, we drove to the beach. 'How nice is this?' I grinned as we stretched out in the sun. Ryszard made me laugh: his sunbathing technique was to time himself for half an hour on one side and then half an hour on the other. 'You're browning yourself like toast!' I ribbed.

In our enthusiasm for some time off, however, we hadn't realized the Volta a Catalunya would be cycling right past the beach, so we kept our heads down, hoping no one would notice our car, even if it did have US Postal emblazoned down the side. But when we returned to where I'd parked, the space was empty.

'Aw, Jesus! Someone must've seen us and pinched the car to teach us a lesson.'

Ryszard howled with laughter, until he realized we needed to find out who'd done it. I called Geoff the mechanic, whom I knew wouldn't tell tales, to see if he could find anything out, but he denied all knowledge of it. An hour later, after a few more enquiries, we realized the car had actually been stolen. Our little day trip was outed, but thankfully Johnny was more concerned about the car, which was found a few days later, dumped, with its starter motor broken, than about his wayward soigneurs.

The next race was in Germany, and afterwards I drove Lance back to the hotel. As we set off, he was ranting about the race's *commissaire* – a cycling official equivalent to an umpire or referee – telling us what a 'fucking useless idiot' he was, then he pulled out his mobile and punched in a number. I listened – that was all you could do when Lance was off on one. Then all of a sudden he said in a loud, clear voice: 'Hein? That you? It's Lance.'

I almost stalled the car. Lance, a rider, was on the phone to Hein Verbruggen. The head of the UCI? I slowed the car a little as Lance spoke, his voice full of indignation.

'That commissaire was fucking useless. A total choad. He's not up to the job, not at all. I hope ya hearin' what I am sayin'? I hope you don't ever use him again.'

I have no idea how Hein responded, but Lance seemed satisfied as he listened, and then said goodbye. This seemed like a friendly chat. These two knew each other, that was clear.

'Lance,' I gasped. 'You're a friggin' nutcase. You're not meant to be doing things like that. You're a rider!'

Lance shrugged and stared out of the window. 'Nah, he needs to know.'

I was dumbstruck. This was Lance being Lance. Doing it because he could do it. Not many riders would even consider trying to call the UCI directly, but of course it was another rule for Mr Armstrong. He made the rules. I didn't see it as a power trip, though. Lance was just keen to 'get things done' and he didn't think the commissaire was doing his job properly, so it needed sorting. Simple. I could see how his mind worked and couldn't help but admire it. Got a problem? Lance'll fix it.

I was genuinely shocked, however, not just that Lance had Hein's personal number, but that Hein even accepted the call. If this was happening, what else was going on behind the scenes?

Back at the hotel, I cracked on with my rubs, and told Lance about a dude called Bart who'd been hassling me for a date. Bald and overweight, he wasn't my type, I laughed. By now, Lance had adopted a big brother role in my life, and that included having a vocal opinion on my dates too.

'Aw, Emma, he's a choad too,' he sighed. 'He screwed Och over.'

Jim Ochowicz, known as Och, was a longtime friend of Lance who had managed the Motorola team when he made his breakthrough into the sport, and he felt Bart had misrepresented their interests in a deal.

'Ah, he's okay really, Lance,' I said. 'But no, I don't want to go out with him.'

A few days later during our massage my phone went. With my hands on Lance's legs, all oiled up, I couldn't reach it in time to answer.

'Oh it's just Bart,' I said, leaning over Lance to spot the caller ID. 'I'll call him later.'

The phone then rang again, but before I could react Lance's arm shot out and he'd answered it. 'Fuck off, Bart!' he yelled, then hung up.

'Lance!' I screamed, mortified. 'What you do that for?'

I looked down at the number – and in fact Bart hadn't rung the second time. It was Auntie Rita back in Ireland.

'Friggin' hell, Lance, that was my auntie, you moron!'

I quickly redialled her number.

'Hello Emma, are you okay? Who was that? Who swore like that?'

She sounded so confused, and I glared at Lance. 'Just some guy who thinks he's funny,' I said, shaking my head as Lance roared with laughter.

8

Tour of Shame

THE BUILD-UP TO THE 1998 Tour de France was full on. The training cranked up, and with it I noticed the riders change. A sense of nervousness pervaded everything like never before.

I was working hard trying to keep up with their demands, although Lance naturally was the most demanding, even if he wasn't up to riding the Tour himself this year. But everything had to be 'just so'. His clothes had to be laid out so he could see everything in one glance; he liked his socks to be black and new (nothing else was good enough); his meals were now strictly controlled; and he still only wanted me to massage him. The attention to detail rubbed off on me, and I aimed to reach his high standards.

During our last massage session before he went off to train alone in the States, I had a little joke with him about always being put upon 24/7. I admitted that I was struggling to keep up. 'Actually, Lance, I'm tired, so from now on the office is closed after ten, end of story. You can friggin' get knotted,' I joked as I pummelled away.

A couple of nights later, at 2 a.m., I got a knock on my hotel-room door and shot up, wondering what had happened. Occasionally a rider woke me at night, but usually only in an emergency. I opened my door to find a self-conscious-looking Tyler Hamilton.

'Hey, Emma,' he said brightly. Whatever the situation, Tyler was always polite, God love him. 'I'm, er, really thirsty. Any chance of some, er, bottled water?'

Then I heard a snigger, and Lance poked his head around the door-frame to show me it was a wind-up.

'You low-life!' I cried. I slammed my door shut, listening to Lance's laughter howl down the corridor. Typical Lance, putting poor Tyler up to that.

But with the Tour ever closer now, there was little mood for any fooling. Riders grew more paranoid, fiercer about their needs. Sickness was one of their main worries. A sore throat, a sneeze, a splutter was enough to put the fear of God into them. Not being on top form could destroy their chances, so hygiene was a major concern. Anxious to reassure them and to assuage their escalating paranoia about air conditioning affecting performance, I bought a fan for each of their bedrooms.

But there were also many superstitions and self-imposed rules among the riders. Some had specific issues. Eki, for instance, couldn't stand the number thirteen, so I couldn't put him in that room or let him race with that number on. All the time new superstitions cropped up, from something particular that a rider liked to eat or drink before a race, to their clothes being laid out a certain way. If one of them became convinced something had contributed to a good performance, they'd try it again.

Of course none of this worked on a logical level, but sport is emotional and events like crashes defied all logic too, leaving the lads desperate to control whatever factors they could. If that meant not shaving your legs the night before a big race, then so be it.

Other teams laughed at me as I walked around, fiddling with fans in rooms. 'Look at her, mammying them,' I overheard one mechanic snigger.

'Ah, shut up,' I replied. 'Plugging a few fans into their rooms is hardly luxurious!' Besides, I hoped the humming noise might help them drift off to sleep. This was another big issue. Before a big race, if a rider was tossing and turning all night there was no time to catch up on sleep. What they expected their bodies to survive each day was barely possible as it was. Try doing it on less than six hours' sleep and you were finished. I'd heard that some riders popped Valium, along with something else to wake themselves up again, but I never actually saw anyone taking it.

Other teams laughed too when they spotted I'd infused the lads' olive oil with garlic and basil.

'What's wrong with that?' I asked a soigneur who was shaking his head at me. 'It's only a bit of garlic in the bottle.' I even got a wheel of Parmesan from another Italian doctor who occasionally joined us. Attention to detail. Lance's ways were being absorbed and my lads were about to attempt the hardest bike race in the world, so they deserved it.

Maintaining the riders' calorie intake was just as hard as keeping on top of their superstitions. They needed up to nine thousand calories a day, but the human body is only capable of absorbing a finite amount in an hour. To help boost energy, I always made sure I had Clif energy bars on me, especially one flavour they all loved: carrot cake.

One afternoon during training, Tyler ducked his head into the camper. 'Any carrot cake left?' he asked.

He looked tired already. Drawn, like he had the weight of the world on his shoulders. Tyler had lost an unbelievable amount of weight since the days in Boulder and I rarely caught him smiling now. His wife, Haven, once told me she knew a race was nearing when she could see her husband's internal organs, his skin was so papery. Tyler had his shirt on, but he didn't look far from that state.

'Oh, sorry Tyler, we've run out,' I said.

His face changed. 'Emma,' he snarked, 'I bet if Lance had wanted one I could have one!'

I almost did a double-take at his churlishness. Always boyishly handsome, I noticed a five o'clock shadow I hadn't seen before, a slightly haunted look in those green eyes of his. This wasn't like Tyler; he wasn't a petty lad.

'I'm sorry,' I began again, but he stalked off, his shoulders sagging with self-pity.

'What's happened to you?' I thought sadly. I assumed the pressure of the race was eating at him. But I didn't just want the best for Lance, I wanted it for all our lads.

The 1998 Tour started in Dublin, so I went home for a few days before meeting the team off the specially assigned ferry to take them to the Dublin Sports Hotel in Kilternan. Arriving at 1.30 a.m. in my team car, I was going to ask the three teams staying there to follow me to the hotel, as it was a pain to find. As I waited by the port, I spotted police milling around. Assuming they were just here to escort us, I went to speak to them.

'What's up, lads? You escorting us? That's good of you,' I said.

'No, we're not police,' one of them replied, flashing his badge.

Customs officers.

'We want to conduct a search on the vehicles,' one said.

I couldn't contain a gasp, knowing what organized chaos lay behind the doors – a whole ton of supplies for three weeks, everything from bikes to spare frames and kit to frangipane.

'Listen, lads,' I said, 'the staff have travelled for twenty-four hours, everyone is dead grumpy before the Tour, and if you try and start pulling all that lot out they're gonna go bananas.'

The customs cop glanced at his colleague as they sized me up.

'If you wanna come to our hotel, there'll be plenty of room tomorrow morning to pull the place apart,' I suggested. 'Try it now and you'll need the riot police.'

Thankfully the officer nodded in agreement. 'Okay,' he shrugged.

The next morning at breakfast, someone pointed out that the head soigneur for Festina, Willy Voet, was missing. Festina were the world's biggest cycling team, with star riders who were favourites to win the Tour. Anything related to the team was going to create gossip, but I didn't think much of it until a mechanic sat down with his toast next to me.

'Have you heard?' he said, leaning towards me. 'About Willy?'

I knew Willy and always had respect for him, as he'd once helped me in a crush at a finish line, spotting before anyone else did that I couldn't get through. He was a nice guy.

'No.' I said. 'Where is he?'

'He's been busted.'

I paused mid-sip. My heart was racing, but not from the coffee.

'For what?' I whispered.

'Drugs. Last night. They found so much his van must've been rattling like a pharmacy.'

While away at races we never read newspapers and rarely watched TV. But Willy's face was soon everywhere. As the personal carer of Richard Virenque, known as 'The King', his arrest was big news. Statements were being made. A police investigation was in full swing. The sporting world was outraged.

Willy had been found with 234 doses of EPO, 82 vials of human growth hormone and 160 capsules of testosterone while crossing the border between Belgium and France near Lille. He was also caught with 'Belgian Pot': a stew of heroin, cocaine and other drugs staff were sometimes known to use to keep them awake on overnight drives. This alone was proof enough to me what a mad world cycling could be. I'd no doubt that using that concoction was playing Russian roulette with your life even more so than most drugs. Our team policy was that no staff were allowed to do overnight drives, thank God, yet I suspected younger soigneurs were tempted. I knew the route where Willy had been caught well; it was a known hotspot for police, so I wondered why such an experienced soigneur had chosen to drive it. In most countries it's not a criminal offence to dope in sport even though it is banned by sporting bodies, but in France it's illegal and of course he was carrying enough drugs to look like a dealer. Heads were going to roll.

Later on, in the car with a few of the riders, still the only topic of conversation was Willy.

'Maybe this will change things,' Frankie ranted. 'I'm sick of it. It's ridiculous. I did my first Tour on spaghetti and water but it's impossible to do it like that now. You just can't. Maybe this will clean it up?'

This was as much of an admission as I'd ever heard. Saying nothing, I stared straight ahead, concentrating on driving, wondering where this would lead. Not that I had to wonder for long. By that evening, it was clear. The knock-on effect was immediate and obvious. The camper door now remained closed all the time, suddenly there was lots more space in the cupboards and fridges, and all the plain cardboard boxes had vanished into thin air. I'd never need to tell a rider off for leaving dirty needles in hotel bins again. Whatever had been going on underground before had now dug down a whole lot deeper.

A few days later we were staying at the same hotel as Festina, the Novotel in Nantes, when I spotted their directeur sportif, Bruno Roussel, stalking across the car park, his face like thunder, occasionally lit by the flashes of news cameras. He'd been sounding off on the news about Willy, distancing himself and the team from him, as if poor Willy was a one-man bandit, keeping drugs for a one-man rave. As I looked at Bruno, I thought of Willy sitting alone in his prison cell, carrying one big can.

'You should be on the phone reassuring his wife, offering to pay his mortgage, asking for his loyalty. Not throwing him to the wolves,' I thought. 'If I was in Willy's position, I'd be singing like a canary.' Where did these guys get off, thinking it wasn't their problem? For what some soigneurs were expected to do, wages were very low, especially given the risks some were taking. Sure, it was their choice, but I couldn't get over the arrogance of it. The pressure to do it came from above.

In any case, at the Grand Départ in Dublin, it was announced that Festina riders Richard Virenque, Alex Zülle and Laurent Dufaux would face questioning when they returned to France. This wasn't a story about to be brushed away. Not this time. The police were involved.

Any feel-good factor and excitement about the Tour were crushed. We were in a constant state of alertness, riders expecting drama at any given moment as news of police raids swept through like wildfire. Stories of riders being pulled naked out of showers and thrown into cells for seventy-two hours, without so much as a phone call, were horrifying. I made sure I went to bed every night wearing a clean pair of pyjamas and that my suitcase was packed, and fell asleep with an ear open just in case. Even the cool and calm Dr Pedro was like a cat on a hot tin roof, something I secretly found amusing. The usually unflappable doctor could break into a sweat after all. Yet for us there were no fists banging on doors. I guessed they didn't want to bring down a US team, not with the potential promise of publicity and income for the Tour from a big new cycling market. Besides, even if the police did come, I assumed they'd not find much. We were not a clean team by now – I wasn't a fool – but surely anything we had wasn't on the scale of Festina?

Something that had become all too familiar by now, however, was the appearance of little thermos flasks along with a new number-one request from riders: ice. 'Ice, Emma? Is there any ice left?' I guessed it wasn't because of a sudden taste for cold drinks. By now riders were expected to carry the 'equipment' themselves and store it themselves, even if the doctor had a hand in administering or advising about the stuff. Once I saw a flask in the fridge, so I picked it up and rattled it. There was a clink of glass inside – a vial, I assumed, of the famous EPO. Ice was needed to keep EPO cool, otherwise, I learned on the grapevine, it could go off and be potentially lethal when injected.

The Festina story built daily during the Tour. By 18 July not only had Roussel admitted to systematic doping in the team, but Virenque left the Tour in tears and the team was expelled. In the end nine Festina riders were arrested and only one of their riders, Christophe Bassons, became 'known' to be clean. With all the added stress and the police clampdown, teams started to complain about the way the whole situation was being handled and nobody was able to concentrate on winning in such an atmosphere, so a strike was announced during Stage 17.

With the riders on strike (they completed the stage, but on a go-slow), Julien and I enjoyed a long day at the hotel. I loved his company, despite his general grumpiness when it came to the job. He owned one of our campers and those four wheels were his pride and joy. He had everything clipped down inside so he could take off at speed, and he never allowed any rider to do a number two in the loo. This was something that was not hard to wind him up about.

'Hey, they've been in there a while,' I joked whenever a rider occupied it for longer than thirty seconds.

'No shitting in the camper!' Julien would yell. My Pepe was always on the cusp of exploding, cussing 'For fuck's sake' in Dutch every few minutes.

With five or six different languages spoken on the team, we picked up on each other's sayings. I'd even heard Eki use my own old Dublin phrase 'Do you know where the five lamps is?' – meaning 'Get stuffed' – when someone asked too much of him. Hearing this in his gruff Russian accent on that particular day made us laugh – a rare moment of respite at a stressful time. By the end of the afternoon, Julien and I were sipping Perrier-Menthe in the sun, but neither of us was relaxed.

'Blimey, Pepe, what do you think's going to happen?' I asked him.

'Who knows?' he replied. 'But things will have to change around here.'

With Julien no subject was off limits; when it came to doping, however, it was always oblique references only. Then he told me what used to happen back in the day. 'Teams got round

87

doping control easily,' he explained. 'Riders would throw rocks at the testers' caravans. They'd get the wife of a mechanic to provide samples. "Congratulations," one rider was told when he got his results. "You're pregnant!"'

We both cracked up at the absurdity of it all.

The next day, the Tour director, Jean-Marie Leblanc, announced he'd negotiated with police that they would limit their tactics and the riders agreed to continue. In the end, out of 180 riders, only 96 finished. All nine of our lads edged over the finish line and the Italian Marco Pantani won the race, but there was little for anyone except him to celebrate.

The Tour, now dubbed the 'Tour of Shame', was over and we couldn't pack up fast enough. As we travelled back to Girona I heard that £15,000 worth of drugs had been flushed down the toilet of our team bus into a field in Le Creusot during the individual time trial, in which Tyler came second, on the penultimate stage of the Tour. Casting my mind back to the lush green fields we'd driven through, I wondered what effect banned substances would have on the vegetation.

'Well,' I mused, 'I guess whatever field it was, you could go back in a few years and find out. I bet that stuff makes wicked fertilizer.'

9

Going Underground

A WEEK LATER WE were off again to the Danmark Rundt, the Tour of Denmark, a six-stage race. While all the fridges had been pretty much cleaned out, I'd noticed that a flask had been left on its own in the door of one fridge, next to the milk. It had (not so) innocently been sitting there for weeks, even during the Tour de France. 'Typical men – think they've cleaned up completely, but look, they've missed a bit,' I thought to myself.

I didn't say a word. With hindsight, this was a sign of my own sickness. Without being conscious of it, I'd started to succumb to the 'crazy little planet' of cycling myself. Rather than just being an observer, I'd become part of the microcosm. Spending months on the road away from home, away from family and friends, we'd developed our own rules, jokes, even our own language. Things I found funny now I would never in a million years be amused by back home.

Granted, I wasn't thinking about this flask night and day, but I was aware it was there and I could have warned someone. After all, there was a risk police would find it in a raid, and yet

I got a twisted kick out of the secret knowledge. The dumbass clean girl soigneur, knowing what numpties some of the lads were. As I say, the sickness had set in.

Later on I got chatting to Johnny Weltz, who brought up the Festina affair, still the main topic on everyone's lips. Jean-Marie Leblanc had even admitted that the increased speed of the Tour peloton was due to doping and the newspapers were still full of reports of witnesses, from journalists to farmers, finding doping products hastily ditched along the route of the Tour in hotels and fields.

'Best thing is we're clean now,' said Johnny. 'Not got a thing on us. Everything's gone. They can search all they like.'

I smiled, then leaned into his ear. 'Oh yeah?' I whispered, nodding to the kitchen. 'Well how comes there's a flask sat in the truck fridge?'

It tickled me to see his face turn whiter than the fridge door itself.

The next day I noticed the flask had disappeared, but failed to register another fact: my humour had now grown very dark.

Perhaps it was being away from home for so long or because I'd been unlucky in love (or a plain avoidant, more like), but just before the Tour ended, when Simon Lillistone, the marketing guy from the helmet manufacturer Giro, asked me to go out with him I said yes. With lots of friends in common, Ryszard approved. 'Much better, Emma. He's more your age,' he winked. He was right, I thought. Simon felt more my equal and I believed we could make a go of things.

By August, Lance was back in the fold.

'Miss me?' he yelled, as he banged on my hotel door. He'd been training hard over the summer and was raving about his new place in Nice. 'I've left Kik to sort it all out. Yeah, it's gonna be amazing,' he said. 'We're redesigning it and having it gutted.'

I was pleased for him; maybe his new sense of confidence meant he'd got some faith back in his cycling too.

'Nice to see ya,' I said, watching him bounce around the room. 'Lance, you know you're like Calvin in *Calvin and Hobbes*, always on the go, wrecking yourself!'

He laughed his head off. The nickname, after the lovable kid cartoon character, just came to me as I watched him doing ten things at once: on his phone, looking at his laptop, chatting to me . . . It was so apt.

Next up we had the Ronde van Nederland – the Tour of the Netherlands – and another director, Denis Gonzales, was covering for Johnny Weltz. Denis quickly earned the nickname 'Speedy Gonzales' as we thought he was so slow. After the race, he was supposed to be giving Lance a lift to the main international airport, Schiphol, but he wasn't around so I stepped in.

The Netherlands had gone well and Lance was in good spirits, his phone clamped to his ear as usual as we drove. Earlier, he had replied to an email about marketing from Simon, adding a PS: 'I hear you're dating Emma, make sure you look after her!' Simon almost died. As ever, though, I secretly liked Lance looking out for me.

As we drew into the airport drop-off area, Lance pulled out a small package wrapped tightly in black plastic from his bag. It was the size and shape of about a dozen syringes tied together.

'Emma, can you dump these on your way?' he asked. 'I don't wanna take them through airport security. Thanks.'

I guessed they were syringes, but for all I knew they were for vitamins, although this was unlikely.

'Sure, leave them with me,' I said automatically, shoving

them in my glove compartment. Lance grabbed his bag and disappeared into the throng of the departure lounge as I drove off, my heart racing a little faster.

I was in a Postal team car and I was worried. Where could I dump them? A service station? No, that was too public. In a split second I decided to keep them on me and drive to Julien's house in Ghent where I was going for dinner that evening. I could chuck them out at his place; he wouldn't mind. I double-checked my seatbelt and pulled on to the motorway, keeping well within the limit. I wanted no excuse for anyone even to consider pulling me over. All the way, I kept checking my rear-view mirror for any car that came too close, or revved a little loudly. My imagination was running wild about unmarked police cars, but I told myself not to be paranoid. Finally I reached the border crossing from the Netherlands to Belgium, allowing myself a little sigh of relief. I'd made it.

Almost precisely at that moment, I spotted a flash of neon blue in my mirrors. A police motorcyclist was looming larger and larger in my rear-view mirror.

Fuck.

I slowed, praying that perhaps it wasn't for me. But yes, the police motorcyclist flashed, indicating I should pull over.

'Oh friggin' hell,' I said through gritted teeth.

My hands were trembling as I spun the steering wheel and changed gear. Pulling on to the side of the road, I took a deep breath. What the hell was I going to say? Why had he pulled me over? He could see I worked for Postal, that was for certain. Did I just fess up? Pretend I knew nothing? I felt sick. I resisted the urge to fumble in my jacket for my phone. I had to remain cool and calm, whatever he wanted. Instead, I thought about who to call in the worst-case scenario, as the officer solemnly dismounted his bike and took off his sunglasses.

I ran my fingers through my hair as he stalked over. I'd tried so hard to stay out of the programme, yet now this? A trickle of sweat snaked down my spine. I drew down my window.

'Hey, officer,' I said, forcing myself to sound bright. I thought speaking first might help. 'I was well within the speed limit, wasn't I?'

The officer was smiling. 'Do you work for US Postal?' he asked.

'Yes,' I replied, my stomach turning watery.

'Do you know Mark Gorski?'

Oh God. I felt my heart drop like a stone into my guts.

'Yes, he's my boss.'

'Ah, I used to race with Mark in the eighties, doing the track with him,' he grinned.

It took me a few seconds to register what he was saying. He didn't want to search my car, or question me, or arrest me. He was a *bike fan*?

'Oh, great!' I beamed back, resisting the urge to laugh out loud.

The officer was leaning on the car door now, just an arm's length from the hidden syringes. 'I've heard his son races too,' he continued. 'Well, if his son ever wants to come to Belgium as well, I'd be more than happy to see him.' He took off a leather glove to pull out his card.

'Thank you, officer,' I said, nodding enthusiastically. 'I'll make sure I pass this on.'

The officer lightly tapped the car roof and told me to take care. I think his words had barely left his mouth before I was drawing the window up again. Waiting until he rode off first, I set off again, this time driving faster. When I pulled into Julien's drive I almost fell out of the car with relief.

'What's up with you, Emmatje?' Julien asked.

'I've just lost a stone of weight in sweat,' I replied.

When I told him and Vera, Julien's face cracked into the biggest smile as he threw his head back and laughed.

'Here's the package,' I said, sliding it across the table. 'Please get rid of it.' I swallowed down my guilt. Dropping my dirty work in Julien's lap wasn't right.

Within seconds it had disappeared. I had no idea where Julien put it, but as long as it was out of my hands I didn't care much either.

The next time I saw Lance he made no mention of the syringes and neither did I. Granted, I wasn't happy about it, but nobody ever spoke openly about anything to do with the programme, and even if I wasn't happy about my impromptu role I wasn't going to break this unwritten rule either.

Along with the ceaseless clinking of ice in flasks, I'd also noticed spaces on walls in hotel rooms where riders took down pictures. Lance laughed about 'liking pictures in his hotel room'. I didn't ask why, but I assumed the picture hooks made convenient places to hang IV bags of saline or whatever they were using. I was also aware that Lance dealt with Dr Michele Ferrari, even if I never saw him or spoke about him. Ferrari was known as a 'dirty' doctor from years back. In 1994 he was under fire for making a claim that taking EPO was no more dangerous than drinking orange juice (his point being that taking copious amounts of anything is bad for you; not exactly a good analogy . . .). Every now and then I'd hear that Lance had disappeared off to Ferrara, where Ferrari lived, for a couple of days, but I never knew what for. Lance nicknamed him 'Schumi' after racing champ Michael Schumacher, and he was also known among other riders as 'The Myth' or 'Dr Evil'. Whatever he was called, I'd heard he saw riders as scientific experiments, there to be tinkered with, like a bike. Knowing Lance, I thought this would appeal.

Whatever was behind Lance's prep, he had another chance at his comeback in the Vuelta a España, Spain's premier road race. We chatted a lot every night and our friendship deepened during this tour, to the extent that I was prepared to be honest about how I was feeling. I hadn't had a pay rise for months and felt I truly deserved one now. Never would I have spoken to Lance about such a gripe before, but now there were no holds barred.

'I'm prepared to walk, in all fairness, if I don't get this,' I said. 'It's been a year.'

'Well just before you do that, speak to me,' he said.

A few days later a mechanic was moaning about his time off. Mechanics missed a lot of the excitement of races and were often stuck outside in the rain fixing bikes. It was no surprise many acted like martyrs at times.

'Emma,' he grumbled. 'You speak your mind. Would you mind saying something to someone? You don't mind speaking up.' Later, I took it to Lance and he cocked his eyebrow.

'Has he spoken to Julien about this?' he asked.

'No,' I said.

'Nah, if he's not prepared to fight his own battles then why should I?' he said. That was Lance. He only fought for people if they were prepared to do it themselves.

Buoyed throughout his time in Spain, it seemed all of Lance's ducks had lined up when he sailed in fourth, after 2,300 miles of racing. I was utterly made up for him and, after such a rocky start, the feel-good factor extended to all the team. This guy's dogged determination not to give up, along with his work ethic, beat any cynicism I felt about drugs in the sport. The question of doping, or his relationship with Dr Michele Ferrari, just didn't enter my consciousness.

I looked on as Lance stood near the podium watching the winners. He belonged there, I knew that much. Needless to say, I felt washed out and stood anywhere but near the podium girls, selected as they were for their looks and figures, but Julien, bless him, spotted me and read my thoughts.

'Don't you worry, Emmatje, they smell up the toilet the same as you and me.'

On my table that evening, every one of Lance's muscles felt empty, but my God he didn't stop talking. I'd barely finished the massage before he was sitting up and firing up his laptop. Unlike many riders, his recovery rate was phenomenal and he needed little attention before another burst of energy.

'Look, Emma,' he said, 'Johan says in this email: "I think fourth was better than you expected. You will look great on the podium of the Tour de France in your rainbow jersey."'

Lance's face was beaming, his eyes absorbing the words on the screen as if he'd fallen in love.

'He's a pure class guy, Johan, isn't he?' he said. 'Next year everything will be sorted.'

Johan Bruyneel was a rider from top team ONCE, and Lance had been speaking about him more and more. The pair had been in talks as Johan, a great strategist and reader of races, was nearing retirement. He was looking for a directorship.

'Well, Lance,' I replied, 'he could be right. You could win the Tour one day, couldn't you?'

'Do you think?' he grinned. 'Y'know, I'm gonna work at this. I'm gonna do everything I need to do. A new direction will be The Bomb. It's what's needed . . .'

As he talked and talked, it struck me how his strength of mind dominated even his body. This dude did everything to the nth degree. He didn't need a catchphrase or good-luck charm, he *was* the catchphrase and good-luck charm.

I thought of the 1997 Tour de France winner, Jan Ullrich. Somehow he was no match. 'Y'know Lance,' I said, 'Ullrich might have the physical strength, but you have the mental strength as well.'

He narrowed his eyes and glanced back at the email. Johan's words were an extension of what Lance's internal voice wanted to hear. Having someone to believe in him from the top had a powerful effect. I don't have full faith in many things, but at that moment I had faith in this man. In my eyes he was a winner already.

'Johnny wouldn't think this big,' I thought as I wiped my hands. 'Lance knows that.'

The Johnny Weltz situation was clearly becoming untenable as more things went wrong – cars breaking down, timetables going missing, pay cheques late – and by now Lance couldn't go for more than an hour without cussing his name.

Was it because my own moral compass had been contorted by the mad world in which we existed, or was it because I saw close up the odds he was battling? Whatever Lance was doing, I didn't see it as cheating. I witnessed a man who worked harder than anyone I knew. Who was still facing check-ups for cancer. Whose endless self-belief and goals inspired me in numerous ways in my own life. He was riding faster than before his illness, and after all his efforts he deserved this.

Meanwhile, we were all gearing up for the Worlds, held that year in Valkenburg in the Netherlands. When I checked the dates, however, I realized Lance's road race was on 11 October, but my good friends Peter and Sarah were getting married in the States on the 10th. Quickly I explained this to Lance, who was keen for me to be at the race. He listened as he tapped out a text message on the phone that seemed permanently glued to his hand. In many ways, staying to help him would show real loyalty to our biggest rider, but at the end of the day a good friend is a good friend. Long after I had left cycling Sarah and Peter would still be friends with me, for life, I hoped. With Lance, once I'd stepped out of Postal, the chances were I'd never hear from him again. That's just how cycling was. You were in. Or you were out.

'Lance,' I said quietly. 'It's Sarah and Peter's wedding when the race is on. I need to be there.'

He went silent. He knew Peter well from years ago too. 'Okay,' he finally said with understanding. 'I'm more likely going to need your help in the time trial rather than the road race. How's bout you stay for that, then go?'

Lance had an answer for everything. Tickets for my return flights were organized so that I was able to be there for the time trial. Job done.

In the end, I was needed in Valkenburg as he'd predicted. First of all, Lance was stressed, as his room was near a common room. 'Is it quiet enough for me to get to sleep?' he asked. 'Can you check?'

I walked into his room and closed the door, listening for sounds outside. Again, attention to detail and forward planning were everything. Then I had to intervene about the dinner. They were serving the pasta with rich, heavy sauces, the type Lance would have a fit over in case he put on weight – an obsession of his that was in overdrive. For Lance, climbing remained his Achilles heel, something he told me that his critics took great store in mentioning. Staying skinny as well as increasing his wattage, his power in pedalling, were his twin hopes for surmounting this. On climbs, cyclists became great poker players. The idea was that the better you could control the contortions on your face when in pain, the more soul-destroying it would be for your opponents. Cyclists had started to don sunglasses too. This had nothing to do with eyesight and everything to do with masking how they felt inside. Another example of crazy Planet Cycling, but it worked.

In the hotel, I ended up going into the kitchen myself to see if I could help keep the calorie count down by speaking to the chefs.

'Hey, this food looks amazing and I'm sure it tastes good, but can we have the bolognese sauce on the side, please? And just the good mince?' I asked.

'Pardon?' cried the chef, looking offended. 'What's your problem?'

'Yeah,' interjected another. 'We spent hours creating this and you've not even tried it.'

'Listen,' I continued, 'you're here to look after the riders. Please save your fancy cuisine for other customers not doing races.'

I knew how hard the lads tried to keep the weight off all year; there was no point in piling on pounds just to please some chef's ego.

After the World Championships Lance was having a house-warming party back in Nice, but I had to dash off to Sarah's wedding. Simon, however, was still keen to go. He liked Lance, and hung out with him when he could, so he asked if he could go without me. Feeling a bit awkward, I asked Lance if it was okay.

'Sure thing, if he wants to.'

I flew to Boulder for the lovely family wedding, made up for Sarah and Peter and pleased I'd put our friendship first. I barely had time to throw confetti and take a sip of champagne before I was back on a flight to France and at work.

A few days later, at our next massage, I asked Lance how his party had gone.

'It was a blast,' he said. 'Y'know what happened after, though? Simon and some lads went off to a strip joint!'

He was incensed on my behalf and so, quite frankly, was I.

'Did you go as well?' I asked, suspiciously.

'Hell no!' he cried. 'And leave Kik at home? Why would I wanna do that? Nah, Emma it's not on what Simon did, y'know?'

I agreed, but changed the subject. I'd have words with Simon when I got home.

10

Up a Gear

A FEW WEEKS LATER, when it was announced that Johan Bruyneel was joining our team as directeur sportif, I knew for a fact who was running the show. Lance must have gone to Mark and Thom to 'suggest' him. Johnny was out, Johan was in. The team once again faced a big shake-up and I, for one, had no idea what that would mean.

That Christmas, I was at my sister Clare's house in Dublin when Johan rang. 'I would like to offer you the job as head soigneur,' he said.

The fact that I'd been doing this job *de facto* but without the extra pay for almost a year suddenly no longer mattered. As a woman, to be recognized as good enough to lead the team on my own merit made me proud. There was one thing I insisted on making completely clear, however.

'That's great news, Johan. Thank you,' I said. 'But please understand I want absolutely nothing to do with the medical programme.'

'Yeah, yeah, sure, no problem. I know that,' he said.

I put the phone down, made up. Years later, when I thought

back to this conversation, I considered how useful it was to the team for me, the head soigneur, to be clean. After all, if anyone grew suspicious it could genuinely be said, 'She knows nothing about our medical programme', because although of course I was aware that things were going on, I genuinely didn't know anything about the specifics of the medical programme or what exactly the doctors were doing. Something was happening, that was obvious, but regarding the ins and outs, I was clueless.

If excitement around US Postal had already been growing steadily, by January 1999 we were about to explode as we ordered new stuff to get set up for the new season. Big companies were now queueing up to provide sponsorship, including Trek, Giro, Visa, Volkswagen and Shimano. The real coup was Nike, who were providing our team clothing. The multimillion-pound sportswear company was not known for supporting cycling, but with Lance's emergence and our improving results, things were changing. Lance was in talks to appear in commercials too.

During training, however, the lads quickly complained that Nike hadn't stitched the chamois on at the appropriate angle, so the riders were ripped to shreds with saddle sores. Quickly, we took them away to be restitched at a tailor's in Spain; saddle sores were the last thing they wanted to endure.

This year we had a guaranteed spot in the Tour, our riders were stronger than ever, and now we had a top strategist in Johan to head up races. My excitement was tempered, though, when I realized we'd be moving from beautiful Girona, as Johan lived in Alicante and had set up a service course in the nearby town of Piles. Compared to Girona, a lively, cosmopolitan city, Piles was a dump. There was nothing in it, nowhere to go and I didn't like it. So I rented a room and then often stayed with Simon in Valras-Plage, across the border in southern France.

The lads had met up earlier at a training camp in Austin, Texas, but the rest of us staff joined them in San Luis Obispo, California. Now there were eight soigneurs (four full-time, including me, Ryszard and a new lad called Jim, a friend of George Hincapie's) and twenty-three riders. On my steady rota now for massage were Kevin Livingston, JV and, of course, Lance.

In California we also met our new doctor, Luis García del Moral, who was replacing Pedro. I hadn't liked Pedro, but the riders did, as apparently he was reassuring when it came to the doping.

Midway through the season one of the riders admitted he was worried about a new drug, PFC (perfluorocarbon), that some of the other teams were said to be using; it mimicked blood transfusion by boosting red blood cells. Pedro had told him he thought it was dangerous and reassured him it wasn't something he'd be prescribing.

'He cares, you know, Emma,' said the rider.

I wasn't sure about that, as a cycling doctor was a cycling doctor, even if he was avoiding the more dangerous drugs.

Lance told me Pedro left Postal to go to work for ONCE, and that he was rumoured to be on $150,000 for fifty days a year. That confirmed to me, as if I didn't know it already, that he was far from clean.

The new doctor, Luis, had a medical centre in Valencia and Johan knew him from ONCE. I instinctively disliked him at first sight. Small, skinny, with the pinched face of a heavy smoker, it was his attitude more than anything that got me. I thought that he was lording it over the rest of us staff, always fussing over something.

'Ryszard,' he snapped a few hours after we'd arrived. 'Where's Ryszard?'

'Why do you need him?' I asked.

'I need someone to carry my bags for me.'

'Eh?' I said. 'We're staff, we carry our own bags.'

He huffed in my face and walked off to find Ryszard, announcing 'I do important work' as his parting shot.

Yeah, I bet you do, I thought.

With the arrival of Luis came the sudden appearance of crushed Coke cans. Luis would emerge from the camper with a rider, the mesh pocket of the rucksack on his back filled with them. I'd no idea exactly what they were for at the time, but they were clearly for something. Coca-Cola was another big Tour sponsor, but suddenly it seemed riders were drinking an awful lot of it, and I'd never known lads so bothered about squashing cans to minimize trash before.

Tyler Hamilton revealed in *The Secret Race* that that was where the lads hid their EPO syringes. Plink, into the appropriately sized hole, and then they just looked like trash.

Alongside Luis was a new sidekick called Jose Martí, also known as 'Pepe'. 'He is a new coach,' Johan had mumbled by way of introduction. After a few weeks I was yet to see any coaching going on. All Jose did was show up once in a while with boxes from the Valencia Institute where he apparently worked. Boxes started appearing again in the trucks or on their way to Luis's hotel room. One day I was chatting with Ryszard and some riders in the car about what Jose was supposed to be, exactly.

'I think he's a courier,' one of the riders shrugged. 'Just comes and goes and gives boxes out, no?'

Boxes filled with God knows what.

While sponsors were bringing in money and kudos, Johan brought in a new atmosphere, one with which I rapidly felt uncomfortable.

Johan, I felt, couldn't be called a man of sophistication. He wore cheap khaki trousers with zips halfway down the legs so they could be turned into shorts. He had an almost permanent scowl on his face. Still in his thirties, he was one of the youngest DSs ever in the Tour, and I sensed an immature aggression with it. His young wife, Christelle, waltzed around in crop tops and tiny skirts, with lots of make-up on, making it known she was the boss's wife. Johan had given her a job too, looking after the logistics, even if Christelle seemed to me to be more interested in her hair than in timetables, and in our busy world we didn't have room for people making mistakes.

Not being a fan of my new boss or his wife didn't seem like too much of an issue, however, as my thirtieth birthday was on the horizon. In my mind I'd not long left working in cycling, so I knew I wouldn't have to tolerate my new bosses for long.

For all Johan seemed to me to lack in people skills, he was a brilliant strategist, obsessed with cycling and with his star rider. Lance's face lit up when he walked into the room and they'd talk with such a passion, I spotted a proper bromance between them.

The Belgians were passionate about cycling; whom they worked for made up their identity and Johan knew his stuff, Lance said. And he was right. Johan had won what was the fastest stage race ever in 1993, and what he lacked in strength he made up for in strategy. He had come up with ideas on training camps too, looking for the toughest climbs to recce for the Tour in the Pyrenees. All this was right up Lance's street.

Just weeks into the season, Johan took me aside and told me that Jim, the soigneur George Hincapie had brought in, wasn't good at his job. 'I got this from Rabobank – it's a soigneur's job description,' he said, handing me a list. 'Go and give it to Jim to try and get him to do his job properly.'

'Why do I have to sound like the patronizing bitch?' I thought to myself. I didn't fancy making the lad feel awkward, even if getting me to do his dirty work did appear to be Johan's management style.

Predictably, when I showed Jim the list he looked at me in a funny way before making excuses and leaving. The next time I saw him things were distinctly cooler between us.

Johan wanted me to point out deficiencies with the other soigneurs too, something I didn't feel was necessary. There was no point speaking to Lance about it, though, as it wasn't my job to disturb riders with my dramas. I was their confidante, but it didn't work the other way round. Also, Lance had bigger things on his mind. Kristin had told me she was undergoing IVF as Lance had been left infertile by his chemo. Beforehand he had stored sperm in a hospital, so fertility treatment was their only option. I was pleased for her. 'I hope it all works out,' I said.

By March 1999, at Paris–Nice, I'd been on the road for a solid ten weeks, a long, tiring stretch. The team were performing well and already there was a sense of a build-up for the Tour. JV, however, was getting the rough end of Johan's temper at times. Over a massage, although as ever we spoke obliquely, he described to me how he was being told off for not being part of the 'programme'. He was a clever guy, a medical student, and had researched what was being tried on the team. He wanted to know what the UCI were doing, what the doping tests were for, why taking what would increase performance. He feared the team being busted, or 'popped', as it was known.

'JV, you're a fully formed human being,' I told him over the massage. 'The rest are two-dimensional and just do what they're told to win. They have no lives outside of cycling. But you're three-dimensional and have a good brain, so don't fit in.'

JV sighed as he flipped over on my table to let me stretch him. He told me how Johan had said he just needed to keep quiet and he was expected to do as he was told. 'One thing is for sure,' he added. 'We're not getting on.'

I felt for JV, because neither was I.

'It's like there's a cool group of riders that Lance goes for and an uncool group, and I'm in that group, the ones who don't toe the programme line,' he said.

I smoothed his calves, thinking about what he was saying. Where was this all going to end?

A few days later I'd just started massaging Lance when he picked up his phone and started giving out to someone.

'Yeah, it's not good enough. They're bloody useless, they're so slow, I'm not having it,' he ranted.

Hearing his cruel words made the bile in my gut rise. We soigneurs worked so damn hard for the riders, to listen to him sounding off about us like that to someone else was infuriating.

'Lance! How dare you speak like that!' I yelled at him. I threw his leg down on the table and turned on my heel. I knew he had his opinions, and my old angst about being a clean soigneur rose to the surface. Perhaps it was more of a problem than I realized? I didn't know. But no, I wasn't going to take this crap, not even from him. I stalked off down the corridor, until I overheard Lance shout: 'Hang on a minute, Kik. Emma's just gone completely mad! I'll call you back.'

I paused, as Lance carried on yelling. 'Emma! I wasn't talking about soigneurs, I was chatting about the builders on our house in Nice. They're being so fucking slow with the finishing touches it's driving me insane!'

'Oh! Ohhhh,' I replied. I felt myself heat up with sheer embarrassment.

'Now come give me that massage,' Lance grinned.

As they were on different schedules, riders usually ate separately to staff, but that particular evening Frankie Andreu, his wife Betsy and I found ourselves sitting together. I'd met Betsy a few times and if her husband was Ajax, she was Ajax-ultra, with her forthright views and no-nonsense ways, but I liked her well enough. As we chatted I relayed my story about yelling at Lance. 'I could've died when I realized it was a builder he was talking about and not me,' I said.

I noticed neither Frankie nor Betsy joined in with my laughter; in fact, they were looking at me, mouths agape. 'What? You shouted at Lance?' Betsy asked incredulously. 'And Lance is still talking to you?'

My own laughter died as I saw how serious their faces were. 'Yeah, sure,' I said, confused. 'Why wouldn't he be?'

Cocking an eyebrow, Frankie gazed at his wife.

'He must be going soft in his old age,' Betsy said, folding her arms.

I shrugged and changed the subject. To me, Lance was Lance. He had a temper and could go off the deep end, but he'd never shown that side to me. Like Frankie, Lance was always straight, but you had to eyeball him, and many were not prepared to do that. From what I could gather, if he was going to attack you he'd do it from the front.

People talked about Lance's habit of staring at you before he spoke, a quirk many found intimidating. I'd never noticed this, although he did always take a deep breath. Maybe because I was a girl he was different or he respected me. I didn't know. I just accepted him for what he was.

Shortly afterwards, with Paris–Nice over, as I worked away on Lance, he asked if I'd heard from home. Like everyone, I missed my friends and family and any news was welcome.

Living and working in the team could be claustrophobic and isolating, and we liked to talk about phone calls or family news.

'My sister Clare rang, actually,' I said. 'She's pregnant and, boy, you'd think she was a gymslip mum with the way my family's reacted.'

I explained how Clare had been with her boyfriend for years but the fact they weren't married meant a pregnancy was controversial. 'Some of my family were even surprised Clare's boyfriend was standing by her,' I said. 'So much prejudice still.'

'I know all about that, yeah,' said Lance, referring to his mum, who had him at just seventeen. 'Hopefully won't be as bad for your sister though!'

Later that day the team had been invited to Lance's house again. Driving up the hill towards it, my mouth fell open. It was understated, but absolutely beautiful, with white bricks and a red-tiled roof; it had the whole Provence thing going on, with a view from the veranda stretching all the way across the city to the Mediterranean. Kristin ushered us in, and while Lance took a few of the guys off for a tour, we wandered out to the pool, where she'd laid out a lovely spread.

'Guess what – I've good news,' she smiled. 'I'm pregnant.'

I gave her a hug, genuinely pleased. I knew Lance would be made up, but felt slightly odd about the fact that he hadn't told me, especially as we'd only been chatting about my sister's pregnancy earlier that day. Later on I caught up with him alone to congratulate him, although I didn't share what I was really thinking. He looked pleased as punch and I thought, 'Lance why didn't you tell me this morning?'

He was a funny guy. I guessed this was his way of not letting anyone get 'too close'. I also thought he hadn't done it on purpose. It was just another quirk of his.

Later that evening, I was sitting and staring across the stunning infinity pool when Kristin came over. 'You look tired, Emma,' she said. 'Why don't you stay the night here?'

Tears of utter exhaustion pricked my eyes. I was sitting in the most heavenly place, yet badly wanted my own bed. I longed to wake up tomorrow and not have to see or deal with any men.

'Thanks, but I'll go,' I replied. 'I need to be by myself tonight.'

After a much-needed few days off, I'd recharged the batteries and set off to cover the Amstel Gold race in the Netherlands. While sorting dinner for the evening I'd heard about a row between Frankie Andreu and Lance in the camper van that was so intense it was to leave their once close friendship never quite the same again. Apparently Betsy had responded to a message left on a cycling forum by a fan, commenting on whether Kristin planned to have a nanny or not. Betsy, being Betsy, decided to wade in and told the fan that Kristin would be a great mum. But when Kristin discovered her life was being discussed online she burst into tears and Lance readily faced down Frankie, telling him in no uncertain terms to keep his wife away. A storm in a teacup blew into a huge row thanks to unresolved but simmering tensions: Lance was already peeved about Kristin being left out of the friendship that had grown up between Betsy and Kevin Livingston's wife, Becky.

Keeping my own nose out of other people's business was another subtle part of my job, but the political side of life in the team made this increasingly impossible. Try as I might to keep my own head cool, things became strained a few weeks later when Johan's wife, Christelle, sent race logistics for the four-day race at Dunkirk to mechanic Geoff's girlfriend, Louise, instead of to me. This needed sorting, so I rang my boss's wife.

'Look,' I said, pulling a face down the phone, 'I really need that list more than anyone else. It's my job to make sure everything runs smoothly, you know that. I have to book flights, hotels, meals . . . the list is endless.'

'Okay,' she sighed, clearly not impressed.

Happy I'd got my point across, I hoped she wouldn't do it again.

Later that night I went into one of the trucks to sort out the bottles for the next day. As I poured the water, humming to myself, the door slammed.

'Who's that?' I whispered.

A tall, brooding figure stalked over. I immediately recognized the zipped-up khaki trousers, and Johan's poker face emerged from the gloom. I shuffled back against the kitchen worktop as he stood right in front of me. Breathing heavily, he jabbed the air between us with an index finger.

'Don't you *ever* question my wife again,' he snarled. 'What my wife says is what I say, is that understood?'

I swallowed hard. I wasn't one to be easily intimidated, but the way we stood eyeball to eyeball, I couldn't look away.

'Uh, okay,' I stammered.

'What Christelle says goes. Is that clear?' he snapped.

His steely gaze lingered on me for few seconds longer, then he gave a curt nod and stalked off. I let out a long breath, freaked out.

'This is really not working,' I thought. Since the start of the year tensions had clearly worsened. Johan's philosophy was divide and rule. I rarely had a laugh with the lads the way I used to, especially with riders like Tyler, who had a haunted look permanently etched on his face even in between races. I took a moment to catch my breath, trying to work out when my next day off was. I was so tired. I was miserable.

111

'You've got to pull yourself together, Emma,' I told myself. 'Crying is not going to help.'

Directly after this race I was to drive down to the Pyrenees to recce the roads with Lance. I was happy to go, until I heard that Johan and Christelle would be coming along too. Enduring the drive would be no mean feat.

'Never mind,' I told myself. 'Just pretend everything's grand.'

I had no desire to tell Lance what was happening with Johan; I kept it to myself. Lance didn't need me whingeing in his ear about a run-in with the boss.

On the drive down, Johan didn't utter a single word in my direction. Trying not to let it bother me, I kept my eyes on the road, taking in the beauty of the formidable mountains. Given the choice, I prefer the majesty of the Alps, but the intense wet green of the Pyrenees is awesome and never failed to take my breath away. We drove carefully, as fresh snow lay on the roads.

'How the hell is Lance going to train on this?' I wondered. It seemed crazy even to try, but what did I know. A bit of snow wasn't going to deter him – that's what made Lance different to anyone else. In spite of the wintry conditions he was determined to recce the course himself. He liked to know every corner, every twist, turn, every gradient and incline. A little bit of snow? Pffft!

We arrived at the Hôtel du Commerce in Saint-Gaudens, unpacked and went for dinner. Lance was as strict as ever with his diet, sticking just to chicken and vegetables. When the desserts arrived, however, he did a double-take at my plate of gooey chocolate pudding.

'Emma, is that good? Sure looks good,' he grinned, clearly tempted, as I licked my spoon.

'Actually Lance,' I replied with honesty, 'it's not as good as it looks, to be fair.'

'So not worth the calories?' he persisted.

'Nah,' I replied.

He looked at me. 'Okay,' he shrugged.

Lance had even vetoed the chocolate HobNobs I brought back from Ireland for the lads, who loved them. Envious riders from other teams accused me of spoiling them, but I just laughed. 'Ach, they're grown men, not children,' I would say. 'It's their livelihood and if they fancy a treat now and again, let them.' I would just put out one packet, though, so each rider had only one or two biscuits.

The next morning I had Lance's clothes and bottles all prepared. More snow had fallen overnight, making the roads even worse. 'If there are any road blocks, I'll just carry the bike over them,' Lance said with a shrug.

Some lads working on an advertising campaign for Nissan were staying in the same hotel but had cried off work for weeks due to the poor weather conditions. Lance set off on a six-hour ride, with Johan following where he could in the car. This was the same route that the riders would be challenged on during the Tour de France, and Johan had worked out precisely at which point Lance needed to increase his wattage. Nothing was being left to chance, which appealed to Lance's perfectionist style. I thought what a team they made: Johan had the mind, Lance had the body and spirit. It was a powerful combination.

The next day we moved to the Mercure hotel in Saint-Lary-Soulan and the regime followed the same pattern. First I made sure Lance had everything he needed, then waited for him to return for his rub. I was hanging out with Kristin when Christelle joined us for lunch and her phone rang.

'Okay,' she said, taking instructions, before turning to me. 'Johan says you're to pretend to be a diabetic and get an IV bag of glucose from the chemist's.'

113

'What?' I frowned. 'Why me?'

I knew deep down what Johan was insinuating. I was knackered after months on the road now and, though there was no room for vanity here, Johan's request offended me all the same.

'Haha,' I laughed. 'No way am I doing that.'

'That's what he asked,' pressed Christelle.

I looked at her and asked what the product was called. Later on, when Johan got back, I simply said to him I'd not been able to pronounce the name of the glucose product in French. 'Someone else will have to get it,' I told him. This was really not what I'd signed up for when Johan had asked me to become head soigneur, even if this time my objection was based less on principle and more on vanity!

11

Courier

THE NEXT EVENING, AS we were preparing to leave Saint-Lary-Soulan, Lance knocked on my room door.

'Emma,' he said, looking at me directly, 'I, ah, need something picked up from the doctor in Spain.'

I knew 'something' might possibly be something I didn't want to know about. But the loyal soigneur side of me appreciated that Lance must be in a fix if he was asking. After all, he never put me in awkward positions unless he had to.

'Uh, okay,' I said. 'Sure, Lance.'

For me, being a clean soigneur was part of my place in the team, however much Johan threw it back in my face. 'What does *she* know?' he'd sneer within earshot if I happened to be around when anything to do with the 'programme' was going on. As the team's only girl, my refusal to be involved in this side of things appeared to be accepted and Lance respected this too, even if it hurt my pride that I wasn't able to provide the 'whole service'. Lance always put in more than a hundred per cent effort and, as the person looking after his wellbeing, that rubbed off on me. I wanted to do whatever it took to help. If he was asking for my assistance now, I automatically assumed I was his last resort.

'Great,' Lance said, beaming. 'You can get it off Johan down in Piles. Then bring it back to me in Nice the next day, okay?'

'Sure,' I said, by now prickly with growing discomfort. 'But don't tell me what it is.'

We both knew this would mean driving across a border with guards, police, sniffer dogs . . . I closed my eyes. I really, really didn't want to know what this 'something' was; it would make me even more nervous.

'Simon's picking me up on the way,' I continued, trying to sound casual. 'I'll probably drive down with him.'

Lance stopped in the doorway and looked up. 'Oh,' he said. 'Emma, don't mention this to Simon. Okay?'

'Okay.' I shrugged. Oh God, now I knew this 'something' was definitely something illegal.

'Just this once, Lance,' I thought. 'Just this once.'

On 6 May, the training week was over and we were packing up to leave when Johan suddenly asked for my keys to our official US Postal team car, emblazoned with our blue and red logo. As his underling I didn't hesitate to hand them over, even if I didn't know why he needed them.

'How am I supposed to get home?' I asked.

Johan just shrugged. 'Where's Simon?' he said.

The previous evening Simon had come down to see me for dinner. He was still working for Giro and living in Valras-Plage so he had left before dawn, taking his company car.

I looked at Johan incredulously. 'Johan, Simon works, he has a job. It's not his job to be following me around whenever it suits you.' I tried to soften my voice. I realized this was speaking a little out of turn, but keeping my temper in check was becoming harder.

Thankfully, Julien stepped in. 'You can come in my camper van,' he said.

'Thanks,' I said with a smile, although I was annoyed that I would now have to hire a car to make the journey to Piles. But for now I was happy to have a lift from my Pepe; we always had fantastic chats. So we set off for the motorway exit where Simon was picking me up.

Aside from Simon's flying visit the night before, we hadn't spent proper time together for weeks now, but finally we could look forward to a proper catch-up. Simon was always very keen to hear what had gone on in the team; he was even crazier about cycling than I was. As I told him about Lance's training and how offended I was about the glucose bag, he listened intently.

'Honestly, do I look like a friggin' patient who needs a drip?' I asked.

Simon laughed. 'I could never see you as the patient, Emma,' he said.

Back at Simon's place in Valras-Plage, Lance's request was playing on my mind and, as much as I didn't want Simon to be involved, I wasn't going to hide it from him either. Taking a deep breath, I told him everything – well, everything I knew.

'You don't need to be part of this,' I insisted. 'Seriously, Simon, if anything goes wrong, I don't want you caught up in it too. Really I'd prefer it if you didn't come.'

Simon wasn't the most expressive man at any time, and barely a ripple crossed his face as I explained my predicament. But he shook his head and said he'd come.

'But if we're caught carrying anything, I will take the rap you know!' I cried.

Simon blew out his cheeks and agreed.

Two days later we set off on the six-hour drive in our hired car to the team service course in Piles. Next door were two small, modest houses where soigneurs and mechanics stayed, and I had sublet a room to myself. Geoff, the mechanic, was away and his girlfriend Louise was alone, so despite being exhausted after our drive, I stayed up with her for a chat before we fell into bed.

The next day Johan arrived. He lived about twenty miles away in Alicante and was already by the team truck as I loaded provisions and equipment for the next race. He looked uncharacteristically cheerful.

'Emma,' he said, his smile open and warm. 'You need these.'

Very discreetly he slipped a brown pill box into my palm. He smiled again – a sign, I felt, that I should conceal the box immediately. I knew I must be doing him a big favour for him to be so pleasant all of a sudden. I excused myself and went to the bathroom, where I slipped the pills into my toilet bag. It felt like carrying kryptonite. They were little white tablets, and it was only years later that I understood what they must have been: cortisone, a banned drug used for masking pain. Lance wanted to train harder than ever, and taking cortisone now rather than during a race meant he would gain all the benefits but was less likely to be caught.

Now I had the drugs in my possession it all felt too real and that night I kept my voice at a whisper as I worked out with Simon what we should do.

'Look,' I repeated, 'I will keep it on my side of the car door, and I will take the blame if anyone stops us.

'Do you know what the stuff is?' asked Simon.

'No,' I replied, and I didn't fancy speculating either. 'If anything happens en route, though, I'll ring Thom. He knows powerful people; he'd get me a good lawyer . . .' More help than Festina had given Willy Voet, I hoped; he was now saddled with a ten-month suspended sentence and a criminal record. But of course the idea that Thom would hire the best lawyers for me was something I just assumed would happen; it wasn't as if I'd actually asked Lance to confirm he would save my skin.

After a bad night's sleep, the next morning we set off, the pills safely stowed on the driver's side. Simon and I chatted as the motorway miles flew by, trying to forget the tiny brown box rattling in my car door. I kept within the speed limit at all times, allowing anyone who wanted to overtake to do so. Finally we arrived at border control.

'Shit,' I hissed, gripping the steering wheel. There was never a queue. Today there was one.

We crawled forward inch by inch, bumper to bumper, as officials in fluorescent jackets roamed up and down. I felt sick, a knot forming in my stomach. Visions of sniffer dogs all over our car and of being handcuffed raced through my mind.

'I'm nothing but a glorified drug smuggler,' I muttered under my breath. I felt annoyed. For me – and Simon – to be in this position just wasn't on, although ultimately it had been my call. My heart was thumping faster than ever. I glanced at my phone, trying to keep calm. Yes, I was sure Thom would help me. Surely he would? That's if I had time to make that phone call.

Finally it was our turn and a policeman started walking towards us. 'Anything happens, you know nothing,' I whispered again to Simon. He nodded his head.

Then we were suddenly waved through, as if the official hadn't a care in the world. I pressed the accelerator a little too hard and breathed out heavily. 'Oh mother of Christ,' I sighed. 'That was no fun.'

Then it occurred to me. Our car looked so inconspicuous. Perhaps Johan had taken my US Postal team car on purpose, knowing we would be less likely to be stopped if I was in an anonymous vehicle?

'Clever,' I thought.

I'd never been happier to see France. When we arrived home, I grabbed the pills and jumped out to get indoors as fast as possible, grateful that tomorrow I'd finally be able to get rid of them.

The next morning Simon went to work and I drove to meet Lance in a car park at McDonald's in Fréjus, three and a half hours away. Traffic was bad on the way and I realized that I was going to be late for our midday rendezvous. Lance hated lateness or inefficiency of any kind, but keeping him in the loop made it less likely he'd be upset, so I called him.

'Lance, I'm about twenty minutes away,' I told him, my foot on the accelerator.

'Hey, no worries, Emma,' he replied breezily. 'Whenever.'

'Oh,' I thought, 'that's not like Lance.'

Spotting the golden arches, I swerved into the car park. Lance's Passat was already pulled up and as I parked next to it he opened the door. I jumped from my seat, clutching the pills in my sweaty hand. Thankfully the box was small enough to look like I just had a clenched fist.

'Hey, Emma!' he said brightly. I glanced over and saw Kristin in the passenger seat. She was wearing tracksuit bottoms and a casual top, as if she'd been to the gym. Their dog, Boone, was on her lap. I passed the pill box to Lance, closing my palm over his.

'Thanks,' he said, swiping it, quick as a flash. 'Catch ya later.'

He leapt straight back into his car and started up the engine. I sat back in my seat, leaning my head against the headrest. The deed was done. I could breathe easy. All the 'what ifs' were quickly shoved to the back of my mind.

'I hope that never happens again,' I thought, as I turned the key in the ignition.

On 17 May Lance began a second pre-Tour training camp that he had arranged, including a stay in Sestriere, an Alpine village in Italy close to the French border. It's a common stage finish in the Tour and Lance wanted to recce the area and train on the climbs. Johan was there examining the course too, so by the end Lance would know every twist and turn like the palm of his own hand.

On the first night, after a seven-hour ride, Lance started talking to me about Betsy Andreu. 'I don't know what her fucking problem is,' he ranted. 'She's fucking going nuts at me.' He picked up his laptop and showed me an email she'd sent him back in April.

Betsy must have been furious when she wrote it. She was telling Lance he was disrespectful to everyone, and so many people put up with it, and he walked over everyone. 'Sorry Lance I'm not going to not stand up to you like so many others,' she'd written.

I thought back to the surprised look on Betsy and Frankie's faces when I'd told them how I'd shouted at Lance while he was chatting about the builders. Maybe Betsy felt now that Lance could take criticism. 'Yeah, she's pissed at you,' I agreed.

'Can say that again,' Lance laughed. 'Who does she think she is?'

Training camp was a success, and on the last night Johan asked me to book a table at the Last Tango, the only restaurant open in the area, serving specialities like wild boar burger and veal fillet. It was a treat after what seemed like a lifetime of chicken and fish salads. After making the reservation for Lance,

Tyler, Kevin, Dr Luis, Johan and myself, I was then asked to reserve an extra seat. When I turned up that evening, I found out who it was for. Dr Michele Ferrari. The Myth. The man Lance called Schumi. With a name and reputation such as his, I hadn't expected him to look as he did: small, mousey, quiet, speccy. Lance was sitting next to him, conversing intensely. What an odd pair they looked, the Texan boy racer and the mad professor, yet I sensed a healthy mutual respect. Michele was about facts and figures; he saw Lance as a machine, and Lance saw Lance as a machine, a winning machine in need of tweaking every now and then.

As we ate, I watched as Luis sat silently fuming. With every mouthful he glanced at Michele, and I could almost see the speech bubble rising above his head: 'Who do you think you are?' I couldn't help but smile to myself. The team doctor's nose had been well and truly put out of joint. Every so often Tyler and Kevin glanced over nervously at Michele. Everyone knew what a reputation this guy had; everyone knew meeting him in public like this might not be the sanest idea. But it was Lance's idea, so we all went with it.

Years later, as I have recalled this meeting many times over, I've mused on how the players in cycling's biggest scandal all found each other. They were a talented trio, Lance, Michele and Johan, a potent mix of minds and bodies, able to cheat the world quite spectacularly.

The next morning I knocked on Lance's door first to wake him up. There was no need to wait for him to shout back; he bounced out of his room already raring to go. 'Let's go to breakfast together,' he said nodding downstairs.

I still needed to wake Tyler and Kevin, but as we approached their doors, before I could stop him, Lance banged on them hard with both his fists. '*Carabinieri! Carabinieri!*

CARABINIERI!' he screamed maniacally, attempting an Italian accent.

I could almost sense the panic through the doors, as Tyler and Kevin flung theirs open, looking stunned, fully expecting to be busted by police. As their shock turned to anger, Lance was almost bent double with laughter. He knew full well they'd been on edge during dinner with Ferrari, and he couldn't resist a bit of fun.

'You fucking bastard!' someone swore, then their doors slammed shut again.

I couldn't help but laugh, even if Lance's humour was sick.

The Critérium du Dauphiné Libéré is an important race in the build-up to the Tour. Set over eight stages in June, its many climbs, like Mont Ventoux in Provence, regularly appear in the mountain stages of the Tour. Many winners of the Tour have been experienced climbers who have won the Dauphiné Libéré in preparation.

And it was during this race in 1999 that, all of a sudden, Johan requested nine little roller suitcases. I went out to look for some, but couldn't find anything suitable. The riders only ever had one suitcase each, but I could guess what this was for. After I came back empty-handed, Johan rolled his eyes and sent Christelle into the town.

'Yeah, good luck,' I thought, knowing she'd have to try exactly the same shops as I had.

Later that day, I bumped into Johan as he came out of my room with a holdall belonging to Simon that I'd been using. 'Simon Lillistone' was scrawled on the side.

'What you doing with that, Johan?' I asked.

'Using it,' he snapped. 'We need bags, this one is empty.'

'No, no,' I cried. 'You're not using Simon's bag for any

"stuff". I don't want that with his name on it. You can't use it.'

Johan shot me a look which almost startled me, then reached into his back pocket for a pen and scrawled out Simon's name.

'There!' he said. 'Now it's not Simon's bag any more, is it?'

You bastard, I thought. I'd no doubt what the new bags were going to be carrying.

Men are just as big gossipers as women, if not more so, and our team was no different. Away from home, isolated from the world, there was plenty of drama between staff and riders. When we weren't racing, we were resting, and what else did we have to do except talk about each other?

When news broke that Marco Pantani had been expelled from the Tour after testing positive for irregular blood levels in the Giro d'Italia, Europe's second-biggest road race, nobody seemed worried or panicked. The general consensus was that if a rider got popped, they just hadn't been careful enough.

By now it was tacitly accepted on the team that we were using Julien's diabetes as a legitimate excuse for prescribed insulin. At the time I didn't realize that insulin has the same effect as testosterone in repairing your body after a race, and yet it also leaves your system quickly and is undetectable.

Although conversations frequently contained allusions to doping, nobody ever came out plainly and told you what they were doing. The only thing riders did discuss were haematocrit levels – an indicator of doping – but never their own, always other riders'. Lance, however, never failed to surprise me. During a massage during the Dauphiné Libéré, on 10 June to be precise, he suddenly blurted out his haematocrit level in the middle of a conversation about race preparation.

'Emma, my haematocrit level is only forty-one,' he said.

We both knew what this meant: he needed to get it higher in order to climb well in the race.

'Oh, Lance, what are you gonna do?' I asked, worried for him.

'Ha, what everyone else does,' he shrugged, turning for me to massage his glutes.

'Uh, okay,' I said, glad he was lying face down and unable to see my expression. For the first time he was openly telling me something, but instinctively I shied away from it. I was a clean soigneur; I didn't need to know and he didn't need to tell me.

As we fell silent I asked myself again why Lance kept me on. He had his trainer, his doctor, and he could easily have had a dirty soigneur, one to complement whatever programme he was on. I didn't quite understand my role in Lance's world, but concluded that perhaps he just liked my massages. I changed the subject and asked how Kristin was doing.

After the race I stayed with Simon and a few of the team at Les Ursulines Hotel in Autun. After a fun night to let off a bit of steam, I woke in the morning, head banging, but with a happy feeling despite a hangover from hell descending. As I opened my eyes, I began to piece my memory back together. Last night, holding my hand across the table, Simon had asked me to marry him and I'd said yes.

However much I loved Simon, we had agreed not to move in together properly until we were engaged, good Irish Catholic girl that I was. No matter where and how far I travelled, I could never escape those roots, such a moral compass had they instilled in me. Little did I know how pivotal this would prove when it came to dealing with Lance years later too.

12

The Big Chance

FOLLOWING THE FESTINA SCANDAL the year before, the media circus surrounding the Tour de France in 1999 was bigger than ever before, the atmosphere more intense than ever, and with Marco Pantani banned and Jan Ullrich now out of the race through injury, the competition was wide open. As exciting as this was, critics were already writing off Lance's chances. He wasn't a gifted climber and had no hope of winning, they claimed. Lance never missed a beat, so I was sure he'd heard the criticisms loud and clear, and that he would use them as ammo to spur him on. He was at the peak of his fitness, he'd left nothing to chance with his strategic planning, and he seemed as buoyed as ever.

This year's event was dubbed the 'Tour of Renewal', with the organizers claiming they were cleaning up the sport, but JV was one rider who wasn't convinced. He was worried what Johan had up his sleeve (or hidden in the camper van) and feared a bust. The fact that we could all end up in the clink if this happened was a stark reality I tried not to think about. I'd no idea what was said between them but, after another run-in with Johan, JV was quick to silence his fears.

By now I refused to dwell on the doping side of things. The riders had to do what they had to do, and as long as I played no part in it, I was prepared to turn my cheek. Yes, with hindsight it was a completely warped philosophy for someone who called themselves a clean soigneur. But having been totally immersed in the cycling microcosm for three years, with all its hopes, dreams, blood, sweat and (lack of) tears, it felt natural. These days cycling was a business, in which, as a team, we had dreamed big, then worked hard and grown. We had reached the dizzy heights of being invited to the Tour and now we were back for a second time, stronger than ever. Whatever the lads had to do, it was a level playing field. There was no way any races longer than a week anywhere in Europe were being ridden *pan y agua*. It was a sad but inescapable fact.

On the morning of the pre-medical at the start of the Tour, when riders are wheeled out in front of the watchful media by the Tour organizers as if to say 'Look how carefully we monitor our riders', Lance called me to his room. I found him in the bathroom.

'Hey, Emma,' he said, pointing to the outside of his arm. 'You got any concealer I could borrow?'

I looked down at the skin on his right upper arm and saw a couple of bluey-green bruises, undoubtedly caused by a needle.

'Whatever it is you girls use?' he grinned. 'Concealer? Foundation?'

My face was most definitely a different shade to Lance's arm. 'My colour will never match yours,' I laughed. 'But I'm going shopping so I'll pick something up.'

He nodded. 'Thanks.'

On the way back from my morning trip to the supermarket, I nipped into the pharmacy, rooted through the make-up counter and, having no clue what would match Lance's arm, bought a few shades. I returned to find him in the bathroom again, his chest puffed out in front of the mirror, rolling his T-shirt sleeve up and down.

'Try this one,' I said, passing him the bottle. As he started smearing it on, I shook my head.

'You're a friggin' nutcase, Lance,' I laughed. 'That's not going to work and you're gonna be in front of all those photographers too.' I could see the headlines now: 'Exclusive – What ARE these tell-tale needle marks on Armstrong's arm?'

Lance laughed. 'Nah, it'll be okay.' He pulled his T-shirt sleeve over the top of the mark. 'How's that?'

'Your sleeve is gonna rub it all off,' I said, pulling it up again.

'Uh, it'll be okay,' he said, shrugging me off.

I hoped so. Half an hour later he was posing with the other riders in front of the world's sporting media. Cameras captured every moment, but not a soul noticed the foundation badly smeared on to the arm of Lance Armstrong.

The prologue to the 1999 Tour was a 6.8-kilometre time trial. Time trials were filled with excitement and drama, and I hated them. Not only were they a nightmare to organize, with riders to-ing and fro-ing at different times, but all of a sudden the camper-van door was permanently slammed shut and Dr Luis and Jose Martí were very busy indeed, making it hard to avoid noticing whatever was 'going on'. And without a doubt something was, just metres away from the throngs of bike fans desperate for a glimpse of their heroes. Equally desperate to keep away from it, I would usually volunteer to organize hotels for the day.

Today, though, I waited at the finish line, barely able to bring myself to watch. Lance had just minutes to prove what form he had, in a flat sprint of around 5 kilometres followed by a nasty uphill section at the end of the time trial. It was the culmination of months of training, of talking wattages and figures with Johan.

Frankie Andreu had already fallen apart on the final climb, after setting off too fast, then Abraham Olano came in with a course record of 8.13, before Alex Zülle, one of the favourites for the Tour, went round in 8.09.

'C'mon, Lance, you can do this,' I muttered. Somehow my guts told me he would. He'd instilled such faith in me by now. Lance losing felt impossible.

I looked at the screen to watch him released from the starters' cage, then, my hands over my mouth, I stood together straining my neck to follow him all the way to the finish line. The chants of *'Lance! Lance! Lance!'* became a cacophony; the minutes felt like hours. Then he appeared, as if flying, and it was over. The crowd broke into shrieks and screams as we looked up to see the clock.

8.02.

A seven-second lead. Friggin' hell.

I felt a lump in my throat and my eyes welled up. 'He did it! He did it! He did it!'

I rarely got emotional when it came to races, but this was different. The biggest cycle race of them all and he'd won the first stage. There seemed to be something so genuinely pure and innocent about what Lance had achieved. Needle marks or no needle marks, I didn't care. He'd done it. The next few minutes passed in a blur of smiles, screams, hugs and cheers. Johan grabbed Lance as he got off his bike and threw his arms around him. His prodigy had won.

With his first *maillot jaune*, or yellow jersey, Lance was leading the Tour de France. He'd defied all the odds – the cancer, the naysayers, the teams who'd let him down along the way – and he'd done what he'd said he'd do. Win.

Later, during the massage, Lance was still flying high. But not only was he determined to win, his little black book was filled with people he wanted to get even with and this was a perfect start. I was so happy for him.

I finished my rubs late and was just having a hot shower before dinner when there was a knock on the door. 'Ah, can I not even have a minute's peace?' I thought. Sometimes I felt riders were like toddlers.

'Yes?' I called, trying not to sound too annoyed.

'It's Mark. We're about to pop open the champagne and we're waiting for you before we do.'

'Coming!' I cried, flattered they were waiting for me. I quickly dressed and rushed to join them, raising my glass high. I couldn't have been prouder to be part of it. Over dinner the atmosphere remained jubilant as the reality of the US Postal team leading the Tour sank in. Lance, always the man of the moment, was super-charged. 'We've still got a lot of work to do,' he kept saying, but I could see in his eyes that being a champion suited him; it was as if he'd come home.

The opening stages sped along open and monotonous flat roads, everyone jostling for position in the peloton, trying to avoid crashes. It was clear how strong our lads were, with Frankie, George and Tyler all proving to be excellent support riders for Lance. They protected our star from the wind and the rain, and on the second stage got him safely over a difficult causeway called the Passage du Gois, a narrow road over a tidal marsh, without being caught in one of the pile-ups. Poor JV did come a cropper, though, crashing and cutting his face wide open. That was why luck was so important: a crash could be caused by something as random as the wind changing.

Five days into the race, Kevin told me he'd been called out of the blue into the medical centre.

'Why?' I asked.

'They wanted to talk to Johan really, not me,' he said. 'Give him the heads-up about Lance. He's been tested positive for cortisone.'

My mouth fell open. It was all so sneaky. The UCI officials needed to speak to Johan, but it would have looked suspicious if he'd turned up at the medical centre on his own, so he took Kevin so as not to arouse suspicion.

Not only was I shocked for Lance, but I also felt incensed on Kevin's behalf. He'd had to have a random drugs test, with the risk attached that he could have been positive too, when the real issue wasn't him but Lance.

'What's going to happen?' I asked.

Kevin shrugged. 'It's sorted,' he said. Nothing else seemed to come of it, so we put it to the back of our minds.

As the Tour wore on, I watched the familiar pattern of the race's brutality kicking in. By Day Seven lads were starting to flag, big time. Tyler, however, was renowned for his ability to 'dig in' and psychologically to go beyond the pale. His role as *domestique* was to set the pace and protect Lance, riding slightly ahead so that Lance was in his slipstream and didn't have to pedal so hard. This forced Tyler to expend far more energy than his team leader, and he did the job remarkably.

With Lance there the other team riders knew the score: they had to put their own ambitions to one side in order to help him to victory. And being on a winning team in the Tour would be momentous for their careers, not to mention their bank balances. However, I could sense a growing unhappiness within Tyler, etched deep in his eyes. The boy who had loved to goof around in Boulder, and had an innate ability to make anyone, whoever they were, feel better about themselves, seemed to have shrivelled up somewhere along the way. All that remained was a cold brusqueness. He barely spoke or looked anyone in the eye. My heart went out to him.

I carried on trying my best to give the lads what they needed, even if what I really wanted to do was just pick them up and put them to bed as they disintegrated in front of my eyes, growing older, smaller and frailer each day. By the end of the evening I used to think, 'They need their mammies to tuck them in their beds' as their bodies cried out for proper rest.

With exhaustion came short fuses. One morning I arrived at breakfast to find tempers frayed over the big pot of jam.

'He's double-dipping, licking his knife and sticking it in and out again,' one rider complained bitterly about another.

I wanted to laugh, but looked concerned. Behind the pettiness they did have a point: if a rider had a cold it would spread like wildfire. Then another rider waded in, accusing someone else of doing it, and I held my hands up.

'Okay, lads, how about if I go and get some small individual pots for yous all and put your names on them?'

That seemed to satisfy them, and Lance nodded approvingly.

Catching a common cold was as potentially lethal to a rider's performance as a serious injury and was treated as such. During a race earlier in the year I had a stinking cold so, feeling sorry for myself, I retired to my room with a box of Kleenex. Shortly afterwards, as I lay sniffing, I overheard Lance outside my door. 'What's she still doing here, then?' he ranted to Ryszard. So I went home for a few days to recover. It was nothing personal. The lurgy was just not wanted anywhere near the riders.

Before the time trial in Metz on the eighth stage, Lance

asked me to recce the course with him. This meant finding an extra two hours in a mad, busy day, but it was my job to be where I was needed. We set off to drive over the 56-kilometre course, with Lance popping in and out of the car on the bends and corners so that he could practise them on his bike. There were two very big climbs: one of 1.5 kilometres and one of 4 kilometres. In the car he was silent for a change, concentrating, looking at his map, working out the route.

During the time trial itself, as always, I turned away from the closed camper-van doors and Luis's comings and goings and kept myself busy elsewhere. The result was incredible. Lance won again, this time beating Zülle by nearly a minute. He was leading the Tour again.

There was much talk about VO2 levels on this Tour. VO2 measures a person's aerobic fitness and maximum rate of oxygen consumption, and in certain circles Lance's was seen as higher than normal. In fact his VO2 wasn't as high as that of some other riders, and wasn't even the highest on the team (Christian Vande Velde held that honour), but this was hushed up. Of course Lance, and indeed our sponsors, were content that people thought he had superhuman strength and was a natural athlete. This eventually became part of his brand; facts like his heart being a third bigger than that of an average man were toted around, whereas in fact many cyclists' hearts were larger, simply down to their exceptional fitness and the brutal demands of the sport.

I don't know what the truth of it was, but three things I knew for sure set Lance apart from others. First of all his lactate threshold was genuinely higher than most people's. Lactic acid is what the muscles produce when they're being worked hard and it causes an incredibly painful, burning sensation during cycling. Lance's body produced it later, meaning he could ride harder for far longer. Another thing was his speed of recovery. After my massage, he quickly got strength back in his muscles and appeared to be energized faster than other riders. His third strength was his mental attitude. To win a three-week race you really have to be able to keep your head together and this wasn't an issue for Lance. His ability to put past failures behind him instantly, focus on the here and now, remain positive and 'can do' whatever was placed in front of him was unique. Any problem he was presented with could be fixed.

I had no idea where all this came from, but these were ingredients of a champion. Of course, at the time I didn't know the full extent of the other ingredients that were in his system.

After the time trial there was a rest day and Lance went to a press conference to face the world's media. And face it he had to. In certain quarters, people couldn't believe how much Lance's performance had improved. Before his cancer diagnosis he'd competed in four Tours, never challenging the leaders. Not surprisingly, the jump from cancer sufferer to Tour leader was puzzling journalists.

Ignorant of the full extent of his doping – and I would never have been able to imagine the sheer scale of it – I'd seen Lance's work ethic and believed he deserved to be leading the Tour. Hearing the stick the media were giving him made me feel nothing but protective. And much of America agreed. For many in the States this was the first time they had tuned into the Tour; Lance had put the sport on their agenda. The French complaining that their Tour was being taken over by a Yank simply sounded like sour grapes.

During the press conference, a journalist from *Le Monde* looked Lance in the eye to ask if he'd doped.

Lance retorted with the now infamous line: 'Mr Le Monde, are you calling me a liar or a doper?', quickly silencing his critic. The question itself, though, made us worry that news of Lance's positive test for cortisone had leaked out. We could only wait and see what would happen next.

And so we'd reached the mountains. The first Alpine stage was to Sestriere, which of course was one of the many we'd recced earlier in the year, a monster of a climb with an altitude of 2,030 metres. It was a dirty day to ride on, too, and Lance would be relying on Kevin and Tyler to set the pace at the front of the bunch and protect him from the hellish winds and horizontal rain. The lads got frozen to their bones, testing their spirits and fitness in equal measure. Yet for the best part of 240 kilometres the team, known now in the press as the 'Blue Train', steamed up the slopes, leaving the competition trailing in their wake.

I was waiting at the finish line, shivering under the cold grey skies as Lance won the stage by thirty seconds from Zülle, opening up a six-minute lead in the Tour. The crowd erupted with deafening screams and shouts; it was so mental, but I concentrated on doing what was needed next – getting the lads into the warm car and back to the hotel.

The atmosphere in the hotel was equally ecstatic. The riders were still obsessed with walking as little as possible to conserve energy, shuffling about like ninety-year-old men, exhausted, but boy, their smiles were those of excited athletes on the way to the top of their game.

Then I heard that Betsy had gone absolutely ballistic at Frankie that evening. She'd watched her husband glide up the mountain easily, barely rising from his seat to pedal, and knew it meant only one thing: doping. Like Lance, Frankie wasn't a natural climber, or as she put rather eloquently: 'Frankie is about as much a climber as the Pope is an atheist.'

I understood where she was coming from, but this was our world now. This was what we were up against. My overriding reaction was: 'Betsy, will you give the guy a break. He's just doing what he needed to do, whatever it was that got him and Lance up there.'

I felt for Frankie. Cross-eyed with exhaustion, he was now contending with the wrath of an angry Betsy too. Given the choice of facing the mountain again or his wife, I bet he'd choose the mountain.

The year before, we'd all heard rumours that Betsy had almost called off their wedding in 1996. While visiting Lance in hospital she had overheard him confess what drugs he had taken before his cancer treatment; he'd openly told the doctors they included EPO, testosterone, human growth hormone and steroids. Presuming Frankie was doing the same, Betsy wasn't happy. Fine if Lance wanted to do what he did, but she didn't want her husband taking drugs and she gave him the ultimatum: promise not to dope or I don't marry you. I thought, fair enough; I respected her point of view as an issue between herself and Frankie.

Later, when he was in my room chatting to some other riders, I saw Tyler openly take out a brown bottle with a pipette and drop oil under his tongue.

'Uh-oh,' I thought.

Tyler was doing what he needed to do, like Frankie, like Lance, and even JV, who questioned everything. That was the thing with doping: I knew they were all at it by this stage, but I also saw it for what it was. Drugs actually made athletes work harder and it was a foregone conclusion that everyone in the Tour had to do it now. It was less about cheating, I thought, and more about survival. Not only were the Postal lads up to their necks in it, but I suspected wives were mainly in the know too. Only later did I learn just how involved Haven was, picking stuff up and dropping it off.

Like it or not, I'd succumbed to the reality of the Tour. Yes, I could tell myself consciously that I was clean and was staying away from it, but subconsciously I'd accepted what was happening and supported my team wholeheartedly regardless.

None is so blind as those who will not see.

Betsy was far from being the only person to notice that her husband was riding more easily. The press, mainly the French again, were now openly gunning for successful teams. Some commentators called it *'deux vitesses'*, a two-speed race, pointing out how strangely relaxed the lads looked. In *L'Equipe*, Lance's face was dubbed 'extra-terrestrial', as if he'd dropped 'from another planet' because he looked so calm. But to the outside world these were just stories. America had found a hero in Lance Armstrong. He was the tabloid story from heaven. Cancer survivor, father-to-be, Texan, on course to win the biggest race in Europe. This wasn't just news, it was the stuff of Hollywood dreams.

13

Une Grande Victoire

THE NEXT STAGE OF the Tour, on the French national holiday of Bastille Day, took us through magnificent mountain pastures in the central French Alps to the infamous Alpe d'Huez. With twenty-one hairpin bends, a maximum gradient of thirteen per cent and the summit looming at over 1,800 metres, this was one of the toughest stages of all. I was again waiting at the top, this time next to the wife of one of Lance's former Motorola teammates, to meet our yellow jersey off his bike. We marked our place and stood our ground in the chaos, which extended even into the staff areas. The atmosphere was like a music festival, with half a million spectators on the roadside, leaving precious little space for the cyclists to ride through.

As we marvelled at the excitement of the Tour and discussed how incredibly well we were doing, I spotted a smart Rolex watch on her wrist. 'Wow,' I said. 'Love your watch. I've been looking for a new one myself.'

'Yes, thank you,' she smiled. 'It cost four thousand dollars.'

Our conversation stalled, so I focused on the race, eventually seeing Giuseppe Guerini win the stage, despite being knocked off his bike by an overeager photographer. Thankfully, Lance conquered the mountain, coming in fifth to increase his lead to a huge 7.42 minutes over Abraham Olano. Victory was within his grasp and team spirits were sky-high back in the hotel.

Gossip was rife, too, about Lance's altercation during the day's stage with Christophe Bassons, the openly clean French rider who was speaking out in a newspaper column, criticizing others' doping. Lance had told him to 'go home' – and a few more choice words besides – after chasing him down. I didn't know Bassons from Adam and, even if I could see where he was coming from, my support lay with Lance.

There was a saying in cycling that you didn't 'cracher dans la soupe' – 'spit in the soup': the unwritten rule that you just did not speak out. You did not disrespect the sport. Above all else, cycling is a huge team effort; no race can be won by a rider not cooperating, so rebellion of any kind couldn't be tolerated on or off the road. This was cycling's omertà – its code of honour. You kept secrets. Those who spoke out risked facing the wrath of the rest of the sport, even of their own team. Now Bassons was openly saying that he believed it was impossible for anyone in the top ten of the Tour to ride clean. His was a lone voice, but even if it was a brave one, I still didn't want him to cause our lads trouble.

During the massage that evening, Lance didn't mention Bassons, but I brought up the implication that I couldn't afford a Rolex. 'I just thought it was rude,' I ranted.

'Fucking hell, yeah, cheeky bitch,' Lance agreed.

'I know,' I sighed. 'Sure, I probably wouldn't actually pay out for a watch like that, but you know, it's the principle . . . I could if I'd wanted to, y'know.'

Lance totally got that.

*

On our final rest day, we caught wind of the news that *Le Monde* newspaper was planning on printing a story about Lance's positive test for cortisone. But however unsettling this was for the riders, we had to keep focus on the Tour, so the next day we just carried on as normal; but as I walked into my hotel room after the stage I found Lance sitting patiently on the end of my bed, waiting for a massage.

'Hey,' he said, looking exhausted. Then, as he stretched out on my table, Thom and Mark strode in.

'Right, we need to talk about the positive cortisone test,' they announced, as I started on Lance's glutes. 'This needs sorting asap. We all need to have the same story before we leave this room.'

A week before the Tour, Lance had won the Route du Sud and had tested clean for cortisone, so he had assumed he'd be okay. But then a new test had come out for the Tour and it was with this one that he had tested positive, so an explanation had to be found. There was a sort of urgent calmness to the conversation, about what could be done, what was 'necessary', and how only one realistic solution would work. Saddle-sore cream contained cortisone, so if they backdated a prescription for Lance, it could be claimed this was how the banned substance mistakenly worked into his system. The fact that Lance hadn't had a saddle sore, nor indeed had claimed one on his exemption form – the list riders submitted before a race of any medications they were using – just didn't seem to be a problem.

I'd never known Lance to have a saddle sore. To be fair, though, riders' bottoms were covered when I massaged them and it wasn't something I expected the fellas would talk to me about either.

Once a Belgian day soigneur came up to me with a huge

tub of chamois cream. 'Emma, whose chamois do you do and whose will I do?' he'd asked.

'Erm, what?'

'Whose chamois do you want me to put the cream on?'

I started pissing myself laughing. 'Listen, my dear boy, the lads' chamois go into the washing machine, not anywhere near my hands. They have a big tub of cream in the camper they can help themselves to, but I'm not putting my hand anywhere near where they've been sitting for eight hours a day.'

The only thing I knew about lads' arses was how tight and small they were, depending on their fitness. The bottom is the only part where fat spreads as you sit on a bike. Riders could just glance at a teammate's backside to make accurate assumptions on how hard he'd trained, how fit he was. A small tight bum told you whether someone could win or lose a race. Now the subject of Lance's bottom could save his career and the team, and indeed the whole 'clean' Tour.

Thom, Mark and Lance were calm as they went through the scenario one more time together and I pretended not to be listening, focusing instead on pummelling Lance's thighs. With the decision made, Thom and Mark left to find Dr Luis and get him to scribble out a backdated prescription immediately.

'Wow, Lance,' I spluttered, 'do you think that'll be okay? I mean, will this sort it?'

'Yeah, yeah, should be fine,' he said, flippantly. 'You know enough to bring me down now, Emma.'

'Yeah, whatever,' I smiled, but I felt a bit embarrassed. Never in a million years, I felt, would I have wanted to bring Lance down, and he knew that.

Years later this quote would be seen as evidence that Lance had confessed to doping and knew I was in a position to topple him. Yet when he said these words it felt nothing like that. It was a throwaway comment, said nonchalantly, and I took it as such. I was that wrapped up in the omertà, and in Lance's fight to win the Tour. To win at all costs.

The massage over, Lance disappeared for dinner and as I tidied my room I thought what a huge wake-up call this was. The UCI had basically put everyone's backs against the wall to ask for an explanation. If they'd wanted to have a clean Tour, they'd have hauled Lance's ass across the coals. But they didn't. They were inviting us to lie. They'd pulled Johan in and given him time to think of a story. The UCI were in on this as much as everyone else. They were turning a blind eye to doping in cycling, end of story. And I could see why. Lance was the star turn, single-handedly bringing untold media attention, American money and sponsorship to the Tour. Without Lance, no way would big companies like Nike, Trek, USPS et al. get as involved in cycling as they had started to do. Cycling needed Lance. Today I could see just how much.

The next day the *Le Monde* story was printed and hot off the press behind it came a statement from the UCI, confirming that they didn't view this as a positive test result and wanted to remind journalists to exercise caution when reporting. They left it at that.

The race continued into the Pyrenees, and another climb of one of the most famous mountains in the Tour, a hard 16 kilometres into the sky of the Col du Tourmalet, where Lance managed to protect his lead. And with Lance on course for the *maillot jaune* in Paris, everyone wanted a piece of him. During our massage he told me he was going to be on the cover of *Time* magazine.

'My God,' I said. 'This is the start of Lance Incorporated. The big old machine is taking over.'

'You better believe it, baby,' he grinned. 'You'd better believe it.'

As I dug my thumbs into the base of his feet, I thought how I wanted to get out of this before it all exploded. Fame and money were monsters I wanted no part in. 'I'm still thinking of leaving next year,' I said. 'I've always wanted to get out of this sport by the age of thirty.'

'You're right, Emma,' he said. 'This is no job for a woman.'

I wholeheartedly agreed – and no, I didn't see Lance as being sexist here; he was just being realistic, plus he'd never treated me as anything other than an equal, unlike many others in the sport.

'What do you think you'll do when you leave cycling?' he asked.

'Uh, dunno,' I admitted. 'I think whatever it is I'd like to live in San Francisco. I love the vibe there.' I started laughing. 'It'll be okay for you, though, Lance. You're sorted now. You won't have to make a living after cycling.'

He laughed. 'You're right, baby. I'm gonna make a wad, that big, then that big,' he said, stretching out his arms. 'And I'm gonna make it worthwhile being in this horrible, horrible sport with these horrible people.'

I looked at him in amazement. Lance was under no illusion what was happening here. Cycling was a hard, cruel sport. This was about money, cover-ups, politics, doctors, doping and pressure. He quite sensibly wanted to get what he wanted and get out.

Or so he said. Signs of the increasing speed of his rising star were everywhere. One afternoon when I went to see him in the camper, the Nike advertising people were there, showing him an advert he'd filmed a few months previously. If I was agog, Lance was cool, taking everything in his stride. This is where he'd been heading for a long time, maybe his whole life, or at least since his mum first 'sponsored' him as a teen.

Being close to Lance suddenly meant I'd become flavour of the month too. With regular access to the big star, people were always asking me if he could sign yellow jerseys for them. He'd happily do it, but it meant another job for me, making sure I picked up the right jersey and got it back to the right person. Journalists were always on my case, catching me at feeding zones or on the start and finish lines, sidling up to me, wanting something.

One afternoon, I turned up with two jerseys and almost forgot to ask him to sign them. 'Oh God, sorry Lance, do you mind?' I said. 'I must remember to get these back to them this evening.'

'Nah, Chicken,' he said, looking at me as I scribbled it on my 'to do' list. 'This is no good. It's stressful for you, running around getting jerseys sorted. Can't they go through my agent? You've got enough to do.'

Lance's final challenge was a 55-kilometre individual time trial through the theme park of Futuroscope. That morning he sat with Johan, deep in conversation over breakfast. The first meal of the day was a big affair – the team would go through more than thirty boxes of cereal, around sixty eggs, and bags and bags of pasta. With his mouth full, Lance beckoned me over.

'Emma, I've told Johan I want you there at my next time trial, okay?'

Sportsmen are superstitious and I knew Lance was only asking me because he'd won the last trial I'd recced. I could see Johan was far from happy, though. His star rider wanting me, a soigneur, rather than him, the directeur sportif, to do the recce? God, was I going to pay for this later . . .

I did as well. After our morning recce, Johan came into the truck as I was cleaning out the bottle-cooler to glower at me and added a few extra tasks for me to do that day.

Understandably Lance was nervous. Even at this stage, things could go wrong and he could lose; after all, anything goes in a Tour de France. One slip-up, one crash, one bicycle malfunction. I had every faith the latter wouldn't happen, however, as Julien was quite incredible at his job. He treated the lads' tyres like cured meats, drying them, hanging them up and storing them for up to two years in his cellar in order to minimize the chance of a puncture. Who knew making tyres involved such a loving process?

Lance's mum, Linda, flew in to watch the Tour's denouement and I met her at the race. She was a petite, young-looking forty-four-year-old and she shook my hand enthusiastically as we met. I was interested to meet this woman who had supported her son all these years and believed in him when the odds were stacked even higher against him. You could see where some of his strength had come from.

I waited at the finish line, eager with anticipation like the rest of the crowd. 'This is it now, Lance,' I thought. 'Do this and you've won.'

All we needed was nothing to go wrong. And Lance seemed to have luck on his side. Unlike other riders, he tended to avoid crashes, and illnesses, and, aside from pulling out of Paris–Nice that time, he had been on a permanent upward spiral since returning to the sport. I held my breath as the crowd's roar grew in volume, many fans chanting his name, others waving flags, everyone straining for the first glimpse of cycling's latest and most unlikely star.

'Lance! Lance! Lance!'

And then he was there. Like a bullet he flew over the line.

Safe and first, winning the stage by 9 seconds from Alex Zülle.

I clamped my hands over my ears for a moment as the screams reached a crescendo. Pushing through the crowds I could have fainted, and I was barely able to breathe in the melee. Lance clambered off his bike, pulling off his helmet, as everyone dived on him. His face shining with sweat and victory, he grinned as his mum gave him a bear hug and kissed him.

'You did it!'

Following his victory, the wheels of Lance Incorporated cranked up another notch, and with incredible speed. Bill Stapleton's phone didn't stop ringing, as every few seconds another invite landed. Journalists from around the world wanted an interview, as did prime-time shows even I'd heard of, like Jay Leno and David Letterman. This wasn't just big for America, it was huge. Lance had already taken a call from his fellow Texan George Bush, and there was now even talk of inviting the former president to the Tour party.

That evening over the massage, neither of us could stop smiling. For a while now Lance had appeared a champion to me, so there was something natural and timely about how it had finally happened. Now that he was the man of the moment, though, there was little time to talk, as our room became crowded with congratulations and more offers of sponsorship and promotional appearances. As always, I focused on my own job, quietly observing the craziness as it orbited around me.

The next day, we had the victory parade down the Champs-Elysées. I wasn't sure if I'd get a look-in, but someone offered me a lift in the back of the US Postal car. Thousands of people lined the streets, cheering, chanting Lance's name and waving the Texan flag. It all passed in a blur from my car window. I gazed, mesmerized, feeling I was a tiny bit-part player in a piece of history. Peering at my reflection in the car window, my

Above and below: Starting out as a soigneur in the States with Shaklee was not always glamorous, but I was so happy to be seeing the world.

Above and below: Along with food bags, the need for water and energy drinks is a huge part of every race, so I was always preparing and handing out bottles.

Above: Some last-minute advice for Kevin Livingston and his fellow Posties before (*below*) a rare moment of relaxation with Juan and Ryszard.

Above: My birthday is on 22 July so it always fell during the Tour de France. That did at least mean I got a nice cake each year!

Left: The end-of-Tour party was another chance to let my hair down and get out of my soigneur clothes.

Below: I was not keen on being thrown in the pool though.

Above: All smiles with Chris and Sip from the Rabobank team. Unfortunately, my time at US Postal didn't end happily.

Below: Among the many jobs I did for Lance Armstrong was to sew his skinsuit for those super-fast time trials.

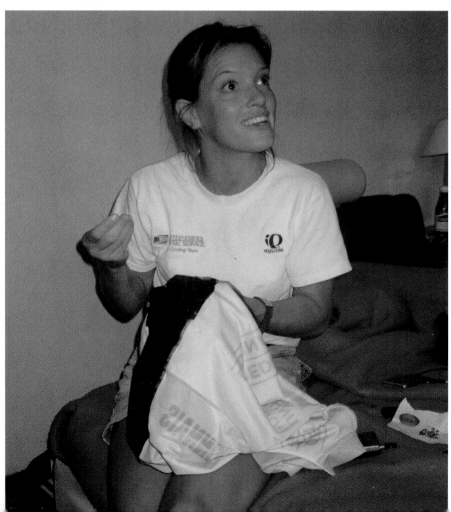

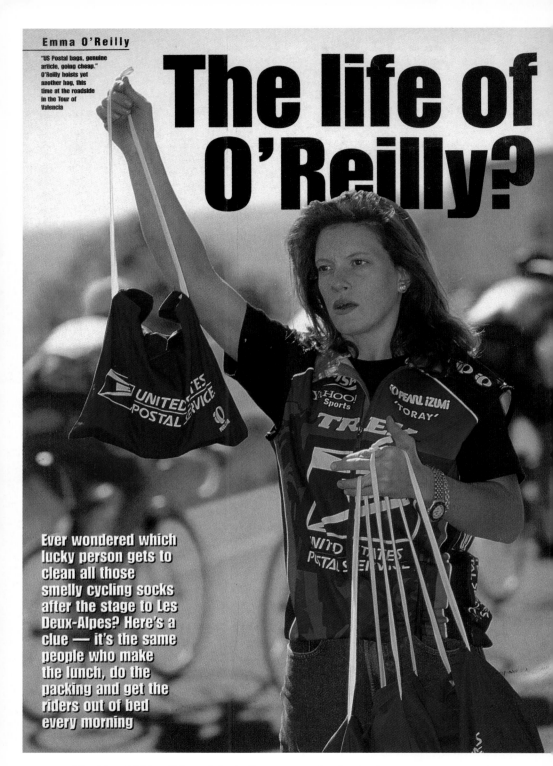

The life of O'Reilly?

Ever wondered which lucky person gets to clean all those smelly cycling socks after the stage to Les Deux-Alpes? Here's a clue — it's the same people who make the lunch, do the packing and get the riders out of bed every morning

The May 1999 edition of *Cycle Sport* magazine had a feature on me – and Lance was on the cover, just before his first Tour de France victory.

Massagesalon Emma

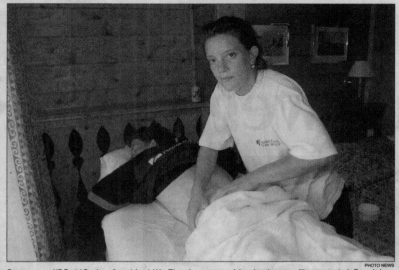

FRIBOURG — Emma, Emma, Emmelie neuriet slava Ekimov zacht vanneer hij de massage-amer van het Au Parc otel in Fribourg binnen-omt. De dagtaak van de us zit erop. Voor Emma egint het laatste luik van en dag die dinsdagmor-en al om zeven uur egon. De Ierse, die isteren haar 27-jarige erjaardag vierde, is het uitenbeentje. Emma 'Reilly is de enige rouwelijke masseur van eze Tour. „Ik dacht dat r bij Festina ook een as die de hotels regelt, jkbaar is ze er nu niet

a boy's club. Dit is een vereldje", lacht ze. „But , maar het is machtig. Ik e nog geen moment be-Voor iemand die niet ge-door de microbe, is dit denleven. Ik lach me s heen. Ik luister naar de ingen van de coureurs, , de vermoeidheid uit de egneem. Ik hou van stroomlijnde exempla-weinig vet. Dan kan je ren perfect laten re-

haal van Emma start in laar broer Norbert, on-

PHOTO NEWS

De renners van US Postal Service prijzen zich gelukkig. Zij worden gemasseerd door de enige vrouwelijke masseur in de Tour: de Ierse Emma O'Reilly.

VANDAAG
17e ETAPPE
WOENSDAG 23 JULI
218,5 km

COLMAR
Neuf-Brisach
Ottmarsheim
La Chaussée
Ferrette
Develier
Pierre-Pertuis
Tavannes
Biel
Kerzers
FRIBOURG

FRIBOURG — COLM

0,0	FRIBOURG	
21,0	Gurbru	3
22,0	Kerzers	
42,5	Biel	3
61,5	Pierre-Pertuis	3
63,0	Tavannes	
70,0	Le Fuet	3
96,5	Bassecourt	
98,0	Develier	
104,5	Develier	3
	FRANKRIJK	
122,5	Ferrette	3
136,5	Folgensbourg	4
155,0	La Chaussée	
170,5	Ottmarsheim	
192,5	Heiteren	
197,0	Neuf-Brisach	4
218,5	COLMAR	

MORGEN
18e ETAPPE
DONDERDAG 24 JULI
175,5 km

Above and below: It was strange to be seen in print across Europe, but there was always plenty of media interest in me as the only female soigneur on the Tour.

BT 1. SEKTION · SØNDAG 10. AUGUST 1997

◆ *Tour-feltets eneste kvindelige massør:*

Emmas flittige hænder

Rolf Work

◆ Rabobank valgte rigtig satse på Won Danmark Ru

I går slutt bedste i klas stian-San S nu fører åre

»Det sme vis, at jeg droppe Dann

Men Won sag, og nu n chance for tops. Jeg sig der, men tro top tree.«

I går sejre lin foran rus kov. Uofficie sen nr. seks val i den Bartoli, form me til mål m

Spænding Næste Worl lerede på lør

Uundvæ
Emma O godt fat i nert. Foto Jens Nørg

Både kolleger og rytternes koner og kærester har set skævt til United Posts kvindelige soigneur, 27-årige Emma O'Reilly. Men rytterne er ligeglade – for hun er knalddygtig.

Af Klaus Moe

◆ Der er et forrygende spil i de-brune øjne. Bevægelserne er målrettede. Hun taler sik-kert og hurtigt. Og de klæde-lige fregner under det kraftige, rødbrune hår, lader ingen tvivl tilbage: 27-årige Emma O'Re-illy er irsk.

Peter Meinerts slanke, sol-brændte krop.

Det er mindre end en time siden han kom i mål på enkelt-starten fredag aften i Danmark

»Jeg fik interessen fra min bror, der var cykelrytter. Jeg tog et massage-kursus – og begyndte at arbejde med ama-tører i ferier og weekends,« fortæller Emma O'Reilly, der

deres kufferter. Ordner vaske-tøjet.

Og tager os af elementær førstehjælp,« fortæller Emma, der oprindeligt er uddannet som elektriker.

jeg vil fortsætte. Jeg har altid sagt, at jeg vil gøre det til jeg fylder 30. Så skal jeg vist få set at få stiftet familie,« siger Emma, der er forbavset over, at der er så få piger i branchen.

positivt.

Det er lid dem kan jeg smiler hun.

»Hun mas Ikke for lur

Above: The reconciliation. After exchanging text messages and then calls, Lance and I finally met up again in Florida in November 2013. It's all about telling the truth.

Below: Chilling at home with my dogs, Cara (*left*) and my dear departed Bear.

eyes, despite their bags of exhaustion, were focused on the seas of smiling fans all cheering for their champion.

'Emma, it won't ever get bigger than this,' I thought.

The Blue Train cruised at the front of the peloton until they spotted the Eiffel Tower, then they fanned out excitedly towards the Champs-Elysées. I jostled my way into the crowd at the finish line and stood on tiptoe to glimpse the Tour crown its overall winner.

First a printer stamped the sponsorship logos of the winning team on to the yellow jersey, then Lance held his arms out as it was deftly pushed on to him and velcroed up the back. Next he stepped up on to the podium to be handed flowers and the traditional cuddly toy lion of the Tour sponsors, Crédit Lyonnais, by the pretty podium girls, each of whom kissed him. Then he took a second to absorb the scene before raising his clenched fists. The crowd roared, hailing their new champion.

Lance Armstrong, winner of the biggest bike race in the world. He'd done what I knew he could do.

14

Loose Ends

BEFORE WE COULD ENJOY the winner's party, there was much to do, sorting out cars, trucks and equipment for the races that followed the Tour. As I dived into the camper to get something, I noticed some of the riders sitting looking at Lance in stunned silence.

'I can't believe you spoke to Mark like that . . .' mumbled one.

'Why not?' Lance snapped. 'He's got no manners.'

'What's up?' I asked.

'Nothing,' Lance said, shrugging. Obviously something was, but he didn't want to say.

With not much time after the victory parade to sort everything, I carried on loading and cleaning as the riders went back to their hotels. Then shortly afterwards Mark called to say we had to join Lance in his hotel.

'What? Now?' I asked. 'We're knackered and covered in crap.'

Lance was staying with Kristin at the prestigious George V Hotel off the Champs-Elysées to celebrate his win.

'He's insisting on it,' Mark said.

I told Julien, who swore and threw down the tyre he was changing. 'This better be good,' he grumbled.

We took a cab over there. In a stained team fleece, my hair a state, my shorts filthy, I wandered, embarrassed, into the fine hotel lobby. The staff took one look at us and frowned.

'*Oui?*'

'We're here to see Lance Armstrong. He's sent for us.'

The receptionist was having none of it and called the manager over. He looked me up and down. 'Mr Armstrong has requested not to be disturbed.'

'Look,' I said, 'we're staff, Lance has asked to see us, and we don't have time this evening.'

'If you know Mr Armstrong, why don't you ring him?' he retorted.

I pulled Lance's mobile out of my pocket. 'I can't ring him because I've got his mobile here,' I snapped.

After much wrangling, they sent a porter up with us to Lance's room. He winced and turned pale when he saw the 'Do Not Disturb' sign, but he knocked quietly.

'What?' Lance barked. 'I said don't disturb me!'

Then, remembering I'd have Kristin's number in Lance's phone, I pulled it out. 'It's us, you moron!' I cried as I dialled.

Just as I thought the porter might have a coronary, the door was flung open. 'Hey, come on in,' Lance grinned.

I thanked the porter and we slipped inside. They had the whole Presidential Suite, opulent in the extreme, with a sitting room and dining room. Lance was having his hair cut by Kristin in the bathroom, so he asked us to wait. Julien and I giggled as we picked up pens and chocolates, all artfully arranged round the room.

'I might steal one and pretend I stayed here myself,' I laughed.

'Ah, it is very nice,' Julien agreed.

Finally Lance came out and sat down on the bed. He pulled out two boxes and handed them to us. We lifted the lids to see stunning gold Rolex watches catching the light so brightly they made my eyes ache.

'Ahhh!' I gasped. 'Lance!'

Julien was speechless, shaking his head. 'Ah, too much,' he muttered.

'A little somethin' to say thanks for everything,' Lance said, chuffed at the looks on our faces. 'I wanted to present them to you in the camper van in front of everyone, but Mark, god-dammit, forgot to bring them down so I gave out to him on the phone.' I nodded, recalling the riders' stunned faces. Nobody dared speak to Mark like that – nobody except Lance.

Rolexes. He had remembered our conversation. This was so cool of him. Then his mobile rang and he picked it up, asking us to wait a sec. Wandering over to the window, he spoke for a while, sounding surprised and cheered, profusely thanking whoever was calling him. A few moments later he was back.

'Hey, that was Al Gore,' he said with a grin.

I threw back my head and laughed. Knowing what a big Republican Lance was, this was hilarious. 'Ahh, sucking up to the Democrats are you? Pragmatic, aren't we?' I cried.

That night the team party was at the Musée d'Orsay, where a whole floor of the famous art gallery had been booked for more than two hundred members and sponsors. I hadn't known what to wear, so I'd asked Simon to pick something up for me. I didn't mind. None of the lads had seen me glammed up before, and even for the winner's do I didn't want to feel conspicuous.

When we arrived in our taxis the party was an awesome sight to behold: guests mingling, champagne everywhere, and all against a backdrop of jaw-dropping works of art. Lance was in a whirl, loving every minute of it, and I barely saw him all night. At the end he made a little speech, expressing his gratitude for our support, and we all raised our glasses. Shortly after that he took a call from President Bill Clinton, who wanted to pass on his congratulations personally.

Not everyone was happy for Lance. I heard that Betsy, who was still furious about the 'not normal' ascent to Sestriere, wouldn't shake his hand. I wasn't surprised, as Betsy seemed the principled type, but aside from her the feel-good factor was second to none. We'd achieved what Thom had said he wanted us to do. Postal had won the Tour. The boy wonder from Texas was the toast of a nation, and of Europe.

As the party broke up in the early hours, everyone tipsy, the riders gathered to go off to find a nearby nightclub.

'Come with us, Emma?' Lance asked.

'No, you go on,' I told him, grinning. This was the riders' victory and, anyway, I was heading to an Irish bar.

While Lance disappeared back to the States to a hero's welcome, the cycling calendar did not stop for us. In August, at the Vuelta a Burgos, the exuberance of Paris tapered off fast as my relationship with one of the other soigneurs, Peter, worsened. I had never got on with Peter, as every time I tried to pull him up on something he ran to Christelle.

So, needing extra staff, I hired an additional English day soigneur, who seemed fine until he accidentally managed to miss a rider's feed. After the race a glowering Johan lost no time in blaming me.

'What the hell do you think you're doing? You could've destroyed the race.'

I bit my lip, desperate not to cry. I waited for the privacy of my car before allowing myself to dissolve. I've always thought that if a job reduces me to tears, then I'm leaving. End of.

Later in the race I was meant to be driving to Belgium with Peter to reach the next stage, but he left me behind and instead took my whole suitcase, with everything I owned in it. I was furious. This was the final straw. There was little sense in approaching Johan with my complaints, so I went to the other powers that be and mentioned what I'd seen and heard about Peter, hoping they'd come to their own conclusions.

The next morning, when Peter didn't turn up I felt a stab of guilt. Even though he was no big loss, the fact that I had been sly in order to get my way showed that a Machiavellian streak had developed within me. This was a meanness I hadn't known I possessed up until now. For the first time a thought occurred to me: is cycling changing me? But I squeezed the worry from my mind and decided to be positive. Peter had gone. Without him, I hoped, my job would be easier.

However, if I'd considered Peter a problem, it was nothing compared to my relationship with Johan. These days whenever our paths crossed he found something to criticize me for. With all his snapping and moaning, things became so untenable that I offered to resign as head soigneur.

'No, I don't want that,' he said, to my surprise, waving me away. 'Just make sure you ring me or Christelle three days before an event and we'll send you flight details or whatever you need. You're staying.'

Simon understandably wanted me to stay too and encouraged me to keep going. Reluctantly, I told myself I just needed to reach my thirtieth birthday and then I could do what I'd promised myself and leave this crazy world behind.

But by the time the Vuelta a España came round in September, even this goal was starting to feel unrealistic. With Lance still away, resting in the States, enjoying his hero status and looking forward to becoming a dad, I was left to focus on other members of the team. I'd always tried to get along with everyone, but now the Flemish-speaking staff started talking in their mother tongue around me. I didn't understand a word they were saying, but their tone and mannerisms left me in no doubt they were chatting pure smut.

I spoke up. 'We're an English-speaking team, lads,' I complained. 'That's the language our riders have to speak and the Americans write our pay cheques. We should talk over dinner in English.'

They just laughed, hard and loud, making me feel very uncomfortable, so at dinner I started sitting in my room and eating cereal instead. At lunchtimes, too, I decided to go out for a run, partly to relieve myself of the stress but also because I was never hungry after the mammoth breakfasts anyway. This brought more aggravation when Dr Luis reported me to Johan.

'Why are you not joining in with the team?' Johan demanded. 'Luis says you're being difficult.'

'I'd no idea a doctor could complain about a member of staff for trying to keep fit and healthy,' I retorted.

Johan glared at me. 'Your attitude needs changing,' he warned.

A few days later, Johan collared me in my hotel room alone. 'We need to talk,' he snapped. 'You're creating a bad atmosphere in the team. You're isolating yourself from everyone.'

I stared at him, not knowing what to say.

'I know you think I'm an asshole,' he continued. 'I know exactly what you think of me.'

I shook my head and opened my mouth to speak but he continued, his voice growing louder.

'You're nasty and abuse your power. I've heard you yelling at Jim!'

I tried to defend myself and explain to Johan how, as the only girl on the team, the atmosphere at the dinner table was making me uncomfortable.

But he didn't seem to hear me. 'You've got mental problems,' he snarled. 'And you'd better be careful, because you're playing with fire.'

I swallowed hard, willing my eyes not to well up. 'As my boss,' I said slowly, trying to control my wobbling voice, 'what do you want me to do?'

'I don't know,' he snapped, running his fingers through his hair. 'Just act like you did earlier in the season – learn to control yourself.'

He glared at me, then turned and left. I wilted again, feeling like a popped balloon, empty, his words echoing in my head. 'You've got mental problems . . . Act like you did earlier in the season . . .'

Maybe he was right? Maybe I had gone crazy? Maybe everyone did hate me? The early part of the season, with all its buzz and vitality, seemed like a very long time ago now. The Tour de France win already seemed like a different lifetime.

I felt more alone than ever in the team, then when I got back to Ghent my Pepe took me aside to give me some advice.

'Emma,' he said in his gruff voice, 'be careful. Johan really has it in for you. He told me how you'd written about me in your diary. Sounding off about something or other.'

I felt sick. My diary? He'd been reading it?

'But how? I mean, I would never say anything bad about you.'

'I know you wouldn't,' he shrugged. 'I didn't believe him. But he's obviously reading whatever you do write down and elaborating it to other staff members. Watch your back, huh?'

That evening I looked in my rucksack, where I kept my diary zipped up. It was mainly lists – timetables, race dates – but on the odd page, when my stress levels were too high, I'd sounded off, and that included a couple of entries about Johan.

'I know more about you than you think I do,' he'd once said to me. It all made sense. I tucked the diary down at the bottom of my bag, glancing at the lock on my room door. I'd always left it wide open, trusting anyone to come and go freely. Now nothing felt safe.

I longed to cut my losses and go. I thought hard about my behaviour and how Johan got me to criticize my colleagues' work or ordered me to get things done faster. 'Go give it out to them,' he'd say.

It was true that I'd had a few run-ins with Jim, so I went and asked him outright: 'Jim, do you think I'm a bitch?'

He shrugged. 'Look, you have been hard on me at times, but I do know where you were coming from. I don't think you're a bad person.'

That evening I spoke to Simon on the phone about it, this time allowing the tears to fall. 'I can't go on,' I cried. 'It's just bullying. Do you think I have an evil temper? Am I mental?'

Simon was very supportive and gentle. 'No, I think you're lovely, Emma. You're not mental at all,' he reassured me.

The fact was, I felt I didn't know any more. I desperately wanted to leave, but Simon had just been promoted to European marketing manager at Giro, and he wanted to spend at least another year in France.

'Hey, I think you should stay. It would be good for me and my career too, and we need the money. What do you say? One more year?' he suggested. 'Go on. You can do it.'

I shook my head. 'I can't,' I said, pinching the bridge of my nose. 'The way this is all going, it's too much.'

'Just one more year, Emma. Not just for you, but for us,' Simon insisted. 'It will be worth it.'

Reluctantly, I agreed.

There wasn't anyone on the team with whom I could occasionally have a moan, except maybe Julien, and sometimes Jonathan Vaughters, so Johan's plan to isolate me had succeeded. JV was also on the receiving end of abuse from Johan and occasionally we swapped stories, complaining together, although this didn't happen very often as Johan's policy of divide and rule was working so well.

At the end of the season, however, JV announced he was quitting US Postal. Doping wasn't for him. He made a moral and personal choice and went with it. Pleased as I was about his decision, I was going to miss our chats, his perspective and his sense of humour.

In October we got a card announcing the arrival of Lance's first baby, a boy, Luke David. I was thrilled for him. Some good news at last. More miracles in Lance's life.

At the end of the season, the Tour winners were all invited to Disney World, Florida, for a few nights to celebrate our success. For once it was a time to chill and catch up with everyone, leaving the stress behind. Even Johan seemed to thaw, throwing the odd grin in my direction. Perhaps being hailed as the youngest-ever winning Tour director had mellowed him. Perhaps the following season would work out after all. I hoped so.

Lance turned up on the second to last day in high spirits, with pictures of Luke, as thrilled with fatherhood as he was with his win. 'Me and Kik are spending all our time now with the little dude in the States,' he told me. 'Emma, do you fancy the keys to my place in Nice? I can arrange for you to pick them up from our caretaker.' Lance seemed to leave a lot of work to this handyman, and said it would be no problem and easy to arrange.

'Lance! Are you sure?'

'Yeah, why not? No point in it staying empty all winter. I'd like you to have it,' he said.

I was living with Simon in St-Etienne, where he now worked, but it would be a far nicer prospect to spend the winter in Nice. 'Thank you!' I cried, happy to take up his offer.

Fame, money, power, success. It's amazing the hold these things have over people and how immediate the effect is. I noticed the shift in the sands straight away as people, sponsors and bike fans alike, around Lance adopted a more deferential air. He had always been the alpha male who acted as if he could walk on water, but now it was as if he *did* walk on water. This didn't happen so much among the other riders, because even as the star rider Lance still needed his domestiques. A champion cyclist never, ever wins a race on his own and Lance knew this. But what did change on the team was the atmosphere. Going from no-hope outsiders to winning team overnight brought with it a responsibility and new-found seriousness. Suddenly everything became more business-like, less fun. Already the new season was being discussed: now we'd won once, we were expected to keep on winning.

On the last day, Johan was leaving early and he sent for me to come up to his hotel room.

'Ah, he's finally going to bury the hatchet,' I thought in the lift. 'This is great. Maybe we can put all this in the past.'

I knocked on his door, smiling in anticipation, but as he opened it the look on his face told me the hatchet wasn't buried at all. In fact, it was about to be slung in my direction.

'Emma, you're fired,' he said smoothly. 'This isn't going to work. Freddy is coming back to be head soigneur.'

I dug my nails into my palms, breathless. Emma. Please. Don't. Cry.

'This has all been discussed,' he went on. 'No point in you calling the Americans behind my back. It's just been left to me to tell you.'

'Okay, fine,' I said firmly, and I turned on my heel to get out of there as fast as possible.

Back in my room, I rang Simon. 'Don't say anything to me because if I start crying I won't stop,' I whispered, 'but Johan has just sacked me. Can you find me an employment lawyer? I can't let the bastard get away with it.'

My head was swimming as I went back to join the others. Sacked. It was over. I'd never do another race again. With con-siderable effort I managed to put a smile on my face, saying nothing to anyone, as the team waved Johan off. I shook his hand firmly and eyeballed him.

'Bye, Johan,' I said, smiling, as if our conversation had never happened. Fuck you, you're not going to break me.

Simon was struggling to find a French lawyer to help me, so once I got home I called JV for help; his dad was a lawyer.

'What the—?' JV gasped, as I explained. 'Does Lance know about this? No way he'd accept this.'

'I don't know,' I said sadly. 'But I'm not bothering him with it.'

It turned out that JV's dad was a criminal lawyer, so couldn't help, but JV was incensed on my behalf. He told me that Johan had sent him a couple of derogatory emails about his perfor-mance, often adding the line: 'There's no point in talking to Mark about this, as we've already discussed it.'

'I bet, Emma, the Americans know nothing about it,' he said. 'You and Lance have a proper relationship. He's different with you than with other people.'

158

I thanked JV for his support and decided I would call Lance after all.

'Can't I leave you alone for more than a few hours?' he cried. 'What the fuck have you been doing in my absence? The last time I saw you, you were best friends.'

'Hardly, Lance,' I laughed. 'That was a long time ago now. I didn't want to go on at you with this stuff.'

'Leave it with me,' he said.

I sat tight for a few more days before Mark rang. 'Emma, I want this to work out despite what Johan says,' he said calmly. 'He took action too quickly. And the action is no longer in effect.'

I thanked him and was relieved, on account of the money if nothing else. But after the whole episode, I seriously questioned how hard returning to work would be. I'd been demoted, and was hated by my boss. Only Simon wanted me to stay still.

'Just think, Emma – one more year,' he said.

'And then we can live in San Francisco?' I asked.

'Yes,' he promised.

15

Closed Book

In January 2000 I turned up to our training camp in San Luis Obispo, now demoted to ordinary soigneur, but with an inflated $45,000 salary and under no illusions as to why. I'd no doubt that they wanted to keep me sweet. Working under Freddy Viaene felt utterly humiliating, and even if everyone was nice to me, that seemed to make it worse. As always, Lance came to me for his massage. We didn't discuss what had happened. He was just looking forward to this year with a renewed determination to win the Tour again. Some people had said his win the previous year was a fluke, and for Lance that was like fire to touchpaper.

'I need 'em to know I'm here to stay,' he said, grinning.

Lance's sparkly new life was filled with exciting news. He had a book deal in the pipeline, adverts, TV shows – he had brought cycling into the spotlight in the States, and the world knew who he was. Seeing him again cheered me up no end. I'd missed him.

About a week into the training camp, I was waiting for Lance but found Kevin hopping on to my table instead. Lance didn't come the next day either, and just as I was wondering if he was being uncharacteristically late, Freddy stuck his head round the door.

'Johan told me you're not doing Lance any more,' he said. 'He's said to Lance "It's either me or her" and so that's it. You're also not to go to any races Johan attends. It will just be the smaller ones from now on.'

I swallowed hard, my face tightening.

'Okay, well if that's what Johan wants,' I shrugged, trying to hold it together.

Me or Johan? This seemed ridiculous. Deep down, though, I understood. Johan hated me around, that much was clear, and he wanted Lance's full attention. Maybe he thought Lance and I had got too close. He relied on me for recces. He stuck up for me. He'd saved my job. This was payback time.

Angered at my treatment, I no longer minded telling anyone who would listen that Johan had tried to fire me and had been overruled. Mr Big Potatoes, the all-powerful Tour de France-winning DS, didn't even have enough influence to sack his own soigneur. He could take Lance away, but not my pride.

The next few months passed in a blur, as I shut down inside and tried to get through it. I regretted coming back, even if it had been for Simon. All the joy of working as a soigneur had been sucked out of me. I survived on the attitude of 'another day, another dollar'.

By April, I'd had enough. I handed in my notice to Mark to leave at the end of the year. I couldn't face giving it to Johan – he'd get too much satisfaction. With so much job insecurity in professional cycling, understandably the other staff members, with just a few exceptions, were also avoiding me when they could. I'd become *persona non grata*. As the female soigneur, the woman in Johan's bad books, nobody dared treat me as a friend.

I rarely saw Johan and, when I did, he refused even to look at me. His tight rules on staff still filtered through, however. This year 'medical passports' had been issued to riders by the UCI in an attempt to try to counter doping, but we staff were told not to carry them, even if we were taking a rider to medical control.

In May 2000 Lance's autobiography, *It's Not About the Bike*, which chronicled his recovery and return to the sport, sailed straight into the bestseller lists, proof of just how much the public had taken this cancer-surviving champion to their hearts. The next time our paths crossed, briefly at a race, I congratulated him on the book, even if I did have something to say about it.

'I've not read it, Lance,' I admitted, 'but I've heard I'm not mentioned anywhere at all. You toerag. That was supposed to be my marketing tool when I leave the sport!'

Lance laughed. 'Aw, Emma, y'know we couldn't get every single person in there.'

'Yeah, right, thanks a lot, Cotton Picker,' I smiled.

By the time the Tour came round, I'd barely seen Lance or any of the big riders. I never texted him either. He was Mr Big and I'd heard from other riders how even Kristin had become Mrs Lance Armstrong too, tailoring her life to his and losing herself in his slipstream – a sad thing to see, as she'd been such an independent sort beforehand.

Although we hadn't kept in touch much, when my engagement had been announced Lance had insisted on getting an invite to my wedding and I'd sent him one. But there was no RSVP from him and Simon was incensed.

'Why's he not coming?' he asked.

'Aw, he's a work colleague, Simon,' I shrugged, rather surprised it mattered that much to him. 'Seriously, I wouldn't expect him to.'

I wasn't keen on inviting the team – not that anyone was talking to me now – and neither did I fancy any press turning up because Lance was at our small ceremony in Dublin. By then Lance might have won his second Tour, anyway, and it would be the busiest part of his year.

I went with Simon and my friends Sarah and Peter to watch one of the mountain stages of the 2000 Tour, at Courchevel. Being a spectator, even just for a few hours, having a picnic on the mountainside, was a wonderful way to remember why I'd fallen for bike racing. Marco Pantani and Lance battled it out on the slopes, the crowd on fire behind them, the Italian winning that stage in a stunning finish as Lance consolidated his hold on the yellow jersey. Little did we know we'd just seen Pantani's last victory as a professional.

As in previous years, scandal was never far away from that Tour. I heard on the grapevine how reporters from the France 3 television network had followed our team doctors and captured them on film dumping medical supplies, miles from the hotel, at a motorway service station. After sifting through the bags, reporters found packaging for a drug I'd never heard of, Actovegin, along with syringes and a pile of bloody bandages. Debate ensued about whether Actovegin was a banned substance, as products similar to it were.

Mark came up with a US Postal team solution, explaining that Actovegin was used for skin injuries and Julien's diabetes. I didn't believe him, but I knew he had to say something. The

UCI went on to give full backing to Lance's version of events when he said openly that he'd no clue what 'Activ-o-something' even was. Another disaster averted.

Nothing was dimming the ascent of Lance, and I was made up when we watched him on TV as he won the Tour again. He'd wanted to prove that his first was no fluke, and now he'd done so. The fact that I'd played no part in it was disappointing in a sense, but as long as Lance was doing what he needed to do, that was all that mattered. I massively respected his work ethic.

Instead of the Postal team celebration, I went to David Millar's big do at the end of the Tour. David had worn the yellow jersey after winning the prologue, and his sister Frances had organized a party for him and other lads at a pub. Simon was friends with David, so got an invitation. We had a lot of fun, and I let my hair down for once. David was a sociable guy who liked to party and holding on to the yellow jersey for a few days had been a remarkable achievement, we thought, considering he was riding *pan y agua*. For a young guy, he had huge potential and commanded a lot of respect.

We left the Tour with hangovers to match our good memories and returned to Ireland for our wedding. On 29 July I married Simon in front of a handful of guests in a tiny church in Leixlip, near Dublin. A fresh start. All I had to do now was see out life as a soigneur until October.

I never showed Postal staff or Johan what I was feeling to their faces, but inside I was broken. Stress and insomnia go hand in hand with me and I struggled through the last few months of my time there. The glory days of my love for cycling had vanished and I thought back to Shott's words three years earlier: 'It's a mad, crazy world.' I missed Lance, Kevin, Frankie and JV especially and, although the director I worked with after my demotion, Dirk De Wolf, was a dream compared to Johan, I crossed off each day like a prisoner marking his release date. Now certain that the sport wasn't for me, I was more aware than ever of how older staff members, who'd made cycling their careers, were treated like old furniture. Let alone the doping side of things. Inevitably, I imagined, if I stayed I'd get drawn further into the dark side of cycling myself. Leaving now was a good thing.

When my final day arrived, I hadn't seen Johan for months and nor had I heard from Lance. He was busy with his young family and it wasn't the place of staff to disturb a rider if you weren't working together. Our lives had simply taken different paths, I accepted that.

As I packed up my massage table for the last time, a couple of the newer soigneurs shrugged: 'Yeah, well, bye then,' as I wheeled my suitcase from our hotel. Ryszard was away at a race, so I didn't even have him to say cheerio to. I told myself it was no big deal. Only my Pepe, bless him, insisted I come to his place for a drink.

'To you, Emmatje . . . and your future,' he said, as Vera uncorked a bottle of champagne and handed me a glass. I let him sweep me into a hug. My five years on the team were over.

I'd barely unpacked my boxes in the apartment we were renting in Santa Cruz when the phone started to ring. Again and again. And again. All the calls were from journalists, all asking the same question.

'Can you tell us why you left US Postal? Why did you stop working with Lance?'

'No comment,' I said.

During the last few months I had often been collared at feeding zones or finish lines by journalists asking why I wasn't working with Lance any more, and I always ignored the questions. By now I was known as the 'clean soigneur', illustrating how rare it was within cycling to have nothing to do with a medical programme. The absurdity of being labelled 'clean' wasn't lost on me either. After all, I'd ended up roped into incidents with banned substances myself. I'd just turned the other cheek, but I felt as tainted as the rest of them.

As far as I was concerned, my departure was none of anyone else's business, especially sports journalists. Surely I was a non-story anyway? I stopped answering unknown numbers and the calls petered out. Perhaps now I could move on with my life in peace.

Despite the bad vibes surrounding my departure from the team, Thom Weisel stepped in and offered his support. My dream was to set up a massage practice and he kindly put the word around his company, so within a week I was fully booked for a month, while Simon carried on working for Giro until his contract finished.

Thom asked for a massage himself and as I left he popped $400 in my bag without my noticing. I felt bad when I discovered it. He might have been stinking rich but, not wanting to rip him off, I quizzed him about it the next time I massaged him.

'Yes, Emma,' he replied, 'I know exactly how much I gave you and how much I can afford.' He paid the same that time too.

Through Thom I also found myself booked to massage Woody Harrelson, who was in town shooting a film. Life, it seemed, had moved on in its own crazy way.

That winter, as we planned our next move to a more permanent place, I got a call from yet another journalist. My day was especially busy, so absentmindedly I asked him to email questions through, hoping it would be enough to get him off my back. That evening, as I grabbed something to eat for dinner, I logged on to my emails, forgetting I'd given my address out. I stopped mid-chew as I read the first few lines of an email sent by a newspaper reporter. As I scrolled down, my eyes popped out. The first few questions were the usual vague ones all journalists asked now and then, the normal suspicions around doping, but further down were more specific questions about Julien, insulin, Actovegin:

1. Have drugs ever been taken by the US Postal team?
2. Did you ever see Lance Armstrong take drugs?
3. Were you sacked because you refused to be part of the programme?
4. Why has Julien DeVries, head mechanic, got an on-going prescription for insulin as covered by the team doctor (why has the team doctor signed it)?
5. Why was Julien using Actovegin?

The list went on and on. Oh my God, I thought, whoever this journalist was, he knew something. I grabbed my phone and rang Mark.

'Listen,' I said, 'this newspaper knows something's up. The questions are far too knowledgeable. They're getting close. What should I do?'

Mark laughed. 'Ah, don't worry about it, Emma. Nobody knows anything.'

I wasn't convinced, but I told myself it wasn't my problem any longer. So I deleted the email and ignored the calls when they chased me for answers. I simply wanted it all to go away.

This proved to be wishful thinking, as shortly afterwards Auntie Cecil rang from Ireland, sounding very confused.

'Emma, a journalist rang me at home the other day wanting to know why you left the cycling team. I didn't have a clue what to say! What were they asking for?'

I was furious. Contacting my poor elderly auntie was a step too far. How did they even get her number? It showed how desperate they were. Whatever journalists wanted from me, they could keep my family out of this. I apologized profusely and told her never to talk to them. 'Just say "No comment", Auntie. You know, like politicians on TV do when they don't want to answer. And give them my details.'

16

Betrayal Bond

As we adjusted to our new lives, it quickly dawned on me that Simon wasn't enjoying America as much as I was. Some people 'get' the great US of A and some people don't, and sadly my new husband didn't. Even when Thom suggested he train to become a stockbroker after he stopped working for Giro, Simon couldn't muster any enthusiasm whatsoever. Saying he was homesick, he wanted to move back to his home town of Shrewsbury.

I was just setting up my dream business and things were beginning to fall into place. Up until now I'd always followed my instincts and tried to live life my own way, but the last miserable year at US Postal had broken something in me. My confidence had been shot to pieces, and when Simon asked me to reconsider my plans yet again over dinner one evening, I felt myself crumble. In desperation, I secretly scribbled out a list of the pros and cons of moving back:

Returning to the UK
Pros: Eating good curries again, seeing my father-in-law [I was really fond of Simon's dad].
Cons: Everything else.

It was hardly a balanced list, and in the end I simply wasn't strong enough to stand up for what I wanted. So on a grey, overcast day in August 2001 we returned to the UK. As we landed at Heathrow my heart sank as fast as the plane's wheels. I was already missing the States.

'Too late for regrets,' I thought, knowing deep down I'd made a huge mistake. Or did I mean too early?

The following weeks were a whirlwind of trying to readjust. Unable to bear the thought of starting my business from scratch again, I decided to have a shot at teaching and landed an interview at a training college in Wolverhampton while Simon looked for work. After I had been offered a place on the course, however, Simon said he didn't think we'd manage with neither of us working, so I got a job in sales to tide us over instead. Even if I was grateful that it was a world away from cycling, I quickly realized that persuading people to buy things they didn't really want wasn't my calling. As I struggled on, Simon went to work for a bike helmet company but cracks in our relationship started to show.

Next Simon volunteered for the women's British cycling team in an attempt to break back into the heart of the sport, he'd ridden in the Olympics twice, after all. He also suggested that we go to marriage counselling. I agreed. I wanted this to work. Still a Catholic girl at heart, divorce was the last thing on my mind.

By now I'd been away from the team for a year and kept in touch only with my Pepe, Julien, on the phone. He liked hearing how I was doing and telling me his own news too. Then one day his tone turned serious.

'Emma, Johan is going around saying you helped a journalist from the *Sunday Times* write an article against the team,' he said.

'Eh?' I asked, confused. 'What on earth?'

'The piece was by a journalist called David Walsh and he's written a few articles criticizing Lance and the team,' he continued. 'Johan's really annoyed about it.'

I'd heard of David Walsh; in 1991 I'd read his biography of Sean Kelly and occasionally I bought the *Sunday Times*.

'Seriously? You're kidding me!' I said indignantly. Old, angry wounds and a sense of unfairness stirred in my guts as I listened to Julien tell me how much Johan had ranted and raved about my disloyalty to the team, about my alleged wrongdoing.

'For God's sake!' I cried. 'This is ridiculous. It's not true!'

'I believe you,' Julien said.

As reassuring as it was that my Pepe trusted me, I worried about my former teammates. I might have left under a bit of a cloud, but speaking to journalists was the last thing I'd consider.

I was pleased that Simon was getting back into the sport he loved; at least he was doing something, even if it was unpaid. Feeling more settled, we got a rescue puppy, a King Charles spaniel and Jack Russell cross, with huge brown bug eyes and a lovely temperament, and we named her Cara. But any renewed hope that our marriage might survive was soon dashed. Within weeks, after one row too many, I moved out of our marital home with a suitcase in one hand and Cara on her lead in the other.

*

They say you find love when you least expect it and, heart-broken from my marriage breakdown, I can honestly say meeting someone new was the last thing on my mind. But, as time passed, I became close to the training director of the sales company I was working for, Mike Carlisle, a straight-talking Mancunian and huge football fan, and I found myself having feelings for him. One of the many refreshing things about Mike was that he knew nothing about cycling; to him it was little more than men on pushbikes in Europe.

Mike walked with a limp, and confided in me that he suffered from progressive multiple sclerosis. He didn't talk much about it, so I looked it up and was shocked to discover that in all probability he would eventually end up in a wheelchair. Always upbeat and a talented training director, Mike, however, was determined that his illness wouldn't stop him from doing anything and I believed him.

Shortly afterwards, still not really knowing anyone in the UK, I moved into Mike's place on the Wirral and he encouraged me to return to the job I loved – massage. Gradually I began to pick up the pieces of my confidence and started working in a clinic, once again reigniting my passion for my original career, but happy not to deal with anything to do with two wheels.

I continued to chat to Julien in occasional phone calls, but I rarely watched races these days, only spotting the latest news on Sky Sports if Mike had it on, or sometimes in a newspaper. After Lance won the Tour again in 2001, I read that Greg LeMond had become the first big former rider to speak out against Lance, questioning his relationship with Michele Ferrari in an article in the French newspaper *Le Monde*:

When Lance won the prologue to the 1999 Tour, I was close to tears, but when I heard he was working with

Michele Ferrari I was devastated. In the light of Lance's relationship with Ferrari, I just don't want to comment on this year's Tour. This is not sour grapes. I am disappointed in Lance, that's all it is.

I quickly turned over the page, knowing that Greg LeMond speaking out could be a big deal, but quite honestly, it bored me. There were more funny goings-on in the cycling world, but when hadn't there been?

A year rolled by, and every now and then something would come up about the sport I no longer followed. I heard how Lance and Kristin had had twin girls, and he won the Tour again in 2002. Then I heard a rumour that Betsy Andreu had spoken to David Walsh. This surprised me, as Frankie was still working with the team, although no longer riding. Betsy had actually gone out of her way and called David herself. That one conversation about drugs that she'd overheard years earlier when Lance was in hospital had eaten away at her, but I was shocked at the level of her anger. What did it have to do with her, I thought? As far as I was concerned, it was odd to diss the very sport that was paying your husband's wage?

Then in June 2003, out of the blue, I got a forwarded email from Simon. We hadn't been in touch, except via lawyers to finalize our divorce, so I was surprised to hear from him; I thought it was best to leave everything between us in the past. I scanned down the email and read:

Dear Emma, a close friend of mine, Paul Kimmage from Dublin, has been trying to contact you on my behalf. I believe we need to talk and I believe it is in both our interests. There will be no strings attached to the

conversation but it would be worth your while to hear me out.
Respectfully yours,
David Walsh

David Walsh, the journalist? What on earth could he want from me? I felt a bit guilty that he'd contacted Simon, who'd put up with enough of me over the years, so I replied to David myself, asking how he thought I could help. He responded, saying he was planning to write a book about cleaning up drugs in cycling and wanted to see if I'd meet him to discuss this, as several other people from the cycling world had come forward to talk too.

My instinct was to say no. Who was I to break the omertà? I'd seen what had happened to Christophe Bassons when he'd spoken out in 1999. He had been humiliated and his career was finished. Although I'd left cycling now, it had already caused me enough grief. I didn't need this. Who was I to spit in the soup?

Before I told him 'thanks but no thanks', however, I agreed to think about it for a few days – and, to my surprise, a gnawing sense of guilt kicked in.

Now that I'd been away from the sport for three years, I'd gained some perspective. For the first time, a growing sense of responsibility began to burgeon in me. The lads couldn't speak out, as they were still part of the mad Planet Cycling, where winning at all costs was the only thing that mattered, regardless of the consequences. They were trapped, whereas I was free. I started to feel that choosing not to speak out was in effect lying. The seeds of principle behind telling the truth had suddenly been planted.

Of course, I knew that Lance openly, brazenly, lied about

doping. Every year he told the same story, pointing out how he'd never failed a test. How tiring it was for him to have to keep denying it, to keep saying how he'd never dope because of his fans. His default setting was to attack those who criticized him and this tactic worked wonderfully. By now the Lance machine was unstoppable. He was the biggest sporting icon of the century. He'd made his 'wad' long ago and was still winning, but he was trapped in his own web of deceit. I'd little doubt Lance would never be able to tell the truth now. To me it was obvious he was the member of the team most comfortable about doping, as we would later discover in lurid detail, but what about the others? I thought of Tyler's haunted face the last time I saw him, the little flasks, the dodgy doctors. Doping in cycling had become less of a choice and more of an absolute necessity for young riders coming into the sport. Let alone what it was doing to the ones already in it.

I sat down and talked it through with Mike, whose eyes always glazed over when I brought up cycling. To him the sport was no great shakes. Whether they'd doped or not, it didn't seem like much of a scandal.

'Mike, this David character wants to write a proper book about it, to be published only in France because the UK libel laws wouldn't allow it. He wants to hear stories from within the team. I don't know much, but I could share what I do know,' I said. 'He's a reputable journalist from a reputable paper. If I go anywhere, maybe it should be to him?'

Not for one second did I think the likes of me would make anything like a difference, but on the other hand, if I refused to say anything and carried on with my life as if nothing had happened, then wasn't I as bad as all the people still covering it up?

'I don't know what to do,' I said.

'If you want to speak out about this,' Mike replied, 'Emma, I will stand by you.'

Over the next week, I decided to meet David and see what he was proposing. No commitment. No promises. Just a chat. He jumped at the chance to go out for dinner and see what happened from there.

Before we met, though, I felt it was important for me to be clear in my own mind about my motivations. If I was ever going to speak out it had to be for the right reasons and not for something like revenge against Johan. I didn't want to be scurrilously speaking behind people's backs, telling tales on my teammates; I wanted to be open about the possibility of revealing what I knew. It was a tough phone call to make, but I rang Julien.

'Aw, Emmatje,' he sighed, 'journalists won't want to hear about cleaning up the sport, they'll just want all the dirt. Why get yourself mixed up in this? Why put yourself in this position? Why? It's not worth it! I'm telling you . . .'

In the tone of his voice I heard my Pepe's disapproval and it pained me. I'd never want to point any fingers or involve him. Despite everything, Julien agreed to pass on the message to Johan, who called me two days later.

'Hey, how's it going?' he started brightly, nothing like the churlish git from years ago. He was doing a good impression of sounding genuinely pleased to speak to me. Yeah, right.

'Good, thank you, Johan,' I said, keen to talk business and get off the phone. 'I just wanted a quick chat, if that's okay.'

'Sure,' he continued. 'Nice to hear from you. Ah, you know you were right all along about Christelle – we're divorced now. Funny how things turn out, isn't it?'

I then explained about David Walsh approaching me. 'Johan,'

I said, 'I wanted to be upfront. You know, tell you what I was thinking about. I want to try to help clean the sport up.'

Johan cleared his throat; somehow I imagined he was trying to keep his temper in check.

'You know,' he said, 'I don't think it's a wise idea to say anything. I mean, what's the point? But, er, y'know, if there is anything we can do, anything at all, all you need to do is ask . . .'

I gripped the phone, feeling sick. Was he implying hush money?

'Okay, well Johan,' I replied breezily, 'as I say, I'm seriously considering saying something. The *Sunday Times* is a reputable newspaper,' I repeated.

He said he'd think about things as well and be in touch.

I put the phone down and felt awful about Julien and Ryszard. Obviously Johan would be furious and he'd take it out on them. I thought of Lance too. He'd worked so very hard for what he'd achieved, doping or no doping, and I saw him as a deserving champion. I liked the guy. Turning him over was the last thing I wanted.

A few days later Johan called back and when I told him David was coming up for dinner, his voice changed mid-sentence. Gone was Mr Friendly; now he was spitting out every sentence.

'Walsh will only want to talk about one thing. If you're the sort of person that goes off and speaks to journalists, then go ahead and fucking do so. If you want to fuck off all your old teammates from years ago, just go ahead. It shows you for the type of person you really are.'

Trembling, I cut the call short and said goodbye. Part of me understood Johan's reaction. He was bound to want to protect his team. Instinctively, too, I was under the impression he didn't believe I knew much anyway. I'd been the clean girl soigneur who'd avoided it all, and perhaps he was right. What did I know? I'd only seen and heard a few bits and pieces. I'd looked the other way when most of it was going on.

Mike and I met David for dinner at Villa Jazz in Oxton, out on the Wirral Peninsula. He was a polite, softly spoken Irishman, and I got the impression he was a true professional. As chief sports writer for the *Sunday Times*, he'd written about a few doping scandals and was a keen advocate of cleaning up cycling. I had been more than a little nervous about meeting him, as I'd no idea what to expect, but as we ordered the food in the laid-back little joint, cycling wasn't the topic of conversation. As soon as David brought up Manchester United, he and Mike chatted animatedly all night.

I was surprised David didn't want to grill me about the team from the off, but I could see he was weighing me up. This was a getting-to-know-you session for both of us, but I did speak to him about my fear of betraying people with whom I'd once loved working, which sat alongside an urge to see the sport recover. 'I just want future generations of cyclists to know they don't have to take drugs too,' I sighed, thinking of poor Tyler and JV.

He listened intently, without a tape machine or notebook in sight, just his light blue eyes absorbing my words. Being Irish too, we talked about how not telling the truth is the same as telling a lie in Catholicism.

'The guilt,' I sighed. 'It preys on my mind, you know?'

David nodded sagely, empathizing with every word. We left the place, shook hands and I promised to call him soon.

Poor Mike suffered over the coming days and weeks. It wasn't so much that I couldn't decide whether to go ahead and speak to David; it was more like every half an hour I changed my mind. I talked to David again about my concerns and he intimated that not only had Betsy spoken out, but also Frankie,

JV, LeMond and a former teammate from Lance's Motorola days, Stephen Swart.

This was reassuring – if the likes of those lads were going on record, I was in good company. Instead of dissing the sport, I'd be part of a brave group of people trying to change things in an admirable way.

'So I'm not the only person speaking out in this book, am I?' I asked David.

'No,' he assured me. 'You're one of many.'

17

Breaking the Omertà

In June 2003, the month that my contact with David Walsh began, I heard that Marco Pantani had made a plea for privacy following his admission to a psychiatric clinic that specialized in drug addiction. Another lad down, I thought. Behind the glory of being at the top of their sport, riders were suffering, no doubt about it. I'd heard of deaths in the 1990s from dodgy EPO and wondered how dangerous the current medical programmes were. Surely it was just a matter of time before things got worse.

All this was pushing me towards speaking out, so I asked David Walsh if I could do an interview, on the proviso that I would need to reflect on it afterwards before giving permission to print anything. This seemed like a good solution for me, and it would also give David a chance to see if I had anything worth listening to. He wholeheartedly agreed and said he'd put a date in his diary.

On a bright, clear, blue-skied, hot summer's day in July, David turned up at our house with his little digital tape recorder and notebook.

'Tea or coffee?' I offered.

I'd never spoken at length to a journalist before and had no idea what to expect. After making drinks, I nervously settled myself on the sofa as David pulled out his pen and pressed 'Record'.

'Let's just start from the very beginning,' he said.

I carefully recounted stories as I remembered them. How a girl from Tallaght decided to become a soigneur. Joining Postal. Our inauspicious beginnings. The hopes and dreams of Europe. Carrying testosterone for George. Throwing out syringes for Lance. Delivering white pills in a McDonald's car park. Buying concealer for needle marks. Overhearing about a backdated prescription for cortisone. To me they were small anecdotes that proved the sport had lost its way. I also spoke about the UCI and how Johan went with Kevin to the control tent so that cycling's governing body could pass on the information about Lance's positive for cortisone and give the lads time to work out a cover-up story.

'You see, if the UCI gave Johan the heads-up about Lance's cortisone, it proves a cover-up. The governing body has a lot to answer for. Doping in the sport comes from the top down.'

As I spoke, David's face remained totally impassive and he nodded, occasionally asking me to repeat myself. As the hours ticked past, crescent-shaped patches under the armpits of his light blue shirt turned steadily navy-coloured. Assuming the summer heat was getting to him, I offered David more water, but he cleared his throat and said, 'No, thank you,' squinting at the red light on his recorder for the umpteenth time.

Seven hours later, my throat was dry and I'd had enough. Pretty sure I'd told him everything, I finally just shrugged. 'That's it David.' I smiled wryly. 'Not much else I can say. As the "clean soigneur", I wasn't privy to much, really.'

David flicked off the tape machine and snapped shut his notebook. 'Thank you, Emma, that was great,' he said calmly.

I wasn't sure from David's blank expression if I'd said anything helpful. The other sources he was interviewing were bound to have more interesting tales to tell. I knew I was pretty small fry in this whole scene. Riders like JV and Frankie were likely to have more to say. As I shook David's hand I looked him in the eye.

'But nothing will be printed until I give my say-so, yeah?' I asked.

He nodded. 'Don't worry, we will talk a lot more.'

As I watched him walk away from my house into the world, with my memories stored on the digital tape machine, suddenly the heat got to me too. I hadn't considered how I'd feel post-interview. Relieved? Peaceful? Like a weight had lifted from my shoulders? I thought for a moment and realized it was none of these things. Not at all. If anything, I felt more tormented than ever. I hadn't just spat in the soup, I'd hoiked up and dropped a gobful in it.

For the next few weeks I had so much contact with David I could have been having an affair with the guy. If he wasn't on the phone, he was emailing, asking me to clarify this or that or to read something over. He seemed decent enough, but his hand of friendship was clearly based on his work.

My torment increased. Despite missing our chats, I hadn't dared call Julien back, as I dreaded what my Pepe would think now I'd spoken to a journalist, even if I hadn't yet given my permission for anything to be printed. My indecisive toing and froing restarted in earnest. 'At least I can pull out,' I said over and over to Mike, as he tried to watch the football or cook dinner. 'At least I have options.'

Mike sighed, as I repeated myself for the billionth time. Then the following night I'd change my mind completely. 'I shouldn't have said anything, Mike,' I told him as he got in from work. 'Who am I to act as judge and jury? I don't even work in cycling any more. No, I'll ring David in the morning and tell him it's all off.'

The next morning I'd wake, having come full circle yet again. 'The thing is, I don't have anything to do with the sport any more, so I *am* in a position to talk. If I say nothing and take all this crap to the grave, what sort of person does that make me? And what if journalists start bugging my family in Ireland again?'

He listened patiently, even if I was driving us both mad.

Despite the turmoil, we were at least both busy with work. I'd bought half of Mike's house and we planned on buying a new place together. Then news filtered through, via David, about more casualties in the sport. José María Jiménez, a great Spanish climber on the Banesto team, who'd previously suffered psychiatric issues, had been admitted to hospital with depression, even though he'd retired the previous year. Also, Frank Vandenbroucke's life was in freefall; he had even attempted suicide. Then that December Jiménez died of a heart attack, aged just thirty-two. He was the fourth cyclist to die in 2003. Andrei Kivilev had died as a result of head injuries sustained during Paris–Nice, but the deaths of two others, Denis Zanette and Fabrice Salanson, had been linked to their use of EPO.

I was horrified. This was my generation. The Postal generation. Who was going to be next?

Tragically, it took only two months to find out. On Valentine's Day 2004, Marco Pantani was found dead from cocaine poisoning in a Rimini hotel room. He was just thirty-four. I thought of him, his energy, his dedication, the way he wore his bandana – which gave him his nickname, 'The Pirate' – and what an inspiration he was to fans. I never knew him well, but when our paths had crossed he'd always been polite, unassuming and gentle.

'To die alone in a hotel room is awful,' I cried to Mike. 'What suffering he must have gone through. In what other sport do champions die like this?'

I thought of Pantani and Lance battling it out on the mountains. Whose life would be destroyed next? It was unthinkable.

Shortly afterwards, I discovered that a twenty-one-year-old Belgian rider, Johan Sermon, had died of a heart attack in his sleep on the same day as Pantani had died. Unbelievable. This was becoming an epidemic. Mike, who still couldn't have cared less about the sport, admitted even he was shocked.

'You know I will stand by your decision, Emma,' he repeated again.

The following morning I woke up knowing in my guts there was only one thing to do. Omertà or no omertà. The senseless, tragic deaths of talented riders was all I needed for the final kick. It didn't matter who thought what about me, what the consequences were. For sure, I was desperate not to hurt my ex-teammates, but I had to look at myself in the mirror every day. If any other riders died, I'd no longer be able to do that. Plus, what was the worst that could happen? I no longer worked in cycling; I had a new life now.

I picked up my phone and punched in David's number. He was delighted at my decision. Clearly the notes he'd scribbled that July afternoon had been burning a hole in his pocket.

'I've got most of what I need, Emma,' he said swiftly. 'But now with your permission we can start right away.'

He wasn't exaggerating. Hours later he was on the phone

to triple-check facts and figures. There were so many emails flying back and forth I could barely keep up.

I believe when inspiration or an idea from nowhere hits you like a bolt from the blue, it's sent by someone up there looking out for you. In this case, the idea of protecting myself and getting indemnified for the book came out of nowhere, and thank goodness it did. Despite not knowing anything about publishing or law, a nagging feeling that I should get myself covered wouldn't go away, so I asked David about it.

'Yes, I'm sure that'll be fine,' he said. 'But I'll have to speak to the publishers.'

'Please,' I replied. 'Without me being indemnified, I'm not doing this book.'

A few weeks later David spoke to me about possible book titles. He and the publishers, La Martinière, had come up with a few by now. As he excitedly reeled them off, I quickly realized they all had one thing in common. The name 'Lance' was in every single one.

'David,' I interrupted, stunned, 'this book isn't about just Lance, is it? We're not just going after Lance here?'

'No we're not, Emma, it's about cleaning up the sport,' he assured me. 'But if we take down the sport's biggest star this will happen automatically.'

I wasn't convinced.

'We're not out to hang Lance, though?' I repeated, feeling uncomfortable. 'The book is about the bigger picture, with all the interviews you've done?'

'Yes. You and the other sources are all speaking from the same page, but Emma, we've got to mention cycling's biggest icon – it makes sense.'

Oh God, Lance was going to go mad. I just hoped my chapter in the book wasn't a big one.

'Publishers need to choose an eye-catching title,' David went on, 'to promote sales.'

Without a doubt Lance's name would promote sales all right. I sighed. I was in too deep now to pull out and, if David was right, as the book's main intention was to clean up the sport then hopefully it would be worth it. Leaving the title aside for now, my focus turned back to the indemnity for which I was still waiting.

'Oh yes,' David said, 'I must chase the publishers for that.' It was rapidly becoming his stock answer.

'Please make sure you do,' I replied.

Weeks later, after more fact-checking, David sent over drafts of my chapter just before the final deadline. They read fairly accurately, except for one thing – David had completely left out my comments about the UCI and how they'd facilitated a cover-up over Lance's positive for cortisone.

'David,' I said, back on the phone to him, 'I definitely want all the stuff about the UCI to go in. It's the cycling governing body. We can't leave that out! This can't all fall on the riders.'

I thought I heard David sigh very quietly. 'I couldn't agree more, Emma,' he said, 'but if we put those accusations about the UCI in, they'll sue and we'll lose. There's just not enough proof.'

'But David, the UCI is behind all the doping culture!' I argued. 'The riders are just pawns in this.'

'Yes,' David agreed, 'but the UCI could sink the book.'

I didn't understand. Surely if the governing body could sue, so could anyone else who was in it? David continued talking, seeming to make sense, but as I got off the phone a familiar feeling after a tussle with David crept over me. I'd leave conversations slightly wrong-footed and unsure that my concerns were being resolved. Still, I was comforted by being one of many sources. Once everyone had said their piece, I was sure the book would pack a punch. David also carefully explained that it was his co-author, the former *L'Equipe* journalist Pierre Ballester, who was dealing with the 'scientific side of things'.

'This book will contain many little-known facts and figures behind cycling,' David said, 'and lots of varying anecdotes.' During the course of his research, David had even spoken to several riders to check my credentials and I was touched by some of their complimentary comments. JV even said to David, 'Make sure you treat her well. I consider her a friend.'

The title David and the publishers plumped for was *L.A. Confidentiel*, and I could see how fitting it was in a sense, although I felt bad about Lance on every single level. I could hear Johan now: 'See, I was right about her all along,' he'd be saying.

After the umpteenth fact-checking evening phone call, I was exhausted by the process. Making money from my interview wasn't on my radar, but faced once again with having to set aside my weekend to read and re-read my testimony felt unfair.

'It's not on!' I complained to Mike. 'David is getting paid for this work, but I am helping for free.'

The next time we spoke I had it out with him. 'Listen, I'm all for helping you, but I'm basically an unpaid researcher working all hours. How's about I get something towards covering my time?'

David went to Pierre and they agreed on £5,000. It seemed a reasonable amount, as I hadn't originally expected or wanted anything, but I would later think it was the hardest five grand I'd ever earn in my life.

Another thing was bugging me. As the publication date, June 2004, drew closer, David grew more vague when it came to my indemnity. Instead of him constantly ringing and emailing me, the tables had turned and I was chasing him now. Pinning him down wasn't proving easy. Sure, he was a busy man with six children and a day job, but it felt wrong. I'd done all this work, been as helpful and compliant as possible and yet when it came to protecting my interests, suddenly he didn't seem as concerned.

The gnawing sense of unease clawed away at me again, but it was too late. All I could do was hope I'd done the right thing. Then finally, at the eleventh hour, the indemnity was granted. 'Thank goodness for that,' I said to Mike, waving my piece of paper. And so all we could do now was wait for the book to be published.

Before publication, David persuaded me to do a couple of interviews to publicize the book.

'It'll be good to put a face to it,' he said. 'All you need to do is repeat what you said to me and answer the questions honestly.'

I couldn't say the idea of being plastered across a newspaper or magazine was a pleasant one, but for the sake of the book I thought it best to cooperate. Besides, the interviews were all for French papers and Norwegian TV, so nobody I knew would see it, I thought. Then *Paris Match*, the French version of *Hello!*, took some pictures of me and our dogs on New Brighton beach – something I found a little cringeworthy, even if the photographers taking the shots were nice enough. All this took time, and taking unpaid days off was something I could ill afford, so after the last interview I said 'No more.' As far as I was concerned, I'd done my bit.

A week before *L.A. Confidentiel* was due to be published, David rang again. 'The publishers want you to go to Paris for the book release date. Is that okay?' he said.

'Er, why?' I asked.

'Maybe just in case any lawyers have any questions, that sort of thing,' he replied.

'I don't think so, David. We're busy with work, so just pass that message on to them, thanks,' I said.

He ummed and ahhed but I stood firm. After I put the phone down I turned to Mike as he clattered around in the kitchen preparing dinner. 'The publishers want us to go to Paris. For the book release. Something's up, isn't it?'

He turned to me: 'Uh-oh, yeah. Sounds strange.'

An hour or so later, David phoned back to see if I'd reconsider.

'Tell them if they want me to stay in Paris, will they put me up in the George V Hotel, please?' I replied cheekily. 'I rather like the irony. That's where Lance stayed when he won the Tour.'

'Er, Emma . . . no, I don't think they will do that,' David spluttered.

I laughed. 'Well then, we won't go!'

Five minutes later he called back again. 'Emma, the publishers are happy for you to stay at the George V.'

I tried to laugh, but this time it wasn't funny. Making excuses, I said I'd call him back later. I had no intention of going to Paris, no matter what they were offering, that was for sure.

'The publishers have agreed to pay for the George V,' I gasped. 'Now I know this is serious.'

Mike's face dropped.

'Okay, well yes – something is most definitely up,' he said.

18

Kill the Pig

O N THE DAY OF publication I was off work, so I set about
doing some chores. The phone stayed silent all morning,
so I assumed all was in hand with the book. In many ways I
was relieved it was over. Being published in France, I hoped
it stayed there. Perhaps the UCI and relevant sporting bodies
would pick up on it and take action?

The living-room floor was a bit dusty, so I grabbed a broom.
Flicking on the TV, Sky Sports was on from the previous night
so I pressed mute. Humming to myself, I pushed the sofa to the
wall as Cara and our new Dobermann, Coco, made hungry
eyes at me.

'Not now,' I said to them. 'Later.'

As I swept, I glanced up as the rolling ticker-tape at the
bottom of the screen caught my eye.

'Breaking news: Former soigneur for Lance Armstrong,
Emma O'Reilly, speaks out.'

At first I thought I was seeing things. My name. On the
frigging TV? 'Emma O'Reilly speaks out' rolled across the
screen again as I dropped the broom.

Oh my fucking God.

Trembling, I unmuted, to hear the newsreader say that Lance Armstrong had instructed his lawyers to sue the publishers of the book and that he strenuously denied all claims of doping.

Diving for the phone, I rang Mike's office.

'Mike Carlisle.'

'Mike, switch on your office TV. Sky Sports. Now. Just. Do. It.'

I heard a clatter as he fumbled for the remote.

'I'm on the fucking news. I'm the main story. My name is on the television!' I choked out.

'Oh Emma, oh no,' he said.

As Mike rushed home, I hit David Walsh's number, only to get his answerphone greeting. 'Come on!' I cried, waiting for the beep. 'David it's me, just ring, okay? As soon as you can!'

I waited for Mike, still in shock, unable to take in what was happening. Then the phone rang. It was a man with a French accent.

'Are you Miss O'Reilly? I'm a lawyer representing La Martinière.'

I wasn't sure what he was on about at first, then I remembered La Martinière were the publishers. A lawyer had never called me at home before and little did I know just how many calls I could expect over the next decade.

'Mr Armstrong has issued legal proceedings to start a process against the book publishers. We are being sued, as are the authors, and you as the named source. There is also an injunction against the book . . .'

Struggling to keep up, the only words I heard were 'sued' and 'named source'. That was me. Then, as he told me exactly how much money Lance was suing us for, my heart banged so hard in my ribcage I thought it would explode. I began to feel like Ralph from *Lord of the Flies*.

By the time Mike got back I was beside myself. 'Seven hundred and fifty thousand euros,' I kept repeating as if in a trance. 'Mike, I'm finished. It's all over. I'm going to lose everything.'

So many questions raged through my mind, I could hardly keep up. Why was I the only named source in the book? Why didn't I know I could be sued? Why was Lance even suing me, when he knew I was speaking the truth? Actually, that last question I could answer.

Lance was Lance. With his back up against the wall, he'd always react in the only way he knew how: fight. Tooth and nail, Lance would go after everyone, except this time I wasn't on his side. He knew and I knew I was telling the truth, but none of that mattered. I'd attacked him in *L.A. Confidentiel*, so naturally he would fight back. I held my head in my hands, wondering what sort of hell my life had suddenly turned into.

Finally David called back.

'Right, David,' I almost screamed, 'am I or am I not the main source in this book? Where are the other sources?' At that moment I wanted to kick myself for not having read the damn thing from start to finish, but I couldn't because it was in friggin' French!

As usual David remained calm and started a lengthy and reasonable explanation. 'Emma, the other sources chose to remain anonymous. Frankie and Jonathan are still in the cycling business; they probably felt the need to protect their names. Stephen Swart was named. He talked about his time in Motorola, doping with Lance in the nineties.'

Once again David made it all sound so palatable, except for the part about Stephen Swart.

'Stephen must've talked about what Lance did years and years ago, so that matters less. He's not criticizing Lance as the Tour de France hero like me, is he?' I raged.

I took a sharp intake of breath as realization struck. I'd put my name to my words because I'd presumed everyone else in the book would have done so too. Yet I could have made the safer choice of remaining anonymous. People giving interviews have that option. I went quiet – a first for me.

'David, what is going to happen next?' I whispered. 'I'm scared.'

'I don't know. Remember, I'm being sued too.'

The next day, another French lawyer, called Thibault de Montbrial, rang. He'd represented Bruno Roussel and Willy Voet after the Festina affair and David assured me he was a man not to be messed with. 'I will be here for you,' he said, as he explained that myself, David, Swart and the publishers were the named defendants to be sued.

'Well at least someone is,' I replied.

Thibault talked me through what would happen next. Lance was claiming everything in the book was made up and as I was the only named source along with Swart, only we could be sued. But that wasn't all. After excerpts of my chapter were reprinted in the *Sunday Times*, Lance was also suing them, along with a French magazine called *L'Express*. This was all very confusing, so I got on the phone to David.

'David,' I gasped, 'I've never given an interview to this *Express* or whatever it's called magazine. I've never even *heard* of them, so how could they sue me for that?'

David went a bit quieter. 'Once you've done an interview it's out there,' he said calmly. 'And it can be reprinted anywhere the newspaper sees fit.' He trailed off as I took another deep breath.

'Is that right, now? I'd no friggin' idea!' I cried.

I wanted to scream. That was the whole problem with this entire fiasco. I hadn't had any idea of how interviews or the media worked, and boy was I paying the price. I cringe now thinking of how naive I was. Not only did I face a huge legal battle, but I was public enemy number one with Lance, stood to lose everything I owned and the phone was ringing off the hook with European journalists wanting to interview me about it!

'*Non, non, non!*'

Throughout my life, whenever something sad or over-whelming happens, the fog descends. This time, along with the numbness came a new, overpowering emotion that ate away deep inside. Guilt.

Part of me longed to grab the phone to ring Lance and tell him how sorry I was. I didn't see him as the big baddie that the book had painted. This had all got out of hand. He was just one of hundreds of cyclists all doping and risking their lives, even if I couldn't deny he was the biggest name in the sport, and therefore doper number one. But what was he going to say? Fuck you! I knew he would. I'd screwed him over royally, and all the others too. I'd become the one thing I prided myself on not being.

Disloyal. A traitor.

Winning the Tour had been a spectacular experience and I'd spat in their soup, spoiling everything for nothing. Lance was going to fight this every step of the way. He'd attack from the front, so I suspected he'd attack me as a woman too. With mounting sadness, I realized I'd probably never speak to Julien again, as I could just imagine what he thought: 'Emmatje, you did wrong.' All the while Johan would be saying to anyone who'd listen: 'I told you so.'

That night I curled up in bed, held the pillow over my head and quietly cried. Mike came to join me, lying down in silence. He didn't know what to say.

'I shouldn't have done it,' I sobbed. 'This was one huge mistake and now I'm going to pay for it. In every sense of the word.'

My phone now rang non-stop from morning till night, often it was the lawyers or David, but the next day a new, urgent-sounding male voice was on the end of the line.

'Keith Schilling, lawyer for Lance Armstrong,' he said.

I felt ill. 'Can I help you?' I squeaked.

Schilling was keen to ask me for a 'conciliatory statement' about Lance. 'You got on well?' he asked. 'You had a good relationship?'

'Well, yeah . . .' I agreed, a bit baffled.

'Well it's time to make this public,' he said.

Actually, despite everything, this was a grand idea. It was very true, and I had never, ever wanted to go after Lance. I hated the fact that *L.A. Confidentiel* was slanted so against him. He may have been the rider most comfortable taking drugs, but I was happy to say publicly what a good relationship we'd had. This was a chance to make it up to him a bit. Maybe he'd even back off.

I got off the phone and dialled Thibault, who was very encouraging about me meeting Schilling.

'Absolutely a good idea,' he gushed enthusiastically. 'Make sure you call me afterwards too.'

So, convinced it was the right thing to do, I gave Keith a buzz back.

'Excellent,' he said. 'I will come tonight.'

'Sure,' I agreed, surprised at how fast this was all happening.

19

Pawned

TRYING TO REMAIN POSITIVE in the face of what I expected to come was tricky. But meeting Schilling was a lifeline, and I hoped it might alter the course of proceedings. If I said something honest about my friendship with Lance, surely it would take the heat off him? Perhaps his legal team would back down too.

Before Schilling arrived I had a chat with Pierre Ballester, David's co-author, for the first time, explaining my fears about where the book was heading. Afterwards he sent me an email, headlined 'We stand by you', telling me I wasn't alone and that it wasn't just my testimony from the book that was important; it was also Stephen Swart's, Greg LeMond's and others', although of course we both knew it was only my name being bandied around now. All very nice, I thought, but somehow I couldn't quite find it reassuring.

That evening, Mike and I waited nervously for Keith to arrive. Leaping up to answer the doorbell, I found a man in a pin-striped suit standing next to a serious-looking young woman. Behind him, a cab was parked up, its meter running.

'Keith Schilling,' he said, squeezing my hand abruptly.

'Who's she?' I asked.

'Oh, she's only a legal assistant,' he said, nodding to the woman, whose face looked as blank and impenetrable as his.

'Fine, well you can sit elsewhere while we talk,' I said to her. She glanced at Keith, who nodded. Already I felt suspicious and under siege.

We sat down as Keith pulled paperwork from his briefcase. Mike spoke first. 'Look Keith, you might think we're very naive here, but we basically believe because Emma is telling the truth, that's our greatest strength.'

Keith nodded, but didn't seem to take the words in. Instead he gazed intently out of the window. 'You not had any paparazzi around yet?'

'No!' Mike laughed. 'Why would we? This is only about cycling; it's hardly a football scandal with David Beckham, is it?'

Keith pulled out a list of questions he wanted answered.

'Was your interview with Walsh taped?' he asked.

'Yes,' I said, trying to sound confident. 'And everything in *L.A. Confidentiel* and in the *Sunday Times* article was true.'

By now, all my intentions of establishing goodwill had evaporated. I wilted inside as he reeled off further questions, but I refused to tell him anything new. Eventually he asked me to write down a list of the questions to which he wanted answers.

'I need this information,' he said, before announcing he was going off to the Lowry Hotel in Manchester. He got up and shook my hand.

'Thank you,' he said.

'Thank you,' I lied, relieved I'd said nothing and agreed to nothing.

As I opened the door for him to leave, he turned to me. 'Did you ever see Lance take drugs?' he asked.

Ah, I thought. The Columbo question, trying to catch me unawares. What a great line that would be: 'Soigneur admits to his lawyer she never actually saw Lance take drugs'. Except it didn't work.

'No. Comment,' I replied.

'Oh, and Lance says to say "Hi",' Schilling shot at me, as he stepped out of the door.

For a split second I felt sad. In a funny way, I missed Lance. But frigging hell, I thought, yeah, I bet he did. I could guess what he'd really said was 'Kill the bitch', and in a way I didn't blame him.

I managed to force a smile. 'Say "Hi" back,' I breathed, before pushing the door firmly shut.

Drained, I looked at Mike; his eyes were like saucers.

'Jesus Christ, exactly what sort of a friggin' mess have I got myself into?'

I stared at the list of questions to which Schilling had demanded answers and swallowed hard.

'I'll need help with these,' I said. I was so frustrated. Mike and I had been planning to try to get away for a few days and now we had to deal with this.

Within an hour the phone was ringing. Thibault. 'How did it go?' he asked, a sense of urgency in his tone. 'Did you see Keith?'

'Yes, he came and he left,' I sighed.

'But he saw you? Brilliant. Can you put this in writing? Send it as an email. I could use it as evidence in court in France as an attempt to hassle a witness.'

'What?'

'Yes. In France, if a witness is visited by the lawyer of the claimant, it can be classed as harassment. I just need you to confirm it in writing.'

I was speechless, then the penny finally dropped. It had all suddenly become painfully clear. I was just a pawn in everyone else's game. The publisher's lawyers were doing their job, but that also meant I was effectively being used to further their own case for the defence, and Lance's lawyers were trying to protect him. Who was actually protecting me?

My worst fears were confirmed when a French radio station, RTL, emailed to request an interview the following evening. My supposedly private meeting with Keith had been leaked. This was big news over there. If Lance's lawyers meddled with a witness it could scupper their case against La Martinière. I was furious, although Thibault flatly denied it was him or any of the French team who'd leaked the info.

I fired off an email to Thibault and to David asking for help in answering Schilling's questions so that I could get him off my back. I also requested a quick response before our few days away, but two days later I had still heard nothing back from either of them.

'It's not on,' I said to Mike. 'The first time I need their help and they stall getting back to me. I just want these stupid questions answered so we never have to deal with Schilling again.' To the best of my knowledge, nothing came of that harrassment issue either.

I rang and rang David, but nobody picked up, so I sat at my computer and typed an email to Thibault, to David and to Pierre, finally giving them a piece of my mind:

18th June 2004

Hi all, the only time I have put you under a heavy time constraint
and you have not SUPPORTED me. I find this absolutely despicable
to leave me so vulnerable, especially in the light of the pressure
you put me under yesterday and this morning to save your book.
WHAT DOES THIS MEAN?

Also you have NO right to turn the visit from LA lawyer into a
media circus and to give our phone number to anyone without
consulting me. Also I want to make it clear you have no right
to answer my allegations that will be put about myself and my
reputation without first consulting and agreeing with me. I have
been used enough to further your media hype around the book. I
do not feel at this stage that you have my best interests at heart,
using me to publicise this book is where your interest lies.

Thanks for nothing,

Emma

I sat and read back my words, my heart banging, my chest so
tight I could barely breathe. 'Mike, what do you think of this?'
I asked as he read over my shoulder.

'Well said, Emma,' he replied. 'In my opinion they're tossers,
the lot of them.'

After barely sleeping for days, Mike and I decided to try to
get away from the whole thing, regardless of what was going
on. I booked a few days' holiday on Teletext, choosing a four-
star hotel in Tarragona, Spain. I planned to lie on a beach, my
phone switched off – although, realistically, I knew I probably wouldn't dare do that. It all seemed like a good plan, until
we arrived at the airport in pouring rain and found our hotel

was so awful it didn't deserve one star let alone the four advertised.

The next day it was still raining, but to top it off, as we headed into town a blur of colours on wheels whizzed by. A peloton. We'd travelled hundreds of miles to get away from cycling and accidentally landed slap bang in the middle of the warm-up for the Volta a Catalunya.

'You're fucking joking me,' Mike sighed, without a shred of humour.

If the lads on the bikes don't kill me, Mike will, I thought. 'I'd no idea!' I protested. We tried to relax, but with more calls coming in from lawyers it was impossible.

Back home, feeling horribly unrested, we discovered that every day brought a new email or a new development, as more people piled in to get involved.

Prentice Steffen, our old team doctor, had been in touch with David with the idea of setting up a whistleblower's case. I'd never heard of such a thing before but, in a nutshell, the US government had passed a law called the 'Whistleblower Statute', designed to encourage individuals to denounce companies for fraudulent actions. Prentice was basically accusing the US Postal Service, and Lance, of defrauding the US government out of $60 million. He argued that as they'd doped, they'd therefore fixed race results, so this counted as fraud given all the sponsorship money they'd gained.

Whoever brought and won the case would 'win' three times the amount of the fraud, in this case a staggering $180 million. And Prentice needed 'direct and independent testimony . . . Lance et al. have done all this for money. It would be nice to see them suffer momentarily for their unscrupulous acts,' he wrote in his email to David, which was forwarded to me.

Initially I was interested, as I believed it might help cycling overall, something the book evidently wasn't doing. But as more emails flew back and forth, doubts gathered. In my mind, Prentice's emails had little to do with cleaning up the sport. This, in my opinion, was all about money.

My gut instinct that Lance would go after me personally was confirmed when I got an email from a total stranger. This time, accusing me of being a grass, the tagline read: 'I'm your ally, Lance is planning to do this to you'. My guts knotted as I clicked it open. 'He is in the process of saying David Walsh is paying you a lot of money to make up lies because you need the money because of your divorce. Godspeed with you Emma. Be strong and courageous.'

Frigging hell, Lance. What was he going to come up with next? I was pissed at David too; in an interview immediately after the book came out he'd claimed, in an attempt to try to deflect any criticism, that I hadn't been paid. Now that had backfired as the news that in fact I had received money had leaked out, making him look like a liar and me a money-grabber.

Frigging hell.

By now I was deleting emails as soon as they came in. Most of them were from members of the public, calling me a traitor, a liar, telling me I shouldn't have been allowed to work with Lance. How dare I speak out against someone so brave? Someone who'd beaten cancer and returned to win? Disgraceful! Many accused me of being penniless, desperate to make a quick buck. As paranoia set in, I felt as if I should walk around the streets wearing dark glasses. Lance had some hardcore fans out there, especially in the States, plenty of whom were keen to tell me how I should be hanging my head in shame, and I was inclined to agree.

Then a journalist I'd known around the sport for years sent

me a transcript of Lance's words at a press conference for the new Discovery Channel Pro Cycling team, into which US Postal had morphed. I'd deliberately been avoiding putting Sky Sports on. If I ever saw anything about Lance anywhere, I firmly told myself 'Switch the shit off, Emma'; this was the only way I could get up in the morning and keep going. But I found myself reading this journalist's words as he gently tried to let me know what was being said about me.

First the interviewer asked Lance: 'The individual that's been quoted the most in the press reports concerning the book was someone you worked with. How stressful is it and do you have any speculation as to why someone like this would want to hurt you?'

Even the way the question was phrased kind of irritated me: 'want to hurt you'. No, I'd not been trying to 'hurt' anyone. I read on.

Lance replied: 'In fact we actually had a very good working relationship. I know that Emma left the team for other reasons . . . um . . . and even as evil as this thing has come out to be, it's not gonna be my style to attack her. I know there were a lot of issues within the team, within the management, with the other riders that were inappropriate . . . and she was let go . . . But to be quite honest, I always had a good relationship with her. I did not work with her very much . . . If you're talking about the year 2004, we're talking about 1999, many many years ago. And this is the first I heard from her in years and years.'

I swallowed hard. Lance was always going to attack me from the front, yeah, I knew that. But insinuating I'd had improper relations with riders? Ah, that was low. That night I tossed and turned. Lance's gloves were off and I didn't expect him to play fair.

If his last comment was bad, the next one hit home harder.

From David and the lawyers came news that Lance had called me an alcoholic at a press-conference interview.

'It's so friggin' unfair,' I ranted to Mike. 'I liked a drink as much as anyone else after the big races, but I could count on one hand how many times we did that in the year. I've never even been out drinking with Lance!'

Mike was furious too. 'He's a cheeky swine!' he cried. 'How does he get away with saying these things?'

I didn't understand either. Lance was chasing me for libelling him, but he could say what he liked about me and the UK libel laws didn't protect me at all.

20

Sticks and Stones

MIKE WASN'T THE ONLY man in my life getting riled either. The following evening I got a phone call from Norbert in New York, where he now worked. I had consciously not told too many people in my life about the book or the legal action. Thankfully my family in Ireland didn't watch Sky Sports or follow anything to do with cycling, so it was only my brother, sister and close friends like Sharon in whom I confided. Even then, my instinct was to protect them from the worst. But Norbert was struggling to contain his emotions.

'Emma,' he fumed, 'I was at work today in the office and overheard a couple of lads talking about you, saying, "Yeah, well that Lance whistleblower is just an old colleague with a chip on her shoulder and she's an alcoholic to boot." Boy, I was so annoyed I followed them into the lift to give them a piece of my mind!'

My big brother was still wanting to protect his little sister, even if he did live across the pond. 'How dare they?' he raged.

'I'm sorry, Norbert,' I said. 'You're having to go through this too.'

I could only imagine what the guys in the lift must have thought when my angry brother approached them, but their reaction didn't surprise me. In America Lance was a hero to millions, not only as a sporting icon but as a humanitarian. They didn't want to hear the ugly side of the cycling story. The side I now represented.

Thibault emailed to assure me he'd provide me with a British lawyer, so the UK side of things could be dealt with properly; hopefully this meant I would understand a bit better what was happening. He sounded rather like a general rallying the troops, telling me to keep my nerves because Lance's lawyers' mission was to have me getting crazy under pressure. He advised me not to fall into this basic trick, that the war would only last for a few weeks, and that no-one would let me down. He then insisted that he needed me and Swart and LeMond and Steffen, 'and EVERYBODY' to stay united. He said the enemy would try everything to weaken us, including psychological warfare and lies, and went on to say 'DO NOT LET THEM SUCCEED!' Finally he told me that Lance was afraid, because we all said the truth, and that we were going to win through this war.

I was rolling my eyes by the time I reached the end. His reaction made me think how I'd become trapped by egos on all sides: Lance, David, the lawyers, all trying to outsmart, argue against, influence and control each other, while I was stuck in the middle of it. How could something so simple as my good (although misguided, I now thought) intentions end up caught in what felt like the crossfire of men's egos? It was insane.

Hot on the heels of this email, Pierre Ballester's wife, Lily, got in touch to tell me she'd never seen her man so busy with another woman but that she admired me so much for standing up for the truth in a man's world. She still worked for *L'Equipe*, the newspaper from which Pierre was fired for speaking out against doping. 'But I fully understand it,' she continued, 'because I understand the righteousness of the cause, the importance of his quest, your quest. And as a woman I also feel very appreciative and very proud of what you did and I want you to know that I'm very supportive. Lily.'

I could see she was trying to be kind but, as far as I was concerned, her husband was part of the team who had roasted me.

Meanwhile, Prentice was growing increasingly excited about my supposed participation in his whistleblower case, but I told him I needed more time to think. He fired an email straight back to apologize, but the whole affair was starting to leave a funny taste in my mouth.

Thibault got in touch again to let me know that someone called Marcus Rutherford from Reed Smith had been appointed as my UK lawyer. I definitely couldn't afford to hire an independent one of my own, so I was essentially at their mercy. Tired of all the emails, I rang David to find out where he stood in all of this. He'd gone terribly quiet, leaving me to wrangle alone. When I eventually got hold of him, he sounded busy, distracted, and said he'd be in touch later. When his email finally did arrive he apologized for not being able to talk when I rang, as it was Father's Day and he'd been busy with his kids. He apologized for how things had turned out and said he felt responsible for it, although he hadn't realized how things would 'unfold'. He went on to try to reassure me about the credentials of my lawyers. Apparently in a previous case, when Thibault had been trying to expose political corruption in France, the life of his daughter had been threatened. If anything, David's email left me even less certain. I'd never met his kids or his wife, but he often mentioned them in conversation now, as if we were all best buddies. Although a dysfunctional friendship of sorts had developed between us, I hadn't agreed to talk because he was my pal; I'd agreed because I believed it was the right thing to do.

Caught in his own whirlwind, David went off to the States to publicize his book. *L.A. Confidentiel* had largely been ignored there by the cycling community and barely got a footnote in the newspapers, aside from headlines about my disloyalty. David had agreed to go on ESPN, the US sports cable and satellite channel, to be interviewed. As the main source (as I was now reluctantly getting used to being called), the producers wanted to know if I would take part too. But the very idea of appearing on American TV to repeat myself brought me out in a cold sweat. I already felt as if I'd done enough to publicize the book, and this would mean taking more unpaid leave from work, so I was reluctant. I became even more so when I realized that, if I did agree to it, Lance could sue me again for repeating the allegations, so I asked David if I could be indemnified. As always, he promised to look into it, but as always, in his own time.

Thoroughly sickened by anything to do with cycling, I cringed if a bicycle so much as crossed my path now. Yet cycling and doping headlines proved hard to escape. And this time, when I spotted a newspaper headline, the name leapt screaming off the page.

'David Millar: In a prison cell for doping'.

I stood and stared at the words, trying to take them in. David Millar. A class rider, openly clean, the UK poster boy . . . I snatched up the paper to read the details, filled with sadness. David had been arrested in a restaurant near Biarritz by plain-clothes police. They'd found empty vials of EPO and two used syringes in his house. He'd spent the night alone in a prison cell.

The last time I'd met David Millar he'd been so sure of where he stood in the madness. Now even riders of his ilk were succumbing. What was worse was that it didn't surprise me in the least. Staying clean and winning races had become impossible.

Thibault kept me in the loop every step of the way, but often I found the whole legal process confusing. Next, news broke that a Parisian court had thrown out Lance's bid to block the book and force the publishers to insert a sheet of paper with his denials into every copy. An irritated judge accused Lance's team of abusing the legal system and David was tickled when Lance was ordered to pay him and Pierre a $1.20 fine – not that I found any of this amusing.

The book had reached number two in the French bestseller list, but the frighteners had been put on every UK publishing house, so nobody wanted to publish it here, although David hadn't given up hope it might happen one day. Quite honestly, I hoped it never would.

Unrepentant, David turned up to face Lance at his next press conference.

'I'll say one thing about the book,' Lance said, eyeballing David. 'I think extraordinary accusations must be followed up with extraordinary proof. And Mr Walsh and Mr Ballester worked for years and they have not come up with extraordinary proof.'

Lance's statement said it all to me. I was easy to brush off as a disgruntled ex-employee, an alcoholic, a divorcee who needed the dosh. Telling the truth wasn't enough.

I tried to keep up with events, but I also wanted to sleep and get on with working, eating, existing with a life outside this madness. I stood to lose everything I possessed, I thought. Although Mike wanted to stand by me, he feared the same consequences. Still trying to do the right thing, whatever that meant, I chased David about the ESPN interview and getting indemnified. Finally he got back to me by email, apologizing again for his slow response and explaining he'd been feeling miserable, shivering with a sore throat. He had been in touch with ESPN, but their company policy didn't allow them to indemnify their interviewees so he had told them to forget about speaking to me. He signed off with: 'Wimp of the week award goes to . . . David'.

I felt pretty wimpish with self-pity too; however, I didn't have the backing of a national newspaper behind me and had to keep up the fight to stay on top of things. Thankfully Mike was more on the ball than myself with so much of it, helping read and compile all these damn emails. He'd also pointed out something else I hadn't thought of.

'Emma, love,' he said, 'if David's publishers decide to publish in the UK after all, could they also sue you here too? I mean, you should look into finding out.'

He was right. I'd no idea of the consequences, so I asked David about it, but, surprise surprise, no quick response. By this point I'd started to despair of the UK's libel laws. The upshot was, if I wanted to be truthful about something – something on which others backed me up – I wasn't allowed to be. Our libel laws imply that if you ask questions – as David did in his book – you are insinuating guilt. But across the Channel, no libel is committed if the questions you raise turn out to be true, or if they are made in good faith, for instance if other people have backed up your claims.

Lance could say whatever he liked about me, and I had absolutely no way of fighting back.

I knew the publishers were insured, so with luck I wouldn't need to pay up in relation to the book itself. But I was much more worried about the *Sunday Times* case, as that was on British soil. If Lance won, he could come after me for everything – my share in the house, any savings I had, anything I owned now or possibly even in the future.

Finally, a lawyer from the paper contacted me asking for a meeting, so I agreed, and she came to see us in Mike's office. Her name was Gill Phillips and the moment we met she reminded me of a civil servant. 'Oh my goodness,' I thought, as she shuffled through mountains of paper, 'I can imagine Lance's lawyers eating this woman for breakfast.'

Worse still, she didn't appear to have a shred of faith in me or my 'evidence', as she kept calling it. I hadn't been named in the *Sunday Times* article, so why, I argued, should I be involved? As she left the building to drive back to the station I looked at Mike and shook my head. I could tell he was thinking the same as me. With Lance's lawyers it would be a case of 'he who blinks first' and this woman seemed to me to be blinking already.

I contacted Marcus Rutherford, my British lawyer, to ask for his advice about the ESPN interview, and also why I was involved in the *Sunday Times* case. After meeting Gill I feared the worst. Marcus agreed I shouldn't make any fresh statements about Lance now (ha – as if I planned to!), but he also told me that, like it or not, I was indeed involved in the *Sunday Times* case and so should cooperate. God, this was so confusing.

As depressing as it was, my friendly journalist kept me up to speed with David Millar's story. By now David had been placed under formal investigation under France's anti-drug laws for possession of dangerous substances, after admitting to a Parisian judge that he had used a three-week course of EPO in 2001 and again in 2003. In a statement issued through his sister, Frances, he said: 'I am deeply sorry for this. I did not want to live a lie any longer. I have told the judge the truth, but the main thing I wish to make clear is that this was my individual decision and I have to take responsibility for my decisions.'

'Good on you,' I said to myself as I read the words. A rider telling the truth. How refreshing. Millar was the ninth member of the Cofidis team, riders and staff, past and present, to be placed under investigation since the Festina affair, yet the team director was insisting they had zero tolerance for drugs. 'Yeah, right,' I thought.

My journalist friend was pretty upset that David Millar had fallen foul of doping, as he was the first Brit to do so in the modern era. I was sad too, but not in the slightest bit shocked. 'It really is a bummer about David,' I wrote to the friend, 'but think the BCF [British Cycling Federation], Cofidis and the Société du Tour aren't being correct and he's just being the scapegoat. I feel that they could have made a better statement still not condoning drugs but at least acknowledging the fact that David's a human being who succumbed to the scourge of cycling.'

To keep ourselves buoyed up, Mike and I attempted to have evenings where we tried (and usually failed) to ban the subject of court cases. 'It could be worse . . .' I began one evening but, when I was unable to finish that sentence, we just burst into a rare bout of laughter. Then, in what had become a familiar pattern, just as I thought bad events had peaked, another letter arrived. This time it was on headed notepaper, from the Home Office. The French Drugs Squad wanted to speak with me.

As I read and reread the request, the words began to swim on the page. Drugs Squad? Of course, by admitting to David

Walsh that I'd crossed the Spanish–French border with banned substances, I had admitted a criminal offence.

I got on the phone to Thibault, who explained that the police, thankfully, were not interested in arresting me. 'They want to ask you about what happened when the Actovegin was found,' he said. 'They never got to the bottom of it and as an insider you could shed light on how things worked over there.'

'I hardly know anything about that!' I cried. 'I wasn't working at the Tour in 2000!'

The very idea that I'd now, after the book ordeal, go running to the police, shopping all the riders and staff, pointing more fingers, was absurd. This wasn't about trying to get my former friends arrested.

'No, Thibault, absolutely no way,' I said.

'Okay,' he replied. 'But think about this. If you voluntarily go to the police, it will look like you have nothing to hide in the face of any criminal trial and the civil case with Lance.'

'But why do they want to talk about the Actovegin?' I asked.

Thibault explained that, during the 2000 Tour, Lance had faced being quizzed by the French police in a criminal investigation but he'd wiggled out of it. He'd told them, 'Listen, lemme just finish the race then we'll all come over, sit down and explain everything about what you found.' But after the Tour Lance hotfooted it back to the States with his yellow jersey. He had no intention of talking to anyone, let alone the police, and they hadn't caught up with him since. Typical Lance.

'Emma, it's the best option,' Thibault said. 'This is unfinished business for them and they won't drop it.'

I had no choice.

21

Digging In

THIBAULT MADE THREE DEMANDS to the Drugs Squad. He requested the right to be there, a guaranteed flight for me
back to the UK on the same day, and a special order to keep my
visit top secret. The squad had experienced leaks recently, so
only three or four officers could know about the meeting.

On 10 July, I flew from Liverpool to Charles de Gaulle
airport, more petrified than I've ever been in my life. I'd left
Mike at home, even though he desperately wanted to come. I
knew the stress was getting to him; God, how could it not – it
was getting to me. But anxiety could make his condition even
worse, and I didn't want that for either of us.

I grabbed a cab to meet Thibault for the first time in a coffee
shop. He recognized me before I did him. Striding over, he
looked every inch the lawyer, fashionable in that distinctive
French way, with his jumper tied over his shoulders.

'Ahh, Emma,' he said, taking my hand. 'You are definitely
better-looking than you are in your pictures . . .'

I was completely taken aback. I was about to be interviewed
by the French Drugs Squad and all he could do was comment

on the way I looked? It was completely irrelevant! I fixed a smile on my face, keeping my thoughts to myself, as he prepped me, trying to be reassuring. I could barely swallow my coffee. I just wanted today to be over.

We took another cab to the Palais de Justice, an imposing but beautiful building near Notre Dame, and we were whisked inside. There was just an interpreter, myself, Thibault and a couple of officers. As we sat down, another man turned up and called one of the officers outside. He started gesticulating at him wildly.

'What's that about?' I whispered to Thibault.

'Oh, it's their boss, wondering why he wasn't told about this secret meeting.'

The Drugs Squad didn't give a hoot about the book or what was said in it. They just wanted me to tell them everything I knew about the Tours. Answering their questions as best as I could, I didn't elaborate much. The clock ticked, hours passed, with everyone – especially me – growing tired of the same old questions. The police were polite, respectful and the whole process just seemed to be a repetition of facts. Keeping my eye on the time, I asked if I could go to get my flight.

'*Non*,' said one. 'But don't worry, we have a helicopter if need be.'

A helicopter? My nerves started to jangle again. I knew very well how French police can hold you for seventy-two hours without so much as a phone call. I could only hope they'd keep their word and let me go. Just an hour before my flight was due to depart, I started to panic, feeling nauseous, but Thibault put his hand up and insisted I should be allowed to go.

Suddenly chairs scraped on the floor and it was all systems go. I was bundled into the back of a police car and we screeched off into the maze of narrow streets. I held on to my seatbelt for dear life as we raced the wrong way down one-way streets, sirens blaring, cutting around corners, ignoring traffic lights. I didn't know whether to try to enjoy it or throw up.

When we pulled into the airport, I said goodbye quickly to the police and rushed in with my bag, my gate about to close. 'Please,' I begged the check-in girl. 'Can I just get on?'

Little did I know, the officers had followed me. 'Are they letting you on?' one demanded. 'We can make sure they let you on!'

I turned to see cops running over, as if we were in a Peter Sellers movie. I half expected the Pink Panther to turn up. These guys meant business, and I wondered again what the hell I'd been caught up in.

'It's fine, lads, I'll just get on,' I said, dashing after the check-in girl.

Just get on the plane, Emma, and get outta here.

I arrived home feeling as if I'd aged ten years in the past ten hours. 'I'm so glad you didn't come,' I admitted to Mike.

The next day Thibault rang to say that the police were happy with my statements and didn't require any further assistance. That was one weight off my mind, but it was soon replaced by Gill demanding a draft witness statement in preparation for the *Sunday Times* case going to court. I rang David, who insisted I trust her. His 'all in this together' chat did little to appease me, though.

The following day Gill sent me an email to say she didn't want to pressurize me but needed to get the *Sunday Times*' defence document together by the end of the week and that my diaries were pretty crucial to this. By now I was in no doubt about my role in this. Not only was I their strongest witness, but they were itching to get me on that stand in court to speak up for them against Lance.

My diaries. Part of me wanted to run into the garden and burn them. I wanted them off my hands. This was beginning to feel more and more as if I was the one on trial, not the newspaper. How could it have come to this when all I did was tell the truth? And wasn't the *Sunday Times* supposed to be on my side? I vented my feelings to Gill.

'I am sorry if I made you feel as if you were on trial,' she said. 'That was not my intention at all, although I hope you will understand that I did need to test your evidence, to reassure myself that what David was telling me was correct and accurate – that is a lot more to do with inherent suspicion of journalists than with you!'

'Great,' I thought.

The idea of taking the witness stand and speaking out publicly against my teammates and Lance in a huge court case was unbearable. I couldn't take the stress and told them I didn't want to do it: I wasn't going to hand over my private diaries or take the witness stand. None of it.

The pressure was also still mounting for me to join the mini-army Prentice Steffen had enlisted for his whistleblower case, which both Greg LeMond and David Walsh were behind. After all, so the reasoning went, if they won their case, it would help the publishers and *Sunday Times*, wouldn't it? This was war, I kept hearing. But my aim was to clean up the sport, not vie for a share of a $180 million pot of gold.

I emailed Prentice to let him know my position. His reply staggered me. 'Emma, please reconsider,' he wrote. 'Think also when in your life you'll ever have the chance to do something so good and possibly earn millions in the process.'

'The chance to do something so good' didn't involve making money in my book. His response reinforced my decision to keep out of it.

*

In a warped way, I admired Lance's guts. In the midst of all his legal battles, defamation cases and trashing his enemies, nothing, absolutely nothing, took his mind off the big job – winning. He had demolished the world's biggest bike race again and won his sixth Tour. Even President George W. Bush rang him to say 'You're awesome' afterwards.

Lance had recently broken up with Kristin, but divorce didn't taint his public image as a family man, even when he seamlessly moved on to someone else: beautiful rock singer Sheryl Crow.

Just when you thought it was impossible for Lance Inc. to get bigger, it did. He was on the red carpet at the Grammys, playing cameos in films; he also teamed up with Nike to promote a mammoth fundraising event, selling yellow wristbands for the Livestrong campaign. The yellow bracelets became a phenomenal success, a must-have fashion accessory, with everyone from Tom Hanks to Pamela Anderson to Matt Damon wearing them. Now a bona fide celebrity himself, Lance's little black book grew and everyone from Bono to Tiger Woods was on his BlackBerry speed dial. A cyclist in Lycra had transcended Hollywood. Unbelievable!

But there were, on occasion, public voices of disapproval, and one of them came yet again from former US Tour de France legend Greg LeMond. In an outspoken interview he told *Le Monde* newspaper that he suspected foul play: 'Lance is ready to do anything to keep his secret. I don't know how he can continue to convince everybody of his innocence.'

Meanwhile, I felt suffocated, enmeshed in a murky web where events were spinning out of control. Fearful of more people judging me, I didn't dare breathe a word at work about what was happening. Thankfully, most people there didn't follow sports news, and those close colleagues who did know respected the fact that I didn't want to talk about it. Poor Mike was the one who got it in the neck most evenings, after I'd checked my emails. As much as I tried to hide my anxiety from him, it wasn't working. Mike had been so strong, had managed his MS so well, but now his limp had worsened. 'It's just a flare-up,' he shrugged. 'It'll be okay. You know it will be fine.'

But within six weeks of *L.A. Confidentiel* being published, he'd started to use a walking stick.

'Mike,' I asked, sick with worry, 'do you need help with this?'

'No!' he shrugged. 'Seriously, I will be fine.'

I wasn't convinced, but I respected his brave stance.

Mike often fielded calls to the house. He'd ask the lawyers, David, or whoever to drop me an email instead. At times it was almost like being under house arrest. Then, one sticky evening in August, my mobile rang and Mike's face told me that for once it wasn't a lawyer or David.

'Um, Emma,' he whispered, waving frantically across the living room, 'quick!'

'Eh? Who is it?' I asked out loud. I'd had it with 'surprise' calls or people urgently needing to chat.

'Greg LeMond!' Mike mouthed.

I grabbed the phone. 'Emma speaking.'

I recognized his Californian drawl from the television and any lingering doubts about it being an imposter were quickly swept away as he started talking, quickly, softly, and with a genuine concern. 'I just had to get in touch, Emma,' he said, 'to say how much I admire you and to tell you to hang in there. We have to be strong and stay strong.'

We talked for two hours, the evening light dimming in my living room as we spoke. Greg knew a lot about coaching and he told me he thought it was physically impossible for Lance to be doing what he did clean.

'I know,' I agreed. 'I don't believe it's possible to win clean either.'

'Lance is out of control.' He sighed. 'It's gone too far.'

Greg's part in the Lance story had grown even darker. After he'd given an interview to David in 2001, casting doubt on Lance's win and on his relationship with Michele Ferrari, he'd been forced into an apology by Trek, who both sponsored Lance and sold Greg's brand of LeMond bikes. Now that he'd spoken out again, Lance's lawyers were once more putting pressure on Trek to sever ties with Greg and cancel all his bike contracts.

'It's a dirty business,' he told me.

I couldn't have agreed more. Greg spoke for so long that the battery on my phone started dying, so in the end I had to say a hurried goodbye. 'It was so lovely to hear from you. I appreciate all your support.'

As the line went dead, Mike just said, incredulously, 'Wow! We just had a phone call from a three-times Tour de France winner.'

Even I, as sick as I was of cycling, felt touched, especially as Greg and his family were having a much harder time than me.

As I went on living in dread of the phone ringing and unable to sleep, it was only a matter of time before more news from the Lance Armstrong vs Times Newspapers libel case arrived via David. On 17 December 2004, the Hon. Justice Eady handed down his judgement, striking out a key defence by the *Sunday Times*. The judge had basically ruled that what was said in the book and serialization was prejudicial to Lance, using the following phrase: 'The overall effect of quotations and the events described in the article is to leave readers with the impression that Mr Armstrong's denials of drug taking beggar belief and are to be taken with a pinch of salt.'

A pinch of salt? According to one of the top judges in the highest court in the land, that's what my truth was worth. On top of this, he refused to cap spending on the case, allowing Lance, who'd already splashed out £140,000 on his legal team, *carte blanche* to carry on. All in all, this judge was ruling in Lance's favour.

Insomnia and anxiety make a potent mix for a man with multiple sclerosis. After a fraught Christmas, the New Year brought an impossible struggle.

'I want to go into work, believe me,' Mike insisted as he tried to pull himself out of bed. Watching the man I loved go through this was heartbreaking. Knowing I had introduced this stress into our lives by speaking out made it even more painful.

Unable to walk properly at all now and in constant pain, Mike decided to give up work. For a proud man, this was devastating, and it tore me in two. We agreed I would bring the money in, while we hoped new medication would improve his condition, but the irony of my boyfriend now needing more drugs than ever just to function wasn't lost on me.

22

The Knock

A SUBPOENA: A WRIT compelling someone to attend a court. The word had never entered my vocabulary before. I'd no idea there were two different types: *subpoena ad testificandum* and *subpoena duces tecum.* Who would? The former is when a person is ordered to testify in court or else face punishment; the latter is when a person is compelled to bring physical evidence to court or else face punishment. I'd had no idea it was a police officer who personally hand-delivered a summons, coming to your front door to make sure you received it.

And I'd had no idea that one day I would suddenly get so many of them. Worries were no longer arriving in the form of emails and phone calls; a knock on the door was our latest dread. And because he was home all day, it was poor Mike having to deal with it. We'd already had several subpoenas from *L'Express,* who were ordering me to testify, and now as I arrived home one freezing January evening I found myself opening another one.

I swallowed hard as I read the letter. 'What the friggin'—!' I spluttered, experiencing a now all too familiar and painful tightness in my chest. I fought back tears. I didn't want Mike to see, but he could tell by my trembling hand that this latest letter wasn't good news.

'Who wants you in court now?' he asked.

'The *Sunday Times*!' I screamed. 'They were supposed to be on our side! Nobody told me they would pull something like this and force me on to the stand. They don't even respect me enough to call and tell me first!'

'Does David know about this?' Mike asked.

That evening we had a serious chat about our finances and how I should try to protect mine. I'd been staring down the barrel of bankruptcy for a while now, but this gun was well and truly loaded. I had to figure out what would happen in the worst-case scenario. Lance had sued La Martinière for 750,000 euros, but at least the publishers were likely to cover this. The *Sunday Times* suit was for almost £1 million and I thought, as a named person, I'd have to chip in. It would finish me completely and then some. No way did we have that kind of money. We discussed the possibility of Mike protecting my finances.

'I'm not sure if it's possible,' he sighed. 'But we have to do something.'

If David had been under any illusion about my feelings before, he definitely wasn't now. I gave it to him with both barrels: 'Your frigging newspaper has subpoenaed me! How could this have happened?'

As always, the madder I got the calmer David became. 'Emma, I'd no idea it would come to this,' he soothed. 'We didn't expect all of this.'

'We didn't expect all of this' was rapidly becoming his new mantra.

'No, David,' I spat, 'I didn't "expect all of this" either.'

'Look, I'm up to my neck in it as well,' he said. 'As you know.'

'But what about me and my life? What about Mike? This is stressful for him and his condition.'

'I am having the same sort of conversations with Mary as you're having to have with Mike,' David replied.

I wanted to scream. 'But David, this is good for you. Good for your career. This has made you! And this is good for Thibault's and Marcus's careers too! This is what you do for a living! I am trying to run my own business, get on with my life. This is not a career for me. This is *not my life*!'

Even though David had left the *Sunday Times* for now, he was still in cahoots with them. His bosses and colleagues still supported him. He still worked in journalism. He was not on his own. Not one jot. He fell silent again. I wanted to scream and tell everyone to leave me be. I'd had enough. I'd made a huge mistake speaking out, even if it was the truth. This was payback time.

That night all I could think was: 'This is precisely why riders and staff don't break the omertà and spit in the soup. This is why nobody ever speaks out. You bloody fool.'

Due to the extraordinary pressure, the twisted fact was that now I felt I deserved everything I got. If I'd just kept my mouth shut, none of this would be happening to my life or Mike's. I felt as if I'd gone mad as I questioned my judgement and lost all sense of perspective.

Contact with David soon tailed off again as he turned his attention to Betsy Andreu, speaking to her at length and comparing notes. At the end of the day they had more in common: a mutual wish to bring Lance to justice. I'd already lost a huge amount of trust in David, but more than that, I saw an unrelenting obsessiveness in the man, the journalist, out to 'get

Lance' at pretty much any cost. That was what mattered to David, not me, nor probably any of his other sources. In my mind, however, I always felt that it wasn't Lance or any of the riders who were the problem. Or Johan, or Thom and Mark, or even 'The Myth' Ferrari. It was the whole culture of cycling. Faster riders, more exciting races and bigger sponsors were all desirable because they made money.

If I thought I was in any way able to limit my dealings with court cases, I was about to have a rude awakening. Someone else who had apparently been keeping an eye on Lance's un-paralleled success was Bob Hamman, the guy who ran SCA promotions, a marketing and insurance company who'd had a policy taken out by Tailwind, the company Lance ran with his manager Bill Stapleton.

Now Lance was owed around $10 million in bonuses for doing the unbelievable, winning six Tours in a row, but Hamman's suspicions about Lance's amazing feat had grown. While the majority of the rest of America ignored the accusations of doping and revelled in their champion, Bob decided to dig deeper.

First his lawyers contacted Betsy and Frankie. Then they came knocking for me. Once again it was all so confusing, so Marcus prepped me beforehand. 'Ask to see any papers filed in the US courts so you know the context, ask if you'll actually be called to give evidence, ask to be separately represented, ask them to pay your expenses,' he said, as I struggled to make notes. In the end I just agreed to speak to Bob Hamman on the phone.

He talked for a few minutes about how he'd had such faith in his system and how let down they'd all been. 'Lance has screwed us out of millions,' he said. 'You could change the face of this case. Help give people back the money they are owed!'

226

Apparently SCA wasn't a huge insurance company but was privately owned and supported about a hundred families through their employees.

'I'm sorry to hear this, but I don't know what it's got to do with me,' I said.

'We want you to testify,' he replied. 'It's going to court and we need witness deposition statements.'

'But this is a business deal between you and Lance,' I protested, confused. 'It's not about cleaning up the sport.' I politely said goodbye to him, hoping that would be the end to it.

In the meantime, news filtered through that after Tyler Hamilton had won the gold medal in the time trial in the Athens Olympics, his victory had turned out to be short-lived. He'd been found guilty of doping and was stripped of his medal. Not only that, he'd gathered so much support protesting his innocence that his family and friends set up a 'Believe Tyler' campaign. When I read about that, I just cringed: 'Oh no, Tyler. No.' I felt unbelievably sorry for him. What a terrible hole to dig yourself into. There was being dishonest, even to yourself, but knowing Tyler as I did, I guessed the burden must have eaten his soul.

As the SCA case rumbled on I heard that Betsy and Frankie had agreed to testify, so I sent an email in support. 'I'm lucky over here,' I wrote. 'I can stay out of it, but it's probably more difficult for you two.'

David confirmed just how hard it was for them. They were under tons of pressure to say that Betsy had lied about the hospital episode when Lance had admitted he'd taken drugs. How their marriage was surviving, I didn't know. Lance even confronted Frankie about it, asking why he was letting his wife do this. What conversations they were having over the dinner table could only be imagined.

Nope, I wanted nothing to do with this. Bob wanted his money back from Lance, fine; don't let me stop him, but it wasn't my battle to pick. I told Marcus this, but he replied, 'Emma, you don't have to get involved, but the publisher believes that the US case is worth supporting as it may knock out the case in France.'

'Right,' I vented at Mike that evening. 'So, let me get this straight. The *Sunday Times* case will help the publisher's case. The publisher's case will help the SCA case, and, now, by me agreeing to help SCA's case, it could throw out the publisher's case . . . Everyone wants me to help them, but who is helping me?'

In February 2005 a lawyer from SCA, Chris Compton, sent an email to Marcus, again requesting my involvement in their case, and, gobsmacked by what he'd written, I read it out to Mike.

He said his nine-year-old daughter had recently come home from school asking if Daddy was still fighting with Lance Armstrong. It seemed her classmates at school were wearing yellow bracelets and she was wondering if he objected to her wearing one. After some uncomfortable conversation, they settled on a pink bracelet which indicated support for breast cancer research. There was nothing he could do to convince his daughter that her father was right about Lance Armstrong except to win the case. Then he finished by saying he hoped I would agree that they deserved every chance to repair their industry reputation and recover those monies – and that there were a lot of children to put through college.

I looked up from the screen and laughed out loud. 'He wants me to get involved in a massive multimillion-dollar case against Lance and all he can talk about is how upset his kid is and yellow wristbands!'

The sentiment behind it was clear, however. Lance was a hero to millions. And yes, he was a liar, a doper, a cheat who'd deceived on the grandest scale, but a business deal set up years ago had nothing to do with me.

In another twist, Marcus had told me he wasn't being paid for advising me on the SCA case; he was there for the publishers. That was all fair enough. I didn't want advice on the SCA case anyway, as I'd made up my mind not to do it. 'Why would I want a company who are trying to persuade me to testify for them to pay you?' I asked him. 'Talk about a clash of interests.'

Then shortly after this conversation, Marcus finally admitted to me that La Martinière were no longer paying his fees, but that SCA had decided to do so – another travesty. My lawyer, the man I was supposed to be trusting, relying on to save my skin, was now being paid by a company who were trying their damnedest to persuade me to testify for them.

That April Lance announced he was riding his last Tour before retiring to concentrate on raising millions for his cancer charity. Then in July – like clockwork now – Lance stood on the winner's podium for his seventh Tour triumph.

Usually I switched the television off if Lance news appeared, but this time I paused to watch the footage of his victory speech. 'I'm sorry if you don't believe in miracles,' Lance said, smiling, his three children and Sheryl Crow close by, 'but this is one hell of a race. This is a great sporting event and you should stand around and believe it. You should believe in these athletes, and you should believe in these people. I'll be a fan of the Tour de France for as long as I live. And there are no secrets – this is a hard sporting event and hard work wins it.'

I allowed myself a hollow laugh. 'Oh Lance, you don't even sound like you mean the words coming from your own mouth now!'

Hard work I agreed with. Self-belief. He'd inspired me all those years ago. Yet now I felt contempt for Lance Armstrong. Here was a man triumphant, but trapped by his own lies, his own hype and myth. As much as I was suffering for telling the truth, I'd never want to swap places.

The rest of 2005 passed in a blur of trying to keep busy in my own life. Now I was the breadwinner, I had decided to take the plunge and turn around a massage business in Cheshire. It was a small practice set up in a converted Victorian railway waiting room next to Hale station and I wanted to rename it 'The Body Clinic'. This was a huge gamble, especially with court cases hanging over our heads, but I refused to let that stop me. Also, I needed the work to support us both. My potential little business couldn't have been further away from cycling and those mountains and fields in France; it was something that suited me perfectly.

As the purchase of the clinic dragged on, in the meantime I took on more work, including massaging local sports teams. One Tuesday in August, I was leaving a training session with the Sale Sharks rugby team in Bramwell when I found my mobile had twenty missed calls. I picked it up and frowned. I recognized only a couple of the numbers, of journalists. I listened to the first voicemail message: 'Emma, can you please call me urgently. We'd like to ask you to make a comment on the *L'Equipe* story. Tests reveal EPO was found in Lance's urine sample from the 1999 Tour.'

I almost dropped the phone.

Breathing deeply, I listened to the rest of the messages. They were all from anxious-sounding journalists, all asking the same thing.

'Wow,' I thought, staring out across the car park. This was

big. The first potential development for years. These tests proved I wasn't lying.

I drove home in a daze. This was quite brilliant. There was no way back. If EPO had been found in samples it would prove to the world that doping had happened. I switched my phone off. Whatever was going to happen with the tests would happen; I didn't need to be speaking to the press about it.

Later I got the inside story. The French anti-doping agency had conducted retrospective tests on urine samples from the 1999 Tour, at which time there had been no test for EPO. Now scientists had developed one and tested supposedly anonymous samples. It was all hush-hush until a journalist from *L'Equipe* caught wind of it and managed to find out whose sample had tested positive. It was Lance's.

Predictably, he vigorously denied the allegations. 'Yet again, a European newspaper has reported that I have tested positive for performance-enhancing drugs,' he said. 'Unfortunately the witch hunt continues and the article is nothing short of tabloid journalism. I will simply restate what I have said many times: I have never taken performance-enhancing drugs.'

So far, so to the script Lance created for himself. Days later, the reaction from the wider world was also disappointingly clear. The US papers barely picked up on the story, and when they did, they stood by their hero. The World Anti-Doping Agency (WADA) said they needed more information, and the UCI announced it was getting an independent inspector to look into it. I just hoped to God they'd do it properly this time.

I lived in hope, but that same month Lance was snapped riding through a field of sunflowers with none other than President Bush. 'Friends in high places,' I thought.

*

Saying a firm 'Thanks but no thanks' didn't work with Bob Hamman; he wasn't taking no for an answer. 'Let's just meet, Emma,' he suggested in another phone call. 'I'll be in London in September for a bridge contest. Will you please allow me to take you out for dinner? Just to talk.'

Out of all the lawyers and head honchos so far, this guy sounded the straightest, and he asked so politely that I found myself agreeing.

So that September we made our way to The Ledbury restaurant in Notting Hill, after checking into the White House Hotel by Regent's Park. Bob had arranged everything and insisted on paying my expenses – something I agreed to, as he had a hell of a lot more money than me and here I was, taking more unpaid time off.

Straightaway I liked Bob. A large man in his late sixties, his voice boomed as we fell into an easy conversation. I quizzed him about bridge, a game I knew nothing about, and he asked me about my massage business. Neither of us mentioned anything about the SCA case or Lance, something I was quite relieved about. After all, what else was there to say? But finally, just as dessert arrived, Bob's face grew serious for the first time that evening.

'Emma,' he said simply, 'will you testify for SCA?'

In a heartbeat, I said 'No' again. 'It's a business decision that went wrong,' I repeated. 'It's about money and not my battle to fight. My life has been full of lawyers and legal wrangling for a year now. I only spoke out to clean up cycling, not to get your money back. Sorry, Bob, but the answer is no.'

Bob nodded, as if he'd fully expected my reply. 'In that case I want to look you in the eye and tell you that we will then sub-poena you,' he announced firmly.

I admired his straightforward manner and smiled back. At least this man had the decency to eyeball me when he said it, showing dignity and guts.

'Fine,' I shrugged. 'You do that.' I knew that as it was a civil case (my knowledge of law at this point was improving rapidly) they'd have to take me to the European Court of Human Rights. But I also knew this guy meant business, and he'd try his damnedest to get me to speak.

'Okay,' he said. His smile was genuine too. I saw in him a world-class bridge player, who basically ran a glorified bookies, and like all gamblers he wanted to win his money back. We changed the subject, finished our meal and headed back to the hotel for a drink together at the bar.

'A pleasure meeting you, Emma,' Bob said as he drained his nightcap. We shook hands; it was all very civilized and adult. This was a business meeting, without emotion, so I felt much more comfortable with that.

While SCA chased me, poor Betsy appeared at her deposition to repeat her hospital story for the umpteenth time. Afterwards she told me all about it, upset that Lance and his old friend Bart Knaggs were allowed into the room with her. Lance apparently just sat and stared at her, then started texting on his phone. His bully-boy tactic worked, as even feisty Betsy found this stressful.

Frankie also testified and my heart went out to him. To do that to his former friend and teammate must have eaten him up inside, but they were in too deep now.

'Well, they're gonna have to drag me through the courts to get me to do it,' I said to Mike.

At least Betsy's story had been backed up by Frankie, which was more than could be said for my ex-husband. When Simon had first been approached by David, during the writing of the book, he'd readily admitted that my account of the journey from Piles to Nice was true. David got this all on tape. Then a few days later, after he'd spoken to a lawyer, Simon refused to get involved. For the *Sunday Times* lawsuit, David had gone after Simon again to ask him to back up my story. If he made a statement agreeing with my version of events, this would be enough to stand up in court. Now the *Sunday Times* were sending him a subpoena.

Although we hadn't parted on amicable terms, I did hope Simon would tell the truth. But he'd got a job again with British Cycling, so obviously he had to look after his own interests. He was thinking of himself, not me, not the sport, but he had a life to get on with and he was fully entitled to do so; I was part of his past now. Eventually the *Sunday Times* had to drop his subpoena. There was no point in trying to force him to testify: he was a hostile witness. I couldn't quite believe how strong Betsy and Frankie's marriage must be to withstand all the stress.

After saying her piece for SCA, Betsy was gutted when she heard that a lady called Stephanie McIlvain, someone she'd been relying on, wasn't going to back up her story. Stephanie was a rep for Oakley, a company who sponsored Lance, and she had also been present in that hospital room. She'd admitted overhearing the same conversation to David for his book and for the ESPN interview, but had remained anonymous. In a showdown with her bosses, they'd told her in no uncertain terms that if she testified, she and her husband would lose their jobs. The web of control and extortion had just grown even more complex.

The following month we heard that Stephanie was grilled for eight hours, and to start with I assumed she must be giving a truthful account if she was in there for that long. Only later did we realize that Betsy's worst fears were confirmed. Stephanie had denied her account.

A few weeks later, on 30 November 2005, it was Lance's turn, but everything went on behind closed doors. Even in private, with everyone sworn to secrecy, the cycle of lies continued to spin.

23

False Dawns

By now, Mike had dealt with so many subpoenas that the police officer who brought them round even rang him beforehand to ask him to put the kettle on: 'I've got another one on its way!'

Poor Mike always dreaded telling me when I got home from work. He'd push the brown envelope with the court order under some magazines on the coffee table and wait to pick the right moment before he broke the news. And it was always bad.

This time Bob Hamman's tenacious plan had worked: he'd won the right from the European Court of Human Rights to subpoena me and now they wanted me to go to the States to testify.

'Over my dead body,' I said simply to Marcus. I neither wanted to be on SCA's territory nor to waste another few days of my life. But I had to agree to it or face prosecution. And as much as I stood for what I believed in, I wasn't going to prison for anyone.

'If I have to speak it'll have to be via a video link or something,' I cried. The thought of travelling to the States terrified me. Although in the cycling community there were growing whispers about Lance's involvement in doping, he was still the all-American hero. I feared being lynched. To my relief, they agreed that I could testify from London.

A new lawyer for the *Sunday Times*, David Engels, came to the house to prep me beforehand. He was from another law firm, a hotshot with apparently more experience than the paper's in-house staff. Despite my run-ins with his newspaper, I liked David, and had more faith in him. He wore a smart suit but was casual with it; he played rugby and wasn't one for messing. He explained the process, how I had to answer the questions one by one under oath and how an affidavit would then be drafted. 'There's going to be a barrister in there with you. He's there to oversee everything, but don't look to him for anything. He can't help.'

I could feel a pain in my chest again.

'Don't worry, Emma,' he said. 'Lance's lawyers over here have about eight partners and we have about eight hundred. We will bury them in paperwork.'

I knew then and there he was going to eyeball Lance's lot, just like he needed to. If it was a case of who was going to blink first, then it wasn't going to be him.

In January 2006, I left to give my evidence in London. Mike wanted to come, but I kissed him goodbye at home. 'You don't need the stress,' I said, realizing as I spoke how fruitless saying this was. Mike was as stressed out of his brain as I was.

The time of my appearance was set for 10 a.m. By 9.30 I was sitting in a side room, clock-watching, the palms of my hands prickling with sweat. With no legal representative yet sent to join me, I was completely alone and felt it. At 10.10 a.m., still with nobody having appeared to get me, I went to find some-one.

'What's going on?' I anxiously asked another lawyer 'over-seeing proceedings'.

'There's been a hold-up. Mr Armstrong's London legal team want to sit in on proceedings, so they've applied for permission in the High Court.'

A sick feeling rose in my guts. 'It's purely designed to in-timidate you, Emma,' I thought. 'But you can't let it.'

'Fucking bastards,' I muttered. I hated bullying of any kind.

'They can't question you,' the lawyer reassured me. 'It's only Lance's lawyers in the States who can, via video link.'

'Fine. Bring it on.'

I was finally shepherded into the room and two of the bozos from Schilling's law firm eyeballed me as I took my seat, but I ignored them, just wanting this over with.

Over the video link, Lance's lawyer Tim Herman started going through the quotes from the transcript I'd given David, asking question after question. They were trying to ascertain what my relationship with Johan had been, and said, 'I believe you called Johan in the book, what you described as "Hit by the ugly sticks on the way down".'

Shifting uneasily on the hard chair, I felt embarrassed. When put like this, I didn't come across at all well. But I nodded and admitted saying it. I'd meant it at the time. In my opinion, Johan had been nothing but a despot.

Then they brought up the money I'd been paid. 'Is it true you received five thousand pounds for your interview for the book?'

'That was the hardest five thousand I ever earned,' I said, unable to bite my tongue. Then, before I could stop myself, I added: 'And how much is this costing you all this morning, then?'

The lawyer didn't seem to have an answer for that.

By the end of the seven-hour grilling, the poker-faced barrister, from whom I'd been warned not to expect any help, explained that I would need to go through the affidavit and sign it.

'We will need to meet again,' he said. 'Perhaps we could do so in a McDonald's car park?'

I couldn't help but laugh. Minutes later I was on the phone recapping the session for David Engels.

'Well done,' he said. 'Especially for asking the lawyer what rate he was on. I couldn't have asked you to say anything more appropriate myself!'

I got on the train home, out of there, annoyed I'd had to do any of this, but relieved it was over.

David Walsh called when I arrived home, clearly thrilled about how the testimony had gone. 'I've heard you were a very strong witness,' he said, his voice rising with excitement. 'I doubt Lance will want you anywhere near the stand when it comes to court for us.'

I sighed. Pleased as I was that it had gone well, I wasn't thrilled about being the star witness. All I'd done was told the truth.

David Engels rang the next day. 'They're talking about putting you and Mike in a safe house,' he said. 'For the *Sunday Times* case.'

'Friggin' hell,' I cried, making sure Mike was out of earshot. Was there no end to this?

Despite the lawyers' excitement, a month after I'd been forced to give my deposition the SCA case was suddenly dropped. All the finer details were lost on me, but it appeared that Lance could have ridden the Tour on a motorbike and he'd have got off. Despite all the evidence from witnesses, SCA couldn't prove he'd doped. The case was going to arbitration but, under Texan law, if SCA lost, they faced having to pay triple damages. Bob and his company would be ruined, so they chose to drop it rather than carry on. Incredibly, though, this case would turn out to be the only time Lance was questioned under oath by a lawyer.

The untouchable Lance train of good luck and fortune rumbled on. In May, the case of the positive EPO test was also dropped after Emile Vrijman, the Dutch lawyer who was acting for the UCI cleared his name. Vrijman concluded that the laboratory didn't 'follow the rules' and they couldn't accept this as a positive test. I was gutted. I had thought that if anything was going to prove watertight, this case would be it. Not so.

And the chain of events didn't stop there. On 30 June 2006, the *Sunday Times* threw in the towel and their case was settled out of court, after Lance won a preliminary court ruling. I got the news from David, who'd assumed someone would have been in touch to let me know.

'No, I've not been told!' I cried. 'What does this mean?'

The lawsuit had been hanging over my head for two years, yet nobody had had the common decency to let me know what was happening. The paper was ordered to pay £600,000 – £300,000 to cover Lance's legal fees and £300,000 for its own costs. David was furious and believed the *Sunday Times* should have fought Lance harder. 'I can't believe they accepted this,' he ranted. 'It's not right.'

A strange mix of emotions washed over me as David spoke, explaining how the High Court had ruled in Lance's favour, saying the article meant 'accusation of guilt and not simply reasonable grounds to suspect'. The paper had tried to argue that it just 'raised questions', but instead they were found to have accused Lance outright of using drugs, something which under UK libel laws wasn't acceptable.

The good news was that there was no longer going to be a trial; I didn't have to be a witness; the case was dropped. Although we still had to worry about the French lawsuit, the chances were we wouldn't face losing our house. My business had a hope of flourishing. We would no longer have to deal with lawyers in this country (this turned out not to be true, of course, but I did hope so at the time).

The bad news was that my name was still mud. Nothing I had said was proven. My reputation was in ruins. Nobody believed my story. Along with Lance, the British justice system had basically called me a liar. I broke the news to Mike, who sat with his head in his hands, absorbing it.

'We're safe now,' he said, his face awash with relief.

'Yes,' I replied.

We held each other silently. Something about this was a huge anticlimax. I questioned even more what the point of it all had been. 'I suppose we'll just have to wait to hear what happens in France now,' I muttered.

One person who didn't sit on the fence with his reaction, of course, was Lance. 'I'm extremely happy with today's judgement,' he said in a statement, 'which is the latest in a series of consistent rulings in our favour.'

Just a week later, Lance quietly dropped the defamation lawsuit against the French publishers and *L'Express* magazine. He waited until he'd exceeded the three-month deadline to chase the case and then let it go; it barely made a footnote in the papers.

Once again it was David who broke the news. 'It's over then?' I gasped. 'It's really all over?' The million-pound-plus bounty on my head had vanished, blink, just like that.

'Yes,' David sighed. 'There's no way Lance would have wanted this to go to court. He's escaped. It means we're off the hook financially, but we don't get Lance in the dock.'

That evening Mike and I should have been popping a cork, but we both felt flat. This was never about getting Lance in the dock; it was about being honest.

'Honesty is the best policy, is it?' I said miserably. 'Well not in this case.'

Lance had said he planned to spend his money on personal causes like his charity instead of litigation. 'I think we're ten–zero in lawsuits right now,' he said. 'My life is not about that any more.'

'What a low-life,' I went on to Mike. 'Lance can go off and carry on like nothing has happened, whereas I'm always gonna be the soigneur who cheated everyone. Who lied. The turncoat who had a chip on her shoulder. The alcoholic, the money-grabber, the—'

Mike shook his head to stop me from going further, then he wrapped his arms around me as I tried to breathe. There was nothing left to do now but try to forget the whole sorry saga.

Sick to death of cycling, I didn't even watch the Tour in 2006, but I heard that Floyd Landis, the thirty-one-year-old from Pennsylvania who won it, was stripped of his victory just days later when he tested positive for testosterone after his performance on Stage 17. It was two years since *L.A. Confidentiel*, lawsuits for defamation had flown around the globe, and yet the sport was as dirty as ever.

In 2007, David Walsh sent me a copy of his book *From Lance to Landis: Inside the American Doping Controversy at the Tour de France*. Inside he'd written the message 'When we

242

learn telling the truth can be a lot of hassle', and I just rolled my eyes. The 'Get Lance' train continued to be a money-spinner for him. I put it on my bookshelf and left it unread for a long time.

It was years before I could bear to have anything whatsoever to do with the sport. I'd stopped watching it completely and no longer spoke to anyone involved. In ways it felt as if my career as a soigneur had never happened, except for the lingering stabs of guilt I still experienced regularly.

Worse still, I now seriously doubted my own judgement. Who had I been to think I could act as judge and jury to the whole cycling industry? Little me speaking out had made not an iota of difference; all it had done was bring stress to our door. I'd made the man I loved more ill and I had wrecked my reputation. The decision seemed nothing but stupid, and knowing I was capable of such an error destroyed my confidence in myself. After all, if I was capable of making such bad decisions, what else could I mess up in my life?

But one good piece of news was that, after a hard slog setting up the clinic, it was growing. I even treated top athletes, although carefully kept my own past hidden. The last thing I wanted was clients to know me as 'The Whistleblower', a failed one at that. When the odd doping story came up, I'd get a call from some European journalist asking me to make a comment, but I refused, and thankfully the UK press left me well alone. David Walsh was still digging, occasionally in touch, but all was quiet on his campaign. Of course Lance was less easy to avoid and occasionally I'd accidentally spot him while flicking through a gossip magazine in a doctor's or dentist's surgery. Once, after he'd split with Sheryl Crow, I caught sight of a snap of him with Mary-Kate Olsen, the petite twenty-one-year-old blonde actress, and I just cringed, turning the page quickly. For two people whose lives had collided with such an impact, our worlds could not have been further apart now.

In March 2009, Lance announced he was considering buying a stake in the Tour de France organization, and planned on coming out of retirement to compete. I had to give him credit; despite everything, his ambition hadn't dimmed. For me, the Tour de France was a world away, some place I knew I'd probably never dare go again. However, when I heard the Tour of Britain was in Blackpool, just an hour's drive away, I decided on a whim to join the crowd.

By now I knew full well how the cycling community felt about me, the former insider and traitor, and I couldn't pretend it didn't hurt. A year earlier, a friend had volunteered me to help the physiotherapy unit in the velodrome in Manchester for the British Cycling team and organize the soigneurs there. I happily said I would, offering my services for nothing, but the negative response I got back made me feel as though they didn't want the likes of Emma O'Reilly there. A pariah in the cycling world, even in the UK, I was right to feel paranoid. My shame was palpable and I had only myself to blame. I resigned myself to knowing this was simply what happened when you broke the omertà.

I decided to take the risk of going along to the Tour of Britain, however, to see if I could feel the warm fuzzies for the sport again now that some years had passed. If anyone from cycling blanked me, so be it, although I decided to take Coco along with me to Blackpool just in case of trouble.

Standing at the edge of the jostling crowd, in anticipation of seeing the peloton's rainbow of colours fly past in a blur,

I found myself smiling, enjoying the energy only a crowd standing a few feet from pro cycling can experience. It proved part of me was still a bike fan, in spite of six years of hell, even if I had to keep my head down to enjoy it. Although British Cycling hadn't been part of my history, I saw people from other teams who looked through me as if I were made of glass.

But I shrugged it off. 'We won't let them spoil our day, will we?' I said to Coco, as she panted back at me.

I went for a wander near the start line, steering through the crowd and waiting for the throng to die down, when a guy in Lycra bowled up to make a fuss of Coco, scratching her ears and patting her enthusiastically.

'Oooh, you're lovely,' he said in an American accent. As I looked down at the mop of curly dark hair, the guy glanced up and then I realized who it was.

'Tyler!' I cried.

'Emma!' he replied. 'Oh jeez, I'd no idea it was you and your dog!'

'It is!' I grinned back. 'This is Coco. Good to see you too.' As wonderful as it was to bump into Tyler, a sudden awkwardness shot through me.

'Hey, if it's best you're not seen chatting to me . . .' I began, looking sideways.

'What are you on about?' he asked, his eyes wide and innocent.

I realized Tyler genuinely mustn't have heard about Lance and the court cases. After serving his ban, he was back racing, so he probably hadn't been reading newspapers. That's not what pro cyclists did.

'Oh, okay,' I said and quickly filled in a few details about the book, how Lance went after me, the court cases, being sued. 'Between myself and Lance,' I said, 'it got personal.'

Tyler's face fell. 'I'd no idea at all, Emma. I'd heard of the book a bit, but not much else.'

Busy with his team, Tyler couldn't chat for much longer, so we wished each other well, had a quick hug and I melted back into the crowd. If nothing else, going to the race had been worthwhile just to see him again.

Buoyed by my visit, I jumped at the chance of going to the Worlds in Switzerland that September, when Alasdair and TC, my old friends from my Irish cycling days, asked me to go with them. It was a repeat of the Tour of Britain when some cycling staff stalked past me, mechanics and riders who'd once always stop for a chat acting now as if they didn't know me. But once again I shrugged it off, and I had a great laugh with the Irish crew, feeling like I was back where I started. At least nobody was attacking me for what I'd done, which was something I'd half expected.

In the pub, after the first race, I spotted Simon. We'd not laid eyes on each other since our divorce, but the least I could do was be civil. TC had a chat with Simon first, then offered to grab me a coffee in order to leave us alone for a few minutes.

As soon as Alasdair had his back to us, Simon's friendly features changed. The stress I'd placed on him was clear to see. 'Written any more articles or books recently?' he asked.

I was a little taken aback by his tone of voice as he leaned towards me. 'Have you any idea just how many subpoenas I was given?' he went on. 'They even called me to reception on the tannoy at work in the British Cycling office. Can you imagine how mortifying that was?'

I swallowed and stared hard at the ground. What could I say? It had all been for nothing. Every last stressful letter, phone call, email, legal threat. The sport was still the same. Without a doubt, doping still existed.

'I . . . I'm sorry,' I spluttered. 'Simon, I really am.' A fresh sensation of guilt lurched through me. Even if he hadn't stuck up for me when I needed it, I couldn't help but blame myself. He hadn't deserved all the hassle my decisions had caused him.

'Yeah, well, it was fucking stressful,' he said.

I tried to apologize again, but I could see it was pointless. He was never going to forgive me for this and I didn't blame him. Maybe I'd never forgive myself either.

24

Old Wounds

M Y PHONE BLEEPED. IT was David Walsh. 'Good news.
Things are looking up.'

I hadn't heard from David in a while. Betsy rang me every
now and then, but I couldn't get caught up in the 'fight' like she
did. Besides, if I got a word in edgeways during each call I'd be
lucky. She'd filled me in on the Floyd Landis affair. Apparently
Lance had blocked Floyd's entry to the 2010 Tour of California
– that's how powerful he had become – and as a result Floyd
had gone nuclear and in early 2010 had begun emailing the
American cycling authorities and the FBI with a full, detailed
confession of cycling's doping culture. Incredible.

Now David had more news. On 20 May 2010 the New York
Daily News had reported that Jeff Novitzky was looking into
Lance's case. Novitzky was an agent for the Food and Drug
Administration who'd been investigating the use of steroids in
sport. He was the man who a few years earlier had exposed the
BALCO scandal. The Bay Area Laboratory Cooperative was
a business that supplied banned performance-enhancing sub-
stances to pro athletes in San Francisco. It was a riveting case,

as Novitzky uncovered corruption on a massive scale, revealing how BALCO started as a sports-supplement company and went on to manufacture banned drugs that remained undetectable for years. The brains behind the scheme, Victor Conte, along with a rogue chemist named Patrick Arnold, created loads of different types of drugs, including EPO. They sold the drugs to athletes on the sly for fourteen years until, in 2002, Jeff and his team came along.

A whole host of top athletes were implicated in using BALCO's services, including track and field gold-medal winner Marion Jones and Barry Bonds, the former San Francisco Giants baseball player. The huge scandal saw Jones sent to prison for six months for lying, despite – like Lance – never having failed a drugs test.

'Do you think anything will come of it?' I asked David with a sigh. There'd been so many false dawns now, I didn't want to get my hopes up.

'Emma, this is the best news in a long time,' he assured me. 'A proper investigation by a man who's caught others bang to rights.'

Later, through David, I heard how Jeff, alongside federal investigators, was bringing in riders one by one. They were asked outright to tell the truth, or to face imprisonment if they lied. Faced with such a stark choice, the riders shattered the all-powerful omertà. There was no room for loyalty in a room with an empty cell next door, waiting for you to fill it. Professional cyclists, capable of enduring excruciating pain on a bike, found themselves sobbing as the truth poured out. Many just confessed everything immediately, perhaps grateful they finally could.

The tidal wave of truth was finally turning. While the Feds were apparently not prepared for seeing such a wave of emotion,

I wasn't surprised. A lie eats away at your soul and these lads had been lying for most of their professional lives. The volume of tears shed proved how painful consistently having to conceal the truth, whatever the cost, could be.

All this, of course, was happening light years away from my quiet life in Hale. Although my business was doing well, Mike's illness had completely taken hold of him and he often needed to use a wheelchair now, making me feel guiltier still. But we just got on with our lives, every now and then getting the odd update from David. I'd no idea if I'd be needed in the Feds' case, or if it was going anywhere. Lance had still not been brought in. I just hoped, one day, I'd get the chance of resolution, a chance to clear my name.

In July 2010 we had been celebrating my fortieth birthday and I was standing outside a disabled toilet at Piccolino's restaurant in Hale, waiting for Mike, when my phone pinged with an email. It was Jeff Novitzky. He wanted to meet me.

'Jesus,' I thought, 'this is one good birthday present.' This meant the case was ongoing, more witnesses were being gathered. It was a slow process, but going somewhere. Hallelujah.

I was planning to head to Florida with Mike that Christmas, so Jeff and I agreed to talk then – we had to wait till I was in the country before speaking officially, he explained, otherwise my input wouldn't be accepted under international law. We had a long chat on the phone and I believed in him from the get-go. He seemed to bring a fresh energy, a renewed sense of steely determination to the scene. And I wasn't wrong: events had already begun to move so fast I could hardly keep up with them. First of all, that July a Grand Jury was formed in LA, under the beady eye of federal prosecutor Doug Miller, who had worked on the BALCO case too, and the ball started rolling . . .

Although I'd never met Floyd Landis, and knew little about him, it was becoming clear that he was a central figure in exposing the extent of doping in cycling. Tyler wrote very eloquently about this in *The Secret Race*:

It was poetic and maybe inevitable that it was Floyd who finally blew the whistle; the Mennonite kid, the one who was Lance's equal when it came to never-say-die toughness. What bothered Floyd wasn't the doping. What he hated – what his soul raged against – was unfairness. The abuse of power. The idea that Lance was purposefully depriving Floyd of an opportunity to compete.

As little as I knew about the Floyd affair, what I was picking up was one defining factor in all this. Lance had made yet more enemies, and the way he was treating people was gradually bringing him down. It wasn't even about the doping; it was his arrogance and lack of emotional intelligence when it came to treating people right. He was too big, too powerful and had not played fair too many times. Eventually someone would crack. David Walsh has said he believes Lance would never have been caught if he hadn't returned to the sport in 2009 after retiring, but I don't think this is true. Lance became a huge bully and eventually someone who could would fight him back. And that was Floyd. And then Tyler.

As well as those two, people who received subpoenas to appear before the Grand Jury included Kristin Armstrong, Jonathan Vaughters, Christian Vande Velde, Frankie and Betsy Andreu, George Hincapie, Kevin Livingston and Stephanie McIlvain. Even Sheryl Crow was on the list. It was incredible: a round-up of all the players in Lance's story. Kevin, one of Lance's oldest friends, was the only US rider who refused point blank to have anything to do with the process. Inevitably, Lance fought back with more powerful lawyers but the evidence was piling up at an incredible rate. Meanwhile, ever savvy, in February 2011 Lance announced he was retiring from the sport for a second time and said he planned to devote himself to his family and charity. By now he had two more children with his girlfriend Anna Hansen: a boy, Max, born in 2009, and a girl, Olivia, born one year later.

I didn't believe for one moment that he would disappear from professional sport, but his comments on the massage table from all those years ago sprang to mind: 'You're right, baby. I'm gonna make a wad, that big, then that big . . .' Lance was now worth a reported $125 million. I wondered if his 'wad' was big enough now.

In the spring of 2011 my brother Norbert came over from the States on a business trip. He hadn't been to visit me yet in the sleepy village of Hale, where Mike and I now lived in a converted Victorian pig slaughterhouse. Norbert was married now, with two daughters, and I couldn't wait to catch up, even though it would just be a flying visit.

But Norbert, being Norbert, barely made it through the front door before he was pulling out his laptop.

'That fucking bastard,' he raged. 'Have you seen it, Emma?'

'Seen what?' I asked, confused. My heart sank. What now? I knew it had to have something to do with the court cases; anything about me and Lance really wound Norbert up.

Norbert already had the laptop open and was fumbling on the keyboard. 'Emma, sit down on the sofa,' he ordered, 'and watch this.'

Mike was giving me a queer look, not knowing if Norbert had gone mad or if it was more bad news.

Norbert clicked on a website, nyvelocity.com, which covered New York bike-racing culture and news. They'd earned themselves a bit of a reputation for breaking stories.

'The tapes of Lance giving testimony to the SCA case in 2005 have been leaked,' Norbert said.

Apparently Lance had annoyed some keen legal eagles for claiming he'd won the SCA case, and as a result the only footage of Lance speaking under oath was now online for all to see.

I shook my head. 'I'm not interested, Norbert. Can't this wait?'

'No!' he cried.

He flicked it on. Lance was wearing a blue shirt, looking shifty, tense, angry. Norbert fast-forwarded until he got to the moment when my name came up. We all fell silent and listened to Lance being questioned.

'Emma O'Reilly was paid for her testimony, and needed the money. Do you believe this was why Emma O'Reilly said these things about you?'

'Absolutely.'

'Because she needed money?'

'I don't know, I am not her financial advisor, but I think, we now know, that Walsh paid his sources, which he denied in the beginning and now admits. I don't think any respectable journalists would find that to be kosher.'

I rolled my eyes. 'Norbert!' I cried. 'For God's sake! Why do I need to hear—?'

Norbert pressed 'Pause'. 'Shhh, Emma, please. Listen to hear what this bastard says next!' He pressed 'Play' again.

'But other than that do you have any other evidence to suggest that Miss O'Reilly was making up this in exchange for money other than the fact that—'

'Emma!' he said, as if my name had slipped his mind. 'Pissed. Pissed at me, pissed at Johan. Really pissed at Johan, pissed at the team. Afraid that we were gonna out her as a . . . all these things she said . . . as a whore or whatever. I dunno . . .'

Norbert paused the video again and almost leapt off the sofa. 'Did you hear that, Emma? Did you hear what that bastard called you?'

I tried to take a breath, but felt as if someone had punched me in the chest. Whore? Lance had actually called me a whore?

If I thought I couldn't have felt worse about the past couple of years, right at that moment I realized I was wrong. I'd got used to being labelled a liar, a pissed-off employee, a money-grabber, even an alcoholic – but whore?

'Lance,' I whispered. 'You low-life.'

Norbert's face was red with fury, stabbing his finger at the screen where Lance was frozen.

'If I ever get my hands on that motherfucker . . .' he yelled.

Mike had gone unusually quiet. I could see he was pale with anger, thinking of what he'd also like to do if he got his hands on Lance. I wanted to reach out and hug him. Watching the two most important men in my life wanting to protect my honour was pretty unsettling.

I stood up. 'Stop it, Norbert,' I cried. 'I never want to see or hear that again. Just fast-forward that part.' I agreed to watch the rest of Lance's deposition, that one word still ringing in my ears.

'Primarily I have to confess I think it was a major issue with Johan,' Lance continued. 'And it wouldn't have been a very good book if it was *J.B. Confidentiel*,' he said, sniggering at his own joke. 'It wouldn't have done that well in sales.'

'You never know, the stories might have been wilder,' the lawyer joked, joining in.

I pulled a face. How great it was to hear the legal team making light of this. Considering the circumstances, I thought they were giving Lance a pretty easy ride. It seemed that even when he was being questioned under oath, people got caught in Lance's slipstream and played his tune, just the way he wanted it.

The lawyer went on: 'Some of the information that was detailed in the book, for example the statements by Miss O'Reilly, alleging these things about you – there has been no public disclosure about anything like that prior to the book. Miss O'Reilly had never talked publicly about you with respect to these allegations, like the syringes and all that kind of stuff?'

'Not that I know of,' Lance replied. He then denied his admission about his haematocrit level, surprise surprise. Next he went on to talk about what the effects would be on his life if he were tested positive for doping, how it would go without saying that he'd be fired, and how he'd lose numerous contracts and sponsorship agreements. The next part was both moving and horrifying in equal measure, proving to me that Lance, my one-time colleague and friend, had sold his soul to doping.

'And,' he said, raising his voice, 'the faith of cancer survivors around the world, everything off of the bike would go away too and don't think for a second I don't understand that. It's not about money for me. Everything. It's also about the faith people have put in me over the years, all of that would be erased, so I don't need you to say in a contract: "You're fired if you're tested positive". That's not as important as losing the support of hundreds of millions of people.'

The lawyer responded: 'It sounds to me in your testimony that you are acutely aware of the importance and significance that you are a clean athlete, but you have not tested positive.'

'Correct,' Lance replied.

I shook my head. 'Hiding behind your cancer charity again!' I cried. 'Okay, I've seen enough.'

That night I again couldn't sleep and turned to notice Mike also struggling. He lay staring at the ceiling, his fists clenched.

'How fucking dare he?' he muttered. 'If I could've laid my hands on that—'

'I know,' I tried to soothe him. 'I know you would, Mike.'

We both knew that would never happen. But like Lance, Mike was a lad's lad. He wanted to punch his lights out. In the darkness, lost in our thoughts, he cleared his throat.

'Emma, I won't judge you on this, but do you, er, need to tell me anything about your past at all?'

I sat up and looked at him in the gloom, shaking my head. Lance had publicly labelled me an alcoholic prostitute and now even my own boyfriend was questioning me.

'No, Mike, no,' I protested. 'It's bullshit. There are no secrets.'

As much as I wasn't surprised that Lance had gone for the jugular like that, I was disappointed. He had never once treated me in a sexist way. While certain members of the team looked down on me for being a woman, that wasn't Lance's style. He respected women, or so I had thought. But I knew what lay behind this. He'd said one of the most hurtful things a man can say to a woman, just to wound me. There was no other explanation for it.

The following day my anger returned and I decided to speak to David Engels about my options. 'He can't get away with saying crap like that, can he?' I cried. 'It's defamation, surely? What if people believe him?'

'It is defamatory, Emma,' he agreed. 'But the time lapse since it happened is too long. You'd need to have taken him to court within a year.'

Engels explained there might be other options for me to consider, but after our discussion it didn't sit comfortably. If I started suing Lance back, where was this ever going to end? That would make me as bad as him.

Later on, the extent to which Lance's side had tried to dish the dirt became clear when I read about it online. Peter, my friend Sarah's husband, admitted he'd been approached around the time of Lance's SCA testimony. Lance's coach, Chris Carmichael, had asked Peter (who'd known Lance for years), 'Was Emma a bit of a slapper back in the Boulder days?' Peter, thankfully, denied this was the case.

'For God's sake,' I thought, 'even if I had been, I was in my twenties and single! I could have slept with whoever I liked and it would've been no one's business.'

As usual, I tried to park my feelings, brush it off, even see the funny side. In a phone conversation with my friend Sharon, I told her how I was feeling.

'I'm choosing not to think of Lance meaning an alcoholic prostitute on the street,' I told her. 'I'll think of myself as a party-going slapper. At least I could be having a good time then!'

25

Tidal Wave

I WAS GRATEFUL FOR a few weeks of peace and quiet, until later
in the spring of 2011 I was shown an article in *Bicycling*
magazine in which my name was mentioned. It examined
evidence for Lance's doping and the writer, Bill Strickland,
argued that if it came down to my word against Lance's, then
Lance should automatically be believed. I stared at the words
until my eyes blurred, then felt a stirring of anger that I'd not
felt for a while.

'Tossers!' I thought. How dare they conclude such a thing!
Lance's word was more important than mine? And how dare
they print such rubbish without even asking me my opinion
directly? I was sick of it. After suffering the humiliation of
Lance's SCA testimony, for the first time in years I decided
to stick my head above the trenches again and stand up for
myself. After all, nobody else was going to do it, and this was a
step too far. Just because I hadn't raised millions of dollars for
cancer didn't make my words worth less than Lance's.

I fired off a letter to *Bicycling* and it was printed in the following month's issue, under the subheading 'The former Armstrong assistant addresses doping allegations'. I've been given permission to reproduce it here in full:

Dear Mr. Strickland

After reading your article 'Endgame,' (*Bicycling*, May 2011), which included a sidebar detailing 10 allegations against Lance Armstrong and your opinion of how each might be viewed by a jury, I felt compelled to reply. Allegation 6, labeled 'The Saddle Sore', involves a dispute over a prescription Armstrong produced in 1999 to excuse a positive result for corticosteroid use in Stage 1 of that year's Tour de France. You note that I, a soigneur for Armstrong's team at the time, told journalist David Walsh that the prescription was illegitimate because it had been created and backdated after the test result was revealed. Then, in the section of that allegation called 'Our Take', you say: 'At this point it's Armstrong's word against O'Reilly's. Unless other witnesses corroborate her story, Armstrong wins this one.'

Years ago I gave an interview to David Walsh, in which I told him the truth of what I had seen and experienced in my years in cycling. Incidentally, I got paid a small sum of money for all the time I put into helping David. Unfortunately, I was somewhat naïve and thought that David's book was about helping to cure cycling of its scourge of drugs. Since I gave the interview, I feel that nothing positive has come from it. All it has led to is pitching people against each other and basically forcing them to choose whose side they are on. The whole subject is much deeper than some spat in the playground. I spoke to David because I felt that by not talking I was a part of a problem that is actually bigger than Lance. The big problem is drugs in cycling.

However, for those in cycling, that idea is way too simple and too many people are making their living out of cycling and feel the need to protect that. When I spoke to David, Marco Pantani and Jose Maria Jimenez had just died. This is what the problem is: People are dying because of drugs in the sport. Because I was prepared to lift my head out of the trenches and say it as it was, I became fair game. This is disgraceful.

But having read your article, I have decided enough is enough. For you to say in relation to that allegation that Lance wins – without you verifying my side of the story – is it because you feel Lance's word is worth more than mine? Is it because the only people you spoke to are still involved with Lance and cycling? I am sure Lance has people to back up his side, but I never got the opportunity to put my side across.

Since I spoke to David Walsh, I have received so many subpoenas that the policewoman who brought them got friendly enough with my boyfriend that she would call before coming and he'd put the kettle on for her. If my word is so worthless, why did I go to France and testify to the French Drugs Squad? I worked the '98 Tour de France, and I know how scary these guys can be, yet I was prepared to go to France, to their territory. I went because I was telling the truth, and also because a certain Mr. Armstrong sued me for a million euros because of my interview with David. If my word is so worthless, Mr. Strickland, why did Lance feel the need to terrorize me for more than two years? Why did Lance feel the need to try and break me? Why did I have his solicitor in my house trying to get me to retract parts of my interview?

Why, if my word is so worthless, did SCA drag me into their case against Lance over their refusal to pay him a Tour-winning bonus because of drug allegations? I did not want to get involved in the SCA case, as that is about a business deal that went wrong. I spoke to David because I wanted to help clean up cycling. I now know how naïve (code for stupid) I was. If my word is so worthless, why did SCA go through a lot of hassle and expense to get me subpoenaed for their case? If my word is so worthless, why did Lance's legal team feel the need to go to the High Court the morning of my testimony for the above case so they could sit in on it? They would have known that I was without my lawyer, another bullying tactic that I had become accustomed to. Unfortunately, it's hard to effectively bully someone who is telling the truth.

I have been called all things under the sun since I spoke the truth – strange that, isn't it? But now I am sick to death of journalists and people in the media using my facts to help whatever point they want to get across. They chase me like dogs in heat when they are trying to get their story, then drop me if they've got their facts or I won't elaborate or embellish their story. I have had their legal people call me at all hours demanding information and to back up what I've said. So I generally get harassment on both sides all because I was stupid enough to speak the truth.

For the record, I might not have achieved anything like Lance has – who has? But I live a nice, quiet life running a small business, with my two dogs and my boyfriend. So Mr. Strickland I would like you and your ilk to know that

I am sick to death of you making judgments of me and my word. You don't know me, I have never met nor talked to you, you have never made an attempt to talk to me. Who are you to make out that my word is worthless? Perhaps you should talk to Lance. He didn't seem to think it was so worthless when he got his legal team to go after me for a couple of years. I also find it interesting to see that you decide the allegation will be in favor of someone who used his privilege of oath to call me disgusting names he wouldn't say without protection.

To finish up, I would like you to know that what Lance has done for cancer sufferers has been phenomenal, and I agree with you that whether he is judged guilty or not he will still be an inspiration and rightly so. I had a couple of my most enjoyable years working alongside him, and really enjoyed his company, no matter what has happened since.

Emma O'Reilly

After the magazine came out, the support I received was phenomenal, catching me totally unawares. Suddenly I had hundreds of extra followers on Twitter, and a huge number of women emailed or sent letters to the clinic with support: 'Hugely courageous'; 'Standing up for what's right'; 'Massive admirer of your strong moral compass'.

I was touched. Aside from the odd voice in the dark, it had always seemed that I'd mainly been criticized for choosing to speak out. However, now that I was standing up for myself against Lance it had struck a chord with people. Perhaps the tide was turning.

*

While I appreciated some semblance of wider support, an epiphany was happening across the pond that was set to speed things up. In May 2011, before he spoke to the Grand Jury, with his back against the wall, Tyler Hamilton made the brave decision to sit down with his lawyer and confess everything, for the first time, fully revealing the extent of doping within the US Postal team. This was a huge moment. Tyler, who'd ridden alongside Lance in 1999 and was up close and personal to everything that went on, was finally speaking out. The man who himself had lied for a decade, who had set up a campaign to clear his own name, was now coming clean.

In his book *The Secret Race*, he described to his co-writer Daniel Coyle the feeling of finally, after so many years of denials, lies and cover-ups, telling the truth, and the sheer sense of serenity it brought to him:

> It sounds strange, but I'd never told it like that, all of it, from the beginning to end. Telling the truth after thirteen years didn't feel good – in fact it hurt; my heart was racing like I was on a big climb. But even in that pain, I could sense that this was a step forward, that it was the right thing to do. I knew there was no going back. I understood what Floyd meant when he said that telling the truth made him feel clean, because now I felt clean, I felt new.

Clean. New. How wonderful that it was Tyler who'd spoken out so eloquently. I'd always liked him. I'd seen how cycling had taken a piece of his soul, and to see him fight back with nothing but the truth was so heartening.

Jeff Novitzky told me that Tyler's testimony before the Grand Jury went on for six hours. He had tested positive after winning his Olympic gold medal in Athens in 2004, and again in the Vuelta a España that same year, but returned to racing in 2009. Even then he tested positive again for a banned steroid. Poor Tyler, caught bang to rights three times. Finally there was no place to hide.

Shortly after his confession, he went on America's *60 Minutes* show to confess to the world. I was stunned as I watched him speak. I saw flickers of the old Tyler beginning to re-emerge. He was so brave. He even gave his gold medal to USADA, saying he wanted them to have it until they'd made a decision. It seemed, as Tyler said in his book, that a bulldozer had been driven into the bike-racing world and there was no going back.

All we could do, however, was wait patiently for the legal wrangling to sort itself out and for the verdict to be reached.

Perhaps it was just irony, or perhaps it wasn't meant to be. The same month Tyler spoke out, my relationship with Mike sadly broke up. Without a doubt the stress of the past eight years had taken its toll, although Mike had done nothing except support, love and stand by me. He was simply my rock. His illness had steadily worsened, however, and we decided it was best for us to live apart. It was a heartbreaking decision.

Thankfully, we parted amicably and have stayed good friends. Mike once admitted that a friend of his asked him during the worst of the lawsuit years, 'Why don't you just ask Emma to stop fighting? It's so tough on you both,' and he simply said it never occurred to him to do that. 'She wanted to tell the truth and I admired her for it,' he replied.

In February 2012, I woke one morning to see that Norbert had direct-messaged me on Twitter. 'The fuckers have got off! It's over. Jeff Novitzky's case has been thrown out!'

What?

I couldn't understand what he was talking about, so I checked the news. It was utterly unbelievable. The US Attorney General for California, André Birotte Jr, had made the astonishing decision, without explanation, that his office was ending the two-year investigation. Snap, just like that.

I emailed Jeff, who was, understandably, gutted. He'd put his heart and soul into this for two years, and with all the evidence they'd collected it had seemed watertight.

'Why has this happened?' I asked.

He didn't know. All he did know was he'd heard of the decision half an hour before it was announced, and it was the day of the Super Bowl, so the story was buried. Unsurprisingly, the FBI and FDA announced they were 'shocked, surprised and angered' at the decision, and they weren't the only ones.

I had to go to work shortly after speaking to Jeff, and had started to wonder what the whole point of any of this was. Lance had truly powerful friends, I knew that, and he was beginning to look a lot like Houdini by now. How he'd managed to get out of this one, I'd no idea.

I felt utterly cynical. Lance was above the law. Cycling was as dirty as ever. Any contribution I'd made to exposing doping had been for nothing. But, I believed more than ever now, if you give in to any strong emotion – anger, resentment or hate – you let the other person win, so I just numbed it all out, throwing myself into my work.

Occasionally I'd speak to David Walsh or to Betsy Andreu, listen to them rant and rave, until I'd had enough and made excuses to end the call. Over the years Lance had called Betsy several spiteful names. While I was the alcoholic prostitute, Betsy had been called obsessed, hateful, vindictive, jealous, and some media outlet even quoted him as calling her fat – all words that seemed to pile the fuel on her rage.

Two weeks later, Travis Tygart, CEO of USADA, emailed me. I'd heard of him through Jeff, and by now Floyd and Tyler had confessed to him. But USADA didn't have any power to press criminal charges. They held a lot of sway over elite sport, so were not completely powerless, but they were no judge and jury. In his email he wrote: 'I've long respected you and your courage' and I rolled my eyes. Fat lot of good that had done me.

Travis wanted me to speak to him, so I agreed to a phone call, but with every intention of not getting further involved.

'Look Travis,' I sighed, 'I have said my piece time and time again. Seriously, what good now can come out of me repeating my testimony for the umpteenth time? I have nothing new to say.'

Travis listened, umming and ahhing.

'Yes,' he agreed, 'this is all true. But this USADA report has only the intention of getting to the truth, of cleaning up the sport, giving a chance for an amnesty to the cyclists of today and protecting future generations. This was what you intended to achieve in the first place, wasn't it?'

My ears pricked up at his words. He was right. Yes, it was.

'Hmm,' I said, still feeling reluctant. I was so tired now of repeating the truth. Was doing it again going to help? I didn't truly believe it now. But this was USADA, who were going to collect the testimony of everyone, cooperating with the Feds. Maybe, just maybe, if everyone joined forces, the evidence would be overwhelming?

'Okay,' I said. 'I've said it all until I'm blue in the face, but I'll do it again one more time.'

In March 2012 I went down to London again to tell the truth for the USADA report. My own testimony was thrown in alongside that of twenty-six other people, including fifteen riders. A tsunami of evidence. After my statement was written up, I needed a notary to authenticate it, but I dragged my heels getting it sorted. In between working and looking after Cara and my new dog Bear, it just stayed on my list of 'things to do'. Travis hassled me to get it signed off. 'Yeah, will do,' I replied. All sense of urgency had been lost; it was hard to care about this as much as I had done over the years.

That summer I heard that Lance had decided not to fight the allegations against him and would therefore be stripped of his seven Tour de France titles and face a lifetime ban. Initially I was amazed that he'd done this but, when I thought of the avalanche that was coming, I wasn't wholly surprised. Essentially, though, I felt almost indifferent towards Lance and his fate. I was sick to the back teeth of the entire process and determined to push any news related to it to the back of my mind as I tried to focus on my own life. I'd spoken to USADA and now I wanted to forget all about it. Mike was ill, my business needed my attention, my life was hectic. Cycling could go and get stuffed.

At the start of October Travis phoned, telling me mine was the last testimony they were waiting on before the USADA report could be made public. 'Yeah, right,' I thought, picturing the affidavit still lying dog-eared in an envelope at the bottom of my bag, but this time I got it done. The day after I posted it off, Travis phoned me. 'Right. It's going out tomorrow,' he said. 'Now, do you have anyone with you?'

'What do you mean?' I laughed, thinking of the dogs. 'Why would I need that?'

'Because this report will kick up a storm,' he said, 'and you might need support. If you do, let me know, and I will be there to help you through this.'

I laughed again. 'Travis, I'm so far down the pecking order of things, I doubt anyone will be bothering me. There's far bigger players in this story.'

The next day I went to work as usual, pushing the report to the back of my mind, still expecting nothing at all to change. After a long day of massaging clients, I saw my receptionist, Jean, still at the front desk. I always told her to go home once the last client was on my table, so I wondered what she was doing. She looked pale, anxious.

'Jean, why are you still here?' I asked. 'Go home!'

She waved at the mass of multicoloured Post-it notes stuck all over her desk, notebook and the wall. 'Emma,' she said, 'the phone's been permanently ringing for the past three hours.'

As we stared blindly at the numbers, a patient I'd just been treating had followed me out of the room to pay. 'What's going on?' he asked.

'You don't want to know,' I said, in complete shock. ITV, BBC, every national newspaper, magazines from all over the country, Europe and America . . . It was crazy. Why were they so interested in me?

I drove home, putting my mobile straight to voicemail. Over dinner, I flicked on the TV and saw that USADA was the big story of the day on the *Ten O'Clock News*. My name and face were again plastered everywhere, alongside Lance's. I don't usually cry – I usually get angry first – but this was too much.

The fall-out from the USADA report was huge and far-reaching. The conclusion was, beyond any doubt, that the US Postal Service Pro Cycling team ran the 'most sophisticated, professionalized and successful doping program the sport had ever seen'. Running to over a thousand pages, the testimony included eyewitness accounts, first-hand, scientific and circumstantial evidence, all to conclude that 'the USPS team doping conspiracy was professional, designed to groom and pressure athletes to use dangerous drugs, to evade detection, to ensure its secrecy and ultimately gain an unfair competitive advantage through superior doping practices . . .'

It continued: 'We have heard from many athletes who have faced an unfair dilemma – dope or don't compete at the highest levels of the sport. Many of them abandoned their dreams and left the sport because they refused to endanger their health and participate in doping. That is a tragic choice no athlete should have to make.'

At long last. This final line was the entire reason I'd spoken out in the first place. And as if to confirm this, around this time Tyler sent me a copy of his book, *The Secret Race*, which had been published in September. He wrote inside: 'I'm so proud of you, Emma'. We hadn't spoken since that chance meeting in Blackpool and I was touched that he'd thought of me. In the book, he laid bare the behind-the-scenes world of doping from a rider's perspective, revealing all manner of goings-on I'd had no clue about.

Eleven of Lance's former teammates gave testimony, including Tyler and Floyd, and they both said Lance had told them he'd also failed an EPO test in 2001, at the Tour de Suisse, but implied it would never come to light. One of the most damning testimonies came from Lance's good buddy George Hincapie, who was, like others, told outright: 'Admit everything and get a six-month ban. Deny everything and you're banned for life.' Poor George confessed to everything he could think of, and I didn't blame him.

The report went on: 'The evidence is also clear that Armstrong had ultimate control over not only his own personal drug use, which was extensive, but also the doping culture of his team.' Christian Vande Velde claimed in his testimony that Lance had told him in no uncertain terms that he had to dope or risk losing his place in the team: 'Armstrong told me if I wanted to continue to ride for the Postal Service team I would have to use what Dr Ferrari had been telling me to use and would have to follow Dr Ferrari's program to the letter.'

In the aftermath of the report, Michele Ferrari and Dr Luis García del Moral were given lifetime bans, as were Johan, Pedro and José Arenas, all three of whom chose to contest the report's findings. Eventually, in April 2014, after taking the case to a three-person arbitration panel, Johan was handed a ten-year ban and Pedro and José both got eight years. To date, Johan says he still disputes the report's findings.

Later, Lance told me that he had been invited to the USADA table in May 2012 but refused to agree to the conditions he'd been set, which he said were different from those of all other riders. After much talk between Lance's lawyers and Travis Tygart, they finally met face to face, in a coffee shop, where they had a heated exchange, Lance asking once again to be treated like other riders, but his request was denied.

The USADA report was staggering, unbelievable. Damning. And something about it made me feel uncomfortable. Most riders got six-month bans, or in some cases nothing, but for Lance it was overwhelming. He was finished.

26

Out

ONCE AGAIN, JOURNALISTS FROM every newspaper and its mother approached me for an in-depth interview to get my reaction. I felt I had little to say, but wanted to do just one of them to get the rest off my back. With a misguided sense of loyalty, I agreed to do an interview with David for the *Sunday Times*, on the basis that he'd covered the story from the start. Only afterwards did I realize I would have been offered some form of payment for other interviews, yet for this one I got nothing (and didn't ask for anything). It's never been about the money (boy, if it had been, I could've been a heck of a lot richer), but once again, after the event, I felt a bit scammed.

Pierre Ballester also asked me to speak to him, but I refused. I did agree to an interview with one big American paper, hoping all the others would leave me be, so I spoke to the *New York Times*. Then I headed into work as normal, ignoring all other calls until after the weekend. The pressure of suddenly being on everyone's hit-list was hideous; I'm not a celebrity and the spotlight is not a comfortable place for me to be. My family and friends, including Sharon, were amazed by how

271

huge the story had become. 'Why didn't you tell us?' she asked.

'Because if I started to talk about it, I knew I'd crack up,' I replied. 'Please understand.'

One request I got was from Craig Doyle's show in Ireland, so, not having seen it, I forwarded the email to Sharon. 'Do you like this show?' I asked.

'Yes!' Sharon cried excitedly on the phone. 'Can I come with you? Can we get tickets to the green room?'

The producers had already emailed me a few times, so I replied, asking if I could bring my best friend and would they mind if she sat in the green room. They said they'd be delighted. Sharon was too. 'I guess if we're gonna go, we might as well have some fun,' I laughed.

But the reality of being caught in a media storm wasn't fun. Two days later, walking through Manchester airport security with Sharon on the way to Dublin to record the show, I began to feel jittery. By the time I got to the departure gate I had over forty missed calls, from more people asking for interviews, making offers. I felt sick. So much for enjoying ourselves.

'Oh God, Sharon,' I gasped, 'I can't breathe. I can't.'

She rubbed my arm for a moment, knowing if she tried to hug me I'd burst into tears. This was all too much. I didn't expect or want any of it.

I got myself together, though, and actually the Craig Doyle interview went really well. I also realized that, with all this attention getting to me, I needed an agent, so when one from London was recommended, I forwarded every single offer to him to be dealt with. Me, with an agent? The idea was laughable, but boy, did I want everyone off my case now.

We agreed that I'd do just one big show in the States, and my new agent flew with me, business class, so I could appear on NBC's *Rock Center*. One excited publicist told me my story was a modern-day version of Samson and Delilah and I could expect book and film rights. Not for a moment did I take her seriously. 'You're one of the central players in one of the biggest sporting doping scandals the world has ever seen,' she said, her eyes lit up.

I shook my head, laughing. 'No thanks,' I said. 'My life is so far removed from cycling these days, it's boring, and boring is exactly the way I like it.'

Dashing across the pond to do a TV interview was more than enough for me; as soon as it was done, I couldn't wait to get out of there and return to work, and normality, simplicity. Back home, though, I struggled through the next few weeks, and by the time Christmas came a fog had descended over my mind and body. Unable to get out of bed, I rang the clinic. 'Jean, you'll just have to manage without me for this week,' I said. 'I can't cope.' She knew something must really be up, as I never took time off. But for three days I barely moved, hardly speaking to anyone. I'd crashed. All the stress needed processing.

Early in January 2013 I finally felt strong enough to go back into the clinic. The publicity and press attention had all died down, everyone had moved on to other stories. My phone had stopped ringing. Peace at last.

The day I went back to work, however, as I was massaging a client, news came on the TV we had in the room. I overheard the words 'Lance Armstrong' and 'Oprah Winfrey' and my eyes shot to the screen.

'Lance Armstrong has announced he is to do an exclusive tell-all interview with Oprah,' the newsreader was saying.

'You tosser!' I groaned. Just as I'd recovered from the last storm, Lance was confessing all to the biggest talk-show host in the world. The whole media charade would start up again. I took a few deep breaths; all I could hope was that the attention wouldn't be like last time.

A few days later I was at home, cooking dinner, when my phone bleeped with a missed call. With terrible reception at my place, this wasn't unusual, but when I looked it was a US dialling code.

David Walsh had warned me that a researcher from *Oprah* may be calling, as they were going to ask Lance about me and the words 'alcoholic' and 'whore' he'd used to describe me. I wasn't sure how I felt about the past being raked over again, although of course it would be interesting to hear what Lance had to say.

The next morning, I was in my treatment room at work when a text came through from the same number.

'Emma – this is Lance. Please give me a call when u can. Thx'

Wow. I stared at the words, hearing his voice as I read them. I resisted the urge to ping back. Lance? It can't be. He only speaks through lawyers. Part of me didn't believe it was him, but then it was the evening before he was going to speak to Oprah, and how good would it look for him to be able to say we'd spoken?

'God, he really must be in trouble if he wants to speak to me,' I thought. I clutched my phone. It was now fourteen years since we'd last spoken. A long time, but somehow not long at all.

No, Lance, I'm not going to be part of your plans now.

Shoving the phone back into my pocket, I continued with my day. My receptionist Jean wanted to talk about time off and, as we sorted the rota, I reminded myself how my life was nothing to do with Lance, cycling or court cases. It was about here, Hale, my clinic, people I loved and cared about.

Predictably, my peace was shattered that evening when the phone went crazy with journalists urging me to make comments about Lance's *Oprah* appearance. I refused to say a word. I'd not seen the interview. How could I pass comment when I didn't know what he was going to say? But this was the madness of Planet Lance; it didn't matter whether it had aired or not, they just wanted a soundbite.

My agent persuaded me to do one UK show, *Daybreak*, thinking it would get everyone off my back. The arrangement was that I would go down to London the night *Oprah* went out in the States, see the tape early the next morning, then pass comment. David had asked me if I would watch it with him. 'I'll only have one person with me,' he promised. 'A good honest journalist!' I just laughed at him.

'No, David, this time I am saying no.'

That night in my hotel room, I flicked through the TV channels and saw the *Oprah* interview was on. Deciding it was fate, I made the decision to watch it there and then, alone.

Hearing Lance utter those confessional words, straight up, no messing, was mesmerizing. Words so many of us thought we'd never hear. One by one, he admitted taking performance-enhancing drugs, with a simple 'Yes'. Shifting in his seat, his eyes wide, staring, and with more than a hint of defiance. This was Lance slightly humbled, I felt, but not broken.

'Oh Lance, you need something in your eyes to make you look a bit weepy, or something,' I thought, realizing it was as much as he could muster. Still, there was part of me that was torn. I'd always liked Lance; I'd liked working with him; and, though it wasn't a popular view, I still knew he had a heart in there somewhere. He was still in fight mode and I wondered how long that would last. I listened, just wanting him to get to my part, if he was going to acknowledge me at all.

Then it came. First Oprah asked if the backdated cortisone story was true and he agreed it was, then she asked, 'What do you want to say about Emma O'Reilly?'

I found myself holding a breath in.

'Hey, she's one of these people that I have to apologize to. She's one of these people who got run over, got bullied,' he said.

'You sued her!' Oprah said.

Lance closed his eyes. 'To be honest, Oprah, we sued so many people, I don't even, um, I am sure we did . . . but I have reached out to her and have tried to make those amends on my own.'

Then he shook his head, as Oprah butted in: 'This is what just doesn't make sense – you were suing people when you know they're telling the truth. What is that?'

Lance hesitated. 'It's a major flaw and it's a guy who expected to get whatever he wanted and to control every outcome and it's inexcusable, and when I say that there are people who will hear this and never forgive me, I will understand that.'

With his words came a sense of release I never knew was possible. All I'd done was tell the truth of what happened. Until I was sick of the sound of my own voice, I'd stuck by my story, even when I questioned my own judgement for speaking out. Lance had come along with his lawyers to bury me, and at times it felt as if he'd succeeded. And now I was completely vindicated. I had genuinely thought this day would never come.

Even as Lance switched into fight mode, to protect the brand he'd become, I always knew deep down that somewhere inside he knew I was just being honest. I'd been brought up to tell the truth, that lying was a sin, and that in the end the truth always wins. For years I had felt guilty, a bit-part player who'd spoken out at the wrong time, who was easy to ignore, easy to run over and stupid for speaking in the first place. In the end I even doubted the values I'd been brought up to believe in: a sense of honesty at all costs. But what Lance was now admitting proved to me that it doesn't matter who you are, or how little you seem, or how long it takes; what's true is bigger than anyone or anything.

I breathed in deeply, my hand on my heart, amazed at how much lighter I felt already, as Lance continued to speak. He went on to talk about Betsy, how he'd tried to make peace with her in a forty-minute conversation, but she'd been hurt too badly. Then Oprah turned back to the subject of me.

'I watched the tape several times and under your breath you implied, you said, the whore word. How do you feel about that today?'

'Not good,' Lance said.

'Were you just trying to put her down? Shut her up?'

'No, I was just on the attack, Oprah. Territory being threatened, team being threatened, reputation being threatened, I am gonna attack.'

I'd had little idea just how painful the weight had been – until now it was gone. After a decade, after all those years, my lost thirties, Lance was telling the world the truth. And somehow I was no longer afraid to feel these emotions, because it was finally, finally over.

I looked at my watch. It was 2 a.m. and I had to be up at 5 a.m. to do a live TV interview, but all I wanted to do was go home and cry.

27

Endgame

A CAB DROPPED ME at the *Daybreak* studios and as soon as I arrived a researcher rushed over with a copy of the Oprah interview on DVD.

'It's okay, thanks,' I said, politely. 'I've seen it.'

'Right,' she said, flustered. 'Well, we need you not to mention the drugs or Lance outright. There's still so many things you cannot say. We're worried about Lance's lawyers.'

I felt like screaming. Rarely do I like making a scene, but the irony of being told I still needed to worry about Lance's lawyers after he'd just confessed wasn't lost on me. I was sick and tired of being gagged. 'Have you not seen the tape?' I cried. 'He's admitted everything. Surely I can say whatever I want now?'

Eventually I calmed down, after sounding off to the poor hair and make-up team, who were very sympathetic. Breathing deeply before I went on air, I thought about everything I'd battled through to get to this point.

'Like Lance, you can stop fighting too now, Emma,' I thought. 'It's over.'

The interviewer asked me if Lance saying sorry was enough, and in my anger I replied, 'Not at all.' I admitted that after I got his text one part of me thought, 'This is great,' but the other part thought, 'You little runt!' I wanted to clip him over the back of the head, drag him up to Manchester and make him apologize to people who were close to me.

Around 28 million people had watched Lance on *Oprah*, and Oprah herself said it was the biggest interview she'd ever done. With people everywhere still talking about it, two weeks later *The Late Late Show* in Ireland asked me to be a guest.

I had so many memories of watching the show with Dad when I was growing up, so I agreed to this one final TV interview. David Walsh was appearing too. There was little doubt I'd lost some respect for him, and little doubt I'd driven the man crackers at times, but he had an underlying respect for me for standing up and being counted. The producers were keen we spoke together. As I sorted tickets, I got some for TC and Alasdair. 'You were there at the beginning,' I said. 'Come to this and it's full circle.'

I told my family about the appearance too, knowing they'd probably tune in. Auntie Cecil sounded excited: 'But Emma, don't you be getting yourself into any trouble now, y'hear me?' she warned.

I laughed. 'Oh Cecil, it's too late for that,' I said. 'I've actually just got myself out of the trouble!'

As we waited in the green room, I nudged David. 'Can you believe how big this whole thing got still? I can't.'

David turned to me, a rare sheepish look flashing across his face. 'At the start, Marc Grinsztajn from La Martinière told me, "You'll need to look out for Emma, make sure she's okay through this." He warned me you'd be the most vulnerable in all of this.'

Sometimes, when someone says something revelatory to you, it can take minutes, hours or even days to sink in. What David was telling me was what I'd long suspected but had now had confirmed. He'd hung me out to dry – but worse than that, the publisher had even openly warned him of the impact this would have on my life and had recommended proper support. Something I feel I never got.

I barely had time to react before a runner shepherded us in front of the audience. Instantly nervous again about going live on air, I managed to smile and walked on, head held high. I just wanted it over with.

During the chat David spoke of his disappointment that Lance hadn't named individuals who'd helped him dope and how the interview wasn't heartfelt. He admitted the interview I'd given him on my sofa that hot July day was the biggest story he'd ever get in his life. 'It was my Christmas,' he enthused, as I found myself rolling my eyes. 'Yes, David, your Christmas was at *my* expense,' I thought, as I controlled myself for the camera.

I was candid, though, when asked my opinions. I didn't think Lance looked sorry enough in the interview; he was sorry he got caught and sorry he couldn't compete. 'It wasn't the body language or verbal language of a contrite man,' I said. 'It was the language of a man who's lost seventy-five million dollars in one day.' My anger still bubbled just below the surface, but I was certain it was visible to the viewers.

The interviewer, Ryan Tubridy asked me about Lance and I told him we had had a good relationship, things were straight up and if he was having a bad day I'd tell him. Then he brought up the whore word and asked me how I felt about that.

'Supply and demand meant there were far fewer women than men in the sport,' I explained. 'I could have had a good time if I'd wanted to. But we'd have conversations like this over the massage table, like moralists, puritanical. While I am giving him a massage we'd be saying, "How good are we?" and for him to attack me in that way, really, really hurt.'

After the show they put us up in the fancy Shelbourne Hotel in Dublin, where the manager came over to me and shook my hand. 'It is a real pleasure and honour to have you staying here with us, Emma,' he said. I was touched. I'd had a few people in the street recognize me too, coming to shake my hand, congratulate me. This all felt surreal and unnecessary; in my mind there were no heroes in this story, but I appreciated the sentiment.

My quiet drive through the flat fields of Cheshire on my first day back at work felt like a blessing. No more court cases, no more drama; I could close my front door of an evening and sleep easy now. Life was simple again. While Lance was being chased for $100 million in lawsuits, I could sink back into anonymity. The truth was out and, as long as I never had to speak with a lawyer again, that was all I cared about. Ever since 2005 my New Year's resolution had always been: 'This year I won't speak to any lawyers.'

It was wishful thinking, though, as unfortunately it didn't take long for another letter to land, this time from Floyd Landis's legal team. They got in touch, wanting me to send an unredacted statement for their whistleblower case, just like the one set up by Prentice Steffen years earlier. Again I refused. None of this was about money and revenge for me. I needed another lawyer to deal with this, though, and with Marcus Rutherford and David Engels long gone and not able to afford one of my own, I felt hugely grateful when one of my clients, who happened to be a lawyer who loved cycling, pitched in to help.

In all honesty, I didn't expect to speak to Lance again. Even if he'd fallen spectacularly from grace and faced having to sell his houses and his private jet, our worlds were so different, our paths unlikely ever to cross again.

But something stopped me from deleting his number from my phone. By March, I'd read and reread his words a million times, wondering whether he actually was genuinely sorry or whether I was just a pawn in his machine, or 'reconciliation tour', as Betsy bitterly billed it.

After he'd defamed me, I'd been asked regularly if I wanted to sue him. For years I'd been labelled a liar, an alcoholic, a whore, and those slurs could have cost him dearly, and I agree that in life sometimes you have to stand up and be counted. Women should not be spoken of the way he spoke of me, and the libel laws gave Lance all the protection but afforded me none, and there's nothing fair about that. However, as lawyers circled, rubbing their hands, offering their services, I realized my decision would be something different. I would show compassion.

Maybe offering an olive branch would encourage Lance to tell the truth? Maybe I'd find peace only by forgiving? Whatever the response from Lance, this felt right to me, so I told the lawyers to get lost and turned the other cheek. Strange as it might seem, I still felt a certain amount of guilt in speaking out so many years before anyone else, and believed the riders, even including Lance, were to an extent victims of a corrupt system.

As flat as I felt about USADA and Lance getting in touch, when I heard that Brian Cookson, Simon's former boss at British Cycling, was throwing his hat into the ring to be UCI president, I decided to email him. At the time Simon was subpoenaed to back up my testimony, Brian had been his superior but had done nothing to help. Now he replied to say he'd be happy to talk with me, and I went to meet him in his offices in Manchester.

'Thanks for agreeing to chat,' I said, trying to be polite. 'If you're serious about cleaning up the sport, why didn't you at least encourage Simon to stand by me?'

'Emma, we thought the situation was a personal thing between a man and his ex-wife. It was our mistake,' he said.

I didn't think this was good enough, so I found myself reeling off one of my all-time favourite quotes. 'Brian,' I said, '*laissez-faire* didn't work during the famine in Ireland. It was hardly gonna work a century later, was it? I needed only one person to back up my story. If in 2004 you'd made Simon come out and admit what had happened, all this could have come out. Cycling could have been cleaned up way back. You could've done something truly great.'

He looked at his hands briefly and nodded, his expression completely genuine. 'I feel ashamed something wasn't done sooner.'

For a moment I fell silent, considering also pointing out that actually Simon had ended up getting the job of cycling manager for the London Olympics, but I bit my tongue. 'How do you think I felt with all the lawsuits on my head?' I sighed.

We chatted for a while longer, then he shook my hand and thanked me for my visit. Whether he'd taken on board what I'd said or not, at least I'd spoken my mind and I knew that cycling must have changed for the better if someone like Brian was prepared to meet me and hear my side of the story.

With the passage of time my anger had receded, but I was still curious about what Lance had to say. Was it conceivable for him ever to go back to being the Lance I'd known before Lance

Inc. took over? What kind of man, after all this, after such a stunning fall from grace, had he become?

Turning the phone in my hands one evening, on a whim, I texted him: 'If you're genuine, let's get in touch.'

Just minutes later my phone vibrated: 'Yes, it is genuine. LA.'

Over the next few weeks we exchanged a few texts, and I missed a few of his calls too, never daring to ring him back.

A few months later I was in America, visiting Norbert on a big family holiday with Sharon too. I'd promised to take his two beautiful daughters for a girlie night out to the pictures when Lance texted again. He wanted to meet in Aspen, or maybe somewhere north, but I put him off; I wasn't ready and besides, I had a hair appointment. 'That's more important than dashing off to see you, matey!' I thought to myself. No, Lance Armstrong could wait.

After I returned home, he started texting me frequently. I was always happy to reply, with upbeat, positive responses. I sensed he didn't know whether I trusted him or if he could trust me, so to prove he could, I was kind, encouraging and chatty, maybe more than I even felt. This circle of mistrust had to be broken somehow. I told him that he was a strong person and could get through this. He said he appreciated this and the fact that I hadn't gone crazy at him like lots of others had.

'It was never just about you,' I texted back. 'It was about the positions you were all in.'

Yes, Lance was the ringleader, he was always fighting to be the best, even at doping, and he won. Yet for him to be blamed so squarely, and to be stripped so completely of all his achievements? No, I didn't think this was fair. Not at all. What about the other Tour de France winners? The podium was full, year after year, of riders who just had to be doping to ride at those speeds and recover so quickly. At the end of the day, if Travis

Tygart and his team were serious about getting to the bottom of the fraud and corruption in the sport, they needed Lance to reveal all, they needed to work out who had facilitated the whole scandal. And the more I heard, the more I thought they didn't want this. It would destroy cycling.

A little earlier, I'd been approached to do a TV drama – something that both staggered and amused me in equal measure. My boring little life? But after meeting a producer I was persuaded to help with a script and we all travelled out to the Tour in the summer of 2013.

Around this time, I pulled out documents and legal stuff I'd kept locked away for years to help with the research. As I read over the *Sunday Times* court summons and paperwork, I looked again at the title: 'Lance Armstrong vs Sunday Times, Alan English and David Walsh'.

I reread the names. 'That's strange,' I thought. 'Where's my name on this?'

I flicked through it, checking and double-checking, reading over the paperwork carefully, until something finally sank in. My name was *not* on this paperwork. It wasn't actually me who was being sued with the *Sunday Times* at all.

Fucking hell.

All those conversations about us being in this 'together', all the references to fears of losing everything, all the meetings, emails, phone calls to David. To me, they'd all insinuated the same thing: I was being sued alongside them. If I had had someone working for me, I'd probably have been told categorically this wasn't the case. But of course it wouldn't have suited their interests. They needed me to testify.

Almost immediately after this revelation, an author researching a book about the doping scandal got in touch asking me to fact-check whether I was sued in the UK too; even those with access to other paperwork seemed to be in the dark about it. When I refused to help her, she went to David Walsh to ask him. Did he actually know I wasn't being sued? David advised her to check with me. He claimed if I had said this had happened, then it must be true.

That was all I needed to know. In my opinion David knew all along I wasn't a named defendant. He never pointed this out because it suited all their needs for me to believe I was. Bitterly confused, I rang Mike. 'Mike, tell me I am not being stupid. Were we being sued in the UK too?'

'Emma, we were definitely being sued in the UK.'

Mike and I had clearly both got completely the wrong end of the stick – as I said, maybe I was just too naive at the time to understand what was going on, David would no doubt say differently, but in my opinion he had acted in a devious way, making me believe one thing to suit his own ends. He wanted his story, he got it, and he got me to back him to the hilt. How stupid had I been?

With the script under way, I found it rather amusing to read an early draft that insinuated I was in love with Lance. I laughed my head off and asked them to rewrite that part.

'Nothing could be further from the truth,' I chuckled.

After much toing and froing with emails, Lance and I arranged to meet in Florida. I was nervous as hell at the idea and wondered about his agenda. Lance, being Lance, would obviously have one. When I heard he was arriving a day early, I grew even more suspicious.

'What have you got planned?' I emailed him, twice. The Lance I knew waited around for nothing and nobody. Both times, however, he denied he had any ulterior motive, saying it was just the way flights worked out, and I believed him. Lance wasn't a liar. By that I mean, sure, he lied about something rather big, but little day-to-day things? It wasn't his style.

Then about ten days before I left for America, while I was tidying the treatment room in my clinic, Lance called again. My instinct was to press divert – fuck, I still wasn't ready to deal with speaking to him directly, not after all these years – but equally I knew if I didn't answer I'd be thinking about it all afternoon. Besides, I was seeing him soon anyway, so best to get this over with.

'Hey,' I said. 'Emma speaking.'

'Emma, it's Lance. How ya doing?'

I stumbled for words, all of a sudden feeling like an awkward teen. 'Just at work. What you up to?'

'Just dropping the kids off at school, then off for a round of golf,' he said.

'Golf? What's your handicap?' I asked, keeping things light.

'Have you never heard the Bob Hope saying? My handicap depends on whether you're betting or boasting,' he laughed. 'Hey, it's nice to catch up. I'll see you in a week or so.'

And he was gone again.

I leaned on the massage table, sick to the stomach. With all that dirty water under the bridge, hiding behind texts was so much easier. Yet the ice had been broken.

I arranged the flights myself and then the *Daily Mail* sports reporter Matt Lawton got in touch and I asked him to come along. Again, I thought that if I put one story out, with the *Mail* this time, then everyone else would leave me alone. The last thing I wanted was to be under siege again.

I told Lance of my plans. 'If Matt is okay with you, he's okay with me,' he said.

Before we flew to the States, I informed Travis that I was planning to meet Lance. 'Would it help if I tried to bring him to your table?' I said. 'He needs to tell you everything.' Travis wholeheartedly agreed, suggesting perhaps that, as I'd known Lance before he'd grown so big and famous, I might be able to get through to him.

By the time we arrived at the airport in Florida, the final arrangements for our meeting still hadn't been made. To add to the confusion, Lance's phone was off and mine wasn't working. Then finally he sent me a text.

'You here?' he asked.

'Are you?' I fired back, adding a smiley face.

Matt's face drained of colour as I showed him my response. 'Please, Emma,' he said, pacing up and down, 'don't do this. Not now. Let's just get the meeting sorted.'

I laughed. This was a big scoop for Matt and I could see how nervous he was. He was about to land on Planet Lance for the first time.

We arrived at our hotel in Celebration where Lance was also staying, but we still didn't know when he was arriving, so Matt and I went to our rooms to freshen up.

'Have you heard from him?' Matt texted after a couple of hours.

'Not yet!' I replied. He was panicking, but I knew Lance would show up. Half an hour later a call confirmed he was on his way from the golf course.

When I finally found him in reception and we had said hello, we went to the hotel restaurant to let a photographer for the newspaper take a few shots.

'I'd no idea if you were coming. I was on the golf course and said to Anna: "Has she done me over?"' Lance admitted.

'Well we're here now,' I replied.

After the lads had finished their pictures, I had to step in and say something as Matt made notes for his story.

'Lance,' I began, 'I took what you said about me on the chin, but what upset me more was the way it hurt my boyfriend at the time. You're a lad's lad, Lance, and if someone had said that about your girlfriend you'd be very upset.'

Lance gazed at me and Matt. 'At the time, what I said about her – I was fighting to protect a lot of positions,' he replied. 'But it was inexcusable. It's embarrassing. I was in a conference room giving a legal deposition and I had no idea it was going to get out. But that doesn't excuse it. I guess you should always assume that, in that setting, the whole world will watch it the next day.'

After our dinner alone together, we walked back to the hotel, reminiscing about some of the silly, fun days, like when Darren Baker was upset by Scott Mercier when he climbed into bed naked with him by accident, mistaking him for his girlfriend.

'There were good times,' I laughed.

'They seem so long ago now,' he agreed.

Back home, the newspaper piece came out and I was quoted as saying Lance hadn't actually said sorry to me over the meal. I wanted to keep part of our conversation private, but Lance read this online and called me.

'It's not what other people think who read the newspaper that matters to me, it's what you think,' he said. 'And as long as you know, Emma, I really am sorry.'

'It's okay, I know you are,' I said.

'The truth will come out one day, you know,' he replied. 'The whole truth.'

I smiled, the irony not lost on me, now that it was Lance Armstrong's turn to say so.

Epilogue

AFTER READING THE USADA report, my overriding feeling was that the riders had been used again. Cycling's governing bodies appeared barely to get a footnote in comparison to the riders and directors. As Lance himself correctly pointed out, he didn't invent the system of doping in the sport; he inherited it. Without a doubt he was a bully, a cheat, a liar – I would never condone him for this or for what he did to me. But for him to carry the whole can, to be banned for life and stripped of everything, is purposeless. Far more practical would be the sport asking him to reveal everything. One thing is for certain – Lance didn't dope alone. He had legions of people in high places aiding him; many people made enormous sums of money from him, and they had a vested interest themselves in keeping his lie going.

And yet Lance and only Lance is being brought down permanently.

In October 2012 I took part in a programme for ABC in which Dick Pound, the former head of WADA, was interviewed. He recounted a conversation with Hein Verbruggen, the former president of the UCI, in which he told Hein he had a doping problem in his sport. Hein responded by saying 'What problem?' He blamed cycling fans for doping: 'If they were happy to watch twenty-five mph rides, then fine, but they want forty mph rides and so riders have to keep up with that.'

Dick replied, 'Like I said, you have a problem.'

When Lance and US Postal landed at the Tour, they brought a whole new audience and more money. That relationship suited cycling for a long time and Lance became the cheat who got out of control, but without a doubt this monstrosity was encouraged from the top.

In 2004 David revealed allegations that after a race Lance spoke to Hein about the commissaire, but Hein flatly denied it. In 2013, he repeated this denial. Then in 2014, after we had met up, Lance finally admitted it was true. Hein Verbruggen was the ultimate facilitator of everyone involved in doping and yet he is honorary president of the UCI. He lied about this, so what else? Ultimately I deserve an apology from him too. Lance and the other wrongdoers have all reached out to me and said a genuine 'sorry', and I do believe it's genuine. I'd go so far as to say that a proper system to help these riders recover needs to be put into place. The pressure to dope has screwed so many people's lives.

A few days after my meeting with Lance was made public, Jeff Novitzky sent me an email to say how he respected my decision to meet with Lance and show forgiveness. One evening, as Lance and I chatted on the phone – we've spoken many times since November 2013 – I told him about this.

'Jeff's probably not your favourite person, Lance, but look what he says.'

Lance laughed. 'No, Emma, he's not my favourite person, but yeah, that's really cool.'

And so I found myself in the strange position of being the

only person actually talking to both sides in this scandal. And Lance, believe me, is humbled. He has made it clear to me several times over that he is 'no longer the boss' and that he trusts me. 'My heart tells me to,' he says.

Happy to try to mediate on his behalf, I went to my own independent lawyer to ask for his direction in bringing Lance and Travis Tygart together. After all, whatever Lance told Travis, he'd need some protection from all the impending multi-million-dollar lawsuits. With my lawyer's help I sent an email to Travis, suggesting a few conditions for their meeting. Lance wanted to tell the whole story, I said, but in a legally protected way for now.

As I write this, I still haven't heard from Travis. This is a pity, as it appears to indicate a reluctance to bring Lance to the table, and to me this smacks of not wanting to face the reality of bringing him in. A central player, Lance would be able to clear up the inaccuracies; he would be able to tell all about who really was involved. It would be something on a greater scale, to clean up the sport. Travis has refused to compromise, however. I can see his point, because of the way Lance behaved – and there's no doubt he behaved as aggressively, as brutally, as a cornered, wounded animal. But if I can put his behaviour to one side, why can't other people? In my mind, this is the ego again, preventing proper discourse. The two alpha males locking horns.

At the end of the day, my point of view is not a popular one, but I still believe Lance has a good, authentic side to him. There should be a determination to get all the facts in this case out unemotionally, and let people decide for themselves. We're meant to live in a civilized democracy, with freedom of speech. Everyone should have a right to tell their story – to tell the truth.

The decision not to allow Lance to compete ever again is one I cannot get my head around. Does it serve a purpose, banning a middle-aged man from competing? But he has told me that in many ways he feels it's odd that people assume he cannot live without competition in his life. 'Emma, I have to ask myself if I'd even want to go back into the madness. Sport is a crazy world, and those who run it.'

Meanwhile, Hollywood came knocking on David Walsh's door and, fair play, he couldn't wait to welcome them in. A biopic was announced, based on his book *Seven Deadly Sins*, starring Ben Foster as Lance and Chris O'Dowd as David. There's a saying a journalist should never become the story, but many say that's too late for David. For the first time, too, it appears he has fallen out with some of his key sources, like Betsy. For my part, I wanted nothing to do with it and have asked that it is publicly declared that I haven't given permission for any material I have given David to be included. Lance, of course, has not been consulted either, even though he is friends with Sean Penn, whose ex-wife is now Ben Foster's partner.

After my reconciliation with Lance, I felt a difference in my everyday life in ways I hadn't anticipated. My confidence was renewed. Knowing past judgements I'd made had not been skewed after all, and knowing I could forgive as well as be forgiven, has been powerful. Spurred on, I tried to get in touch with others to extend this.

Catching up with Tyler was wonderful, and over a mammoth two-hour phone call we laughed and almost cried. 'I can't believe we haven't done this before now, Emma,' he enthused. I agreed; it was wonderful to hear his voice again.

Tyler had got divorced for a second time and was rebuilding his life, finding himself again. Cycling had shattered his world, his moral compass had been corrupted, and now he needed to find who he really is. We spoke of old times and all the fun we had, but when I pointed out how much he changed, he didn't let me get away with that lightly.

'But Emma, so did you! I saw the same cynicism, the same stress in the end. You were not the same person either by the end of your time in Postal.'

And he was right, I changed too. I was right in the centre of the doping world, and party to it.

I told Tyler how incredibly brave and moving I thought *The Secret Race* was. He thanked me and said, 'I feel bad about some of it, however; people like the doctor, Pedro, and how he was portrayed as the big villain.'

I laughed and recounted my story of how Dr Pedro tried to get me sacked over the denim-shirt incident. 'He wasn't all nice, Tyler, and don't forget, those soft brown eyes and big talks he had with you were all about persuading you to dope!'

We spoke about my reconciliation with Lance. For Tyler, things were far more strained, especially after their encounter at a restaurant in Aspen, Colorado. Tyler was left with the impression Lance would have done anything to silence him.

Personally I've never seen that side of Lance, although I don't doubt Tyler's account for one minute. Lad to lad is a different story. Still, without a moment's hesitation, I urged Tyler to forgive him.

'Don't do it for Lance, do it for you,' I said. 'Forgiveness brings peace. You'll truly be able to move on with your life then.'

Tyler agreed it might be possible, especially since the confession. 'What's Lance like now?' he asked. 'Is he like he was in the training camp in '98?'

'Yeah, he is,' I said. 'He's become human again.'

Tyler admitted he'd lost all the money he earned from cycling, but wouldn't have wanted it any other way. 'It wouldn't have felt right to have it still,' he said. 'I like my simple life again now.'

'Me too,' I agreed.

In January 2014 I met with my old nemesis Johan, the man who brought me to the edge of my sanity. He was keen to do it away from any cameras, away from the spotlight, and we sat down in Manchester for a five-hour lunch. With his ten-year ban currently in place, he plans to fight it every step of the way. Other directors with doping histories, like Denmark's Bjarne Riis, are still working in the sport. I cannot understand why Johan is being treated differently.

Before I could say anything to Johan, though, it was he who put first things first. 'I was a dick to you, Emma,' he said. 'I'm sorry.'

We talked about the pressure of the Tour, the pressures from above, and how Johan was so inexperienced in the role at that time.

'I can't have been easy to work with at times,' I laughed. 'Afterwards some staff congratulated me for never backing down to you, Johan. My own part in the rebellion was noticed!' Not that it is something of which I am proud at this stage of my life.

In many ways, Johan struggles with his image as the big baddie in the scandal. While Lance accepts there is a lying, cheating side to him that grew out of control, Johan doesn't accept that so much blame should be heaped on him.

'I might've been part of a medical programme,' he told me, 'but I never, ever forced anyone into it.'

While it's a fact that Johan and Lance developed a culture within their team that if riders did not follow the medical programme, it meant a lack of 'commitment', I believe them when they say there was no coercion. Nobody put a gun to a rider's head. It was down to their own discretion and some, like JV, decided to leave because of it and some, like Christian, didn't. Facts like these need to be looked at again, and it needs to be remembered that each of us has to take responsibility for our decisions in life.

My next phone call was to George Hincapie. George, I hope, won't mind me saying that the fact is he doped for at least as long as Lance, and yet was offered just a six-month ban. While Lance was in hospital with cancer, George was doping, yet he didn't get such a harsh sentence. I apologized to George for dobbing him in it all too, and asked him if he felt able to speak up for the sport again.

'I have been caught cheating,' he said. 'You have more credibility than me. All you did, Emma, was tell the truth.'

With phone calls to riders out of the way, my thoughts turned to what was potentially the hardest call I had to make . . . to Julien, my Pepe. Out of everyone, the loss of his friendship was the hardest to bear. I knew full well how strongly he'd felt that I should stay away from speaking to David; in hindsight, perhaps he was being protective, knowing just what a burden breaking the omertà could be. Ever since that phone call when he told me to say nothing, I'd felt as if I'd betrayed a loyal, good man whose career spanned five decades.

But, with my new-found confidence, I took a deep breath and dialled his number, deciding to risk whatever the wrath thrown in my direction would be.

'Julien?' I said softly. 'It's Emma O'Reilly speaking.'

I squeezed my eyes tightly shut as he took a moment to register. Then he simply gasped: 'Ahh, it's your Pepe!' And straight away I knew I'd been forgiven.

'Emmatje, you shouldn't have spoken to those assholes!' he cried. 'Look at what happened! Look what a mess it brought to you! I told you not to say anything, didn't I? Didn't I!'

And for thirty seconds or so I laughed, simply because at long last I could.

Index

301

ABOUT THE AUTHOR

Emma O'Reilly was born in 1970 in the working-class Dublin suburb of Tallaght. She trained to be an electrician before becoming interested in sports massage and therapy.

Emma worked for the Irish National cycling team for three years and then for professional teams in the United States, joining US Postal in 1996. Confronted by a doping culture she despised, she resigned her position in 2000 and began to speak out about what was happening in the sport.

She now runs The Body Clinic in Hale, Cheshire, treating Olympic athletes and professional sportspeople as well as members of the general public.